Wildfowl Carving

Wildfowl Carving

VOLUME 1

ESSENTIAL TECHNIQUES FOR CARVING, TEXTURING & PAINTING WILDFOWL

Jim Pearce

Foreword by
HRH The Duke of Edinburgh

GUILD OF MASTER CRAFTSMAN PUBLICATIONS LTD

First published 1995 by
Guild of Master Craftsman Publications Ltd
166 High Street, Lewes
East Sussex BN7 1XU

ISBN 0 946819 53 X

Designed by Gellatly Norman Associates.

Typeface: Garamond ITC Book

Paper: Fineblade Cartridge 115 gsm

Printed and bound in Great Britain by the University Press, Cambridge

Fig 3.9 courtesy of Cliff Benton; Figs 5.1 and 5.45 courtesy of Joe Blossom; Fig 1.3 courtesy of the National Museum of the American Indian, Smithsonian Institute, USA; Figs 1.11 and 1.12 courtesy of Sophie Ridges; Figs 1.4 – 1.9 courtesy of the Ward Foundation, Salisbury, MA; Fig 1.1 courtesy of the Wildfowl and Wetlands Trust.

TO ELISABETH, LOUISE AND ANDY,

DEBBIE AND NICHOLAS

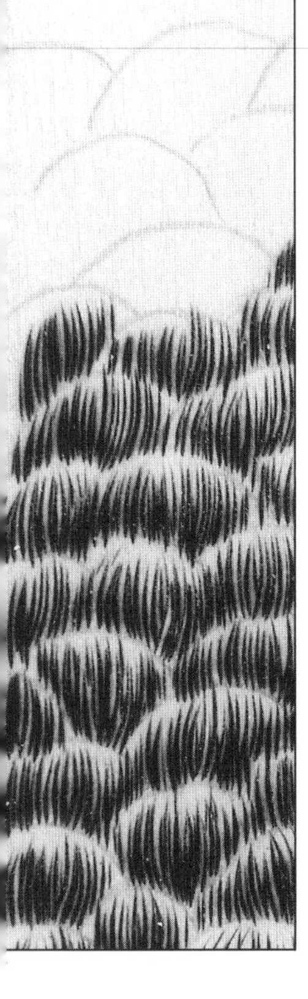

CONTENTS

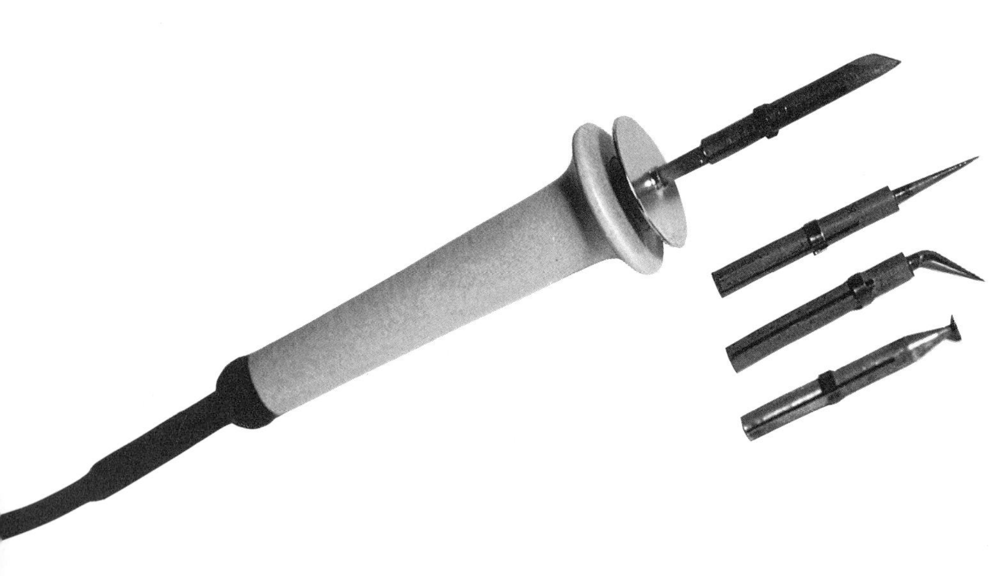

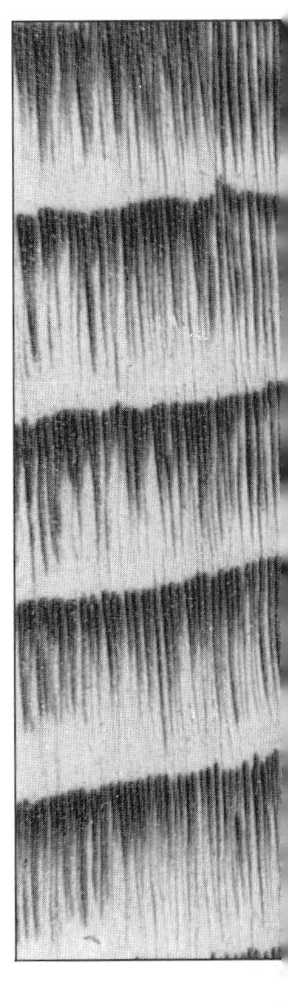

Foreword by HRH The Duke of Edinburgh

Many human activities have been the inspiration for the work of artists and craftsmen. High on the list is humanity's relationship with wildlife in general and to hunting and trapping in particular. One of the oldest ruses is to attract wildfowl into a decoy pipe by the use of imitation birds, usually carved in wood. These 'decoys' were frequently made with great skill and have since become objects of interest to collectors. This, in turn, has led artists and craftsmen to fashion such imitations as works of art in their own right.

The carvers of the 'working' wooden decoys were concerned more with giving the right impression than creating an exact imitation. The artist or craftsman in wildfowl woodcarving takes a particular pride in reproducing exact details. This requires special techniques and anyone interested in practising this art, or who wishes to know how these carvings are made, can do no better than read this book.

Acknowledgements

I am deeply indebted to all those carvers who responded so willingly to my requests for help by sending me photographs of their work.

Special thanks are due to my long-suffering wife, Elisabeth, not only for her moral support throughout the time spent in the preparation and writing of this book, but also for her hitherto latent talent as a photographer. Called upon frequently and nearly always at very short notice, she succeeded in capturing all the many decisive moments on film for me with uncanny skill.

I would also like to express my gratitude to Liz Inman, my editor at GMC, for all her sound advice and patience. The book would not have been possible without her help. Thanks also to Joe Sheehan and Jon Ingoldby, desk editors at the Guild of Master Craftsman Publications.

My thanks must also go to all those who responded to my letters seeking information and photographs, in particular:

Trevor Adams	Watford Observer
Peter Bacon	BDWCA
Ken Beynon	BDWCA
Diane Fowler	The Wildfowl and Wetlands Trust
Melvyn Hagger	PDQ Ltd, Watford
Cathy Hart	Wildfowl Carving and Collecting Magazine
Shelley Olsen Kelly	The Ward Foundation
Allan Knotts	Knotts' Knives
Pauline McGowan	Old Hall Farm Decoys
Sophie Ridges	The Decoy Arts Gallery
David Tippey	BDWCA
Tony Walker	Robert Sorby Ltd

About the Author

On graduating from the Royal Military Academy, Sandhurst, in 1949, Jim served in the Royal Engineers until he retired in 1962. After studying for three years at the Polytechnic of Central London he won a City and Guilds Gold Medal for photography and a scholarship to study advanced colour photography at Eastman Kodak in New York. He worked for four years as a professional photographer before moving into education. He obtained a Master's Degree and became a Principal Lecturer in the Faculty of Art and Design at the Harrow College of Higher Education until 1987.

His interest in wildfowl carving began in a dentist's waiting room in 1984 when his wife spotted an advertisement in a magazine for one of Bob Ridge's courses in the West Country. A week working with Bob confirmed that interest, which has now developed into an incurable addiction. Jim later spent some time learning more advanced carving and painting techniques from Jim Sprankle in the States.

He has been a successful professional wildfowl carver since 1988 and is currently a tutor at Missenden Abbey and Denman College, and an active member of the British Decoy and Wildfowl Carvers Association.

Introduction

This book is for those who are fascinated by ducks, geese or swans and who would like to learn the art of carving them in wood. The act of taking a block of wood and carving, texturing and painting it to create a duck or other wildfowl can seem daunting. However, as a wildfowl carving instructor I have witnessed at first hand that the basic skills can be learnt easily and tackled by anyone.

I have structured this book just as I do my classes. All materials, tools and techniques that you will need for your first wildfowl carving are covered fully in the preliminary chapters. The rest of the chapters break down the stages of carving, texturing and painting into simple and progressive steps. Each and every step is fully explained and photographed. Additional reference material is provided by way of line drawings.

A note about tools

Many books on wildfowl carving share a single shortcoming:, they assume the beginner has available to them expensive carving machinery such as flexi-shaft grinding equipment etc. In my classes, I have found that a great majority of students drawn to wildfowl carving are complete beginners to any sort of carving at all! And these students are happily relieved to discover that wildfowl carving can be undertaken with, apart from a woodburning device for creating feather texture, the most simple of hand tools and straightforward techniques.

Wildfowl Carving: Volume 2

The second volume of this work covers advanced techniques for the more experienced carver, and more sophisticated equipment and tools are dealt with in detail. However it must be stressed that wildfowl carving can be practiced to a high standard using very simple tools and no special facilities.

Reference features

Volumes 1 and 2, taken together, are meant to comprise a handbook of the techniques, tools and materials of the wildfowl carver. Moreover, I have designed it to function as a general reference source for the field as well. To this end I have included various appendices, in which you will find the following information:

- Body sizes and eye sizes and colours of nearly 400 different birds, including waterfowl, birds of prey, game birds, songbirds, shorebirds and seabirds.
- A chart detailing the characteristics of various woods a carver might be interested in using. This contains an assessment of how each of these woods can be expected to perform when used for wildfowl carving.

The information in these appendices is the result of a long process of collecting and sorting bits of information from various sources and compiling them into what I hope will be a useful format for all wildfowl carvers. As reference material is so important to the carver who wishes to portray his subject with accuracy, I have included an extensive bibliography.

Techniques and skills

All of the carving and painting techniques covered in the book have been applied using as a subject the common goldeneye drake *(Bucephala clangula)*. The goldeneye is found in most parts of the world, and is an excellent duck on which to learn the basic carving techniques.

The reader will soon discover, however, that the skills involved in carving a duck are readily transferable and can easily be applied to the carving of other birds and wildlife. The carver is limited in his choice of subject and pose only by his or her own imagination.

CHAPTER *1*

History and Background

The decoy

Evidence exists showing that the Greeks and the Egyptians, when hunting, used rudimentary lures fabricated in the shape of birds, which they then tethered to live birds to attract other birds. The Greeks are known to have towed realistically carved and painted wooden decoys to attract ducks into netted tunnels as long ago as 500 BC. Casks, sealed in a tomb in about 1400 BC, containing crudely made decoys of mud and feathers, were most probably used to hunt ducks along the edges of the Nile.

However, it was not until a wicker basket containing 11 canvasback ducks made from mud, reeds and feathers was discovered by archaeologists in a Nevada cave in 1924, and estimated to be between 1,000 and 3,000 years old, that it was confirmed that decoys had been used by native Americans.

The word 'decoy' is believed to be derived from the Dutch word for a cage or trap, 'de kooi'. In the seventeenth century, the Dutch used a method of luring ducks into a large netted hoop, or 'pipe' which narrowed down

Fig 1.1 Mallard 'flushing' down a decoy pipe.

to a small diameter tunnel from which the ducks were then taken (see Fig 1.1).

The success of the method relied partly upon the natural curiosity of the duck, for, in addition to live duck lures and a liberal distribution of grain in the water, a terrier dog was an essential member of the hunting team (see Fig 1.2). The dog's task was to arouse the curiosity of the ducks by appearing periodically from behind reed screens erected along the sides of the 'pipe', and gradually lead them, in this hide-and-seek manner, further into the tunnel. Since the effectiveness of the operation relied on the ducks believing the dog to be a predator, e.g. a fox, and therefore instinctively drawn to 'mobbing it', some decoy men would use a brown ferret on a string, or even a ginger cat!

This system of hunting ducks was first introduced into England in the latter half of the seventeenth century and together with other methods – involving spring-loaded nets and of course guns – continued for many years.

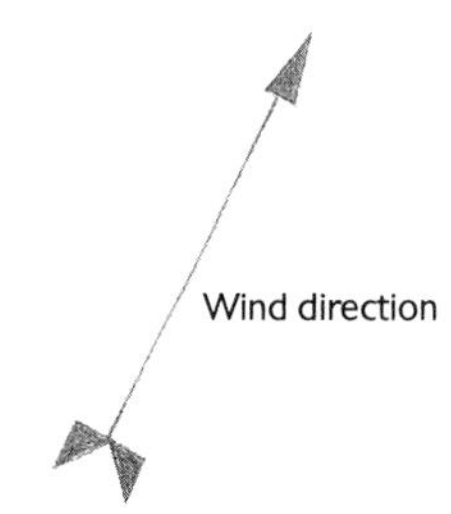

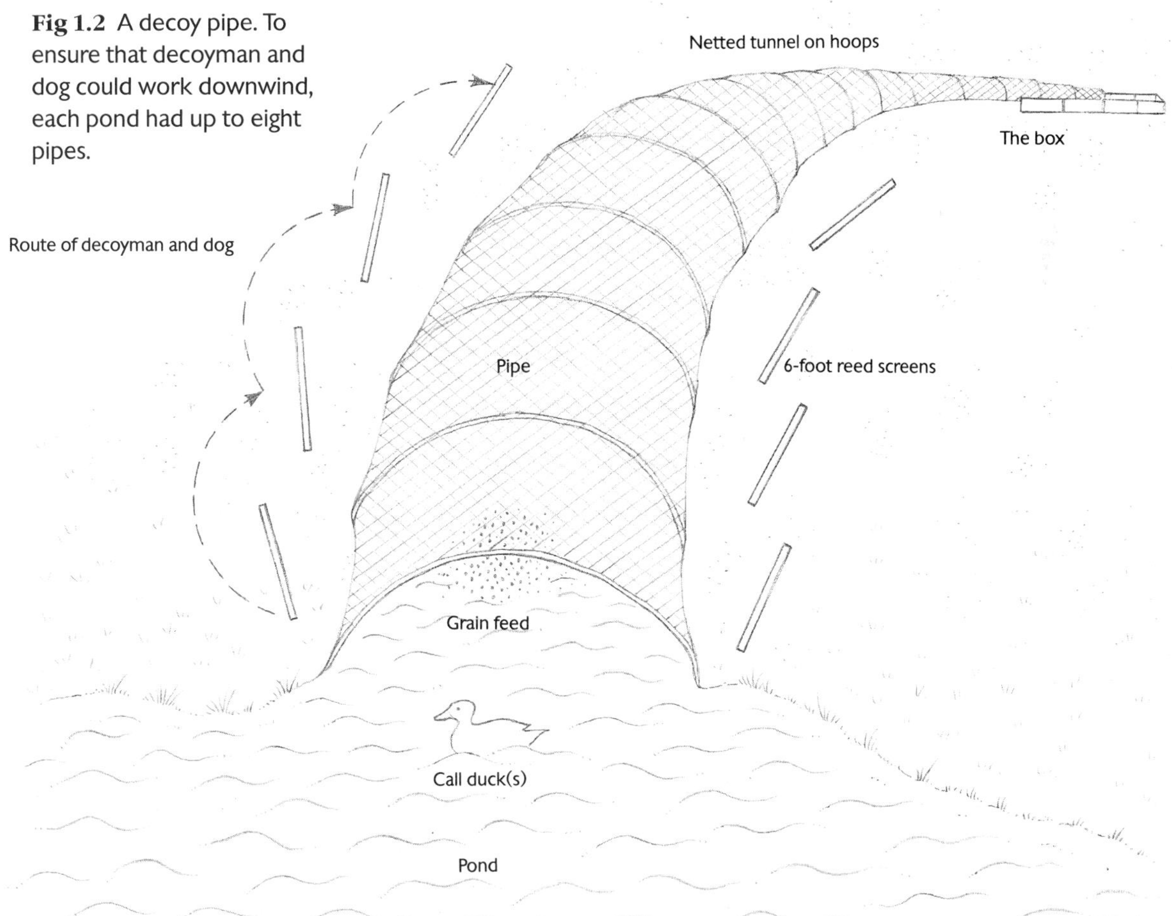

Fig 1.2 A decoy pipe. To ensure that decoyman and dog could work downwind, each pond had up to eight pipes.

One of these tunnel net decoys can still be seen at Borough Fen in Cambridgeshire, England, and although no longer used for hunting it is used to catch wildfowl for ringing purposes and scientific research.

American settlers

The history of the craft of wildfowl carving has been almost wholly determined by events and circumstances in the USA. The first settlers in America, having to hunt to survive, soon found that their weapons were relatively ineffective, unless they could bring the quarry within range. From the native Indians, they discovered how to make and deploy decoys for this purpose (see Fig 1.3).

Fig 1.3 Early American Indian decoy made from rushes and feathers.

Market hunters

Hunting continued as a survival exercise throughout the seventeenth and eighteenth centuries, and as the demand for wildfowl increased and the guns improved, more and more hunters turned professional.

These market hunters were making thousands of decoys, and by the early 1900s were shooting over them and killing millions of birds every year. The first decoys to be made on a large enough scale to meet this demand were carved by watermen who, having seen the lucrative trade expand, became market hunters themselves. From simple tools, such as knives and hatchets, they fashioned decoys having a crude likeness to the ducks they were hunting. In time, the demand for decoys became so great that some of the hunters found it more profitable to abandon the shooting altogether and turned to carving decoys as a full-time occupation.

Migratory Bird Treaty 1918

The wholesale slaughter of millions of ducks every year ended with the passing of the Migratory Bird Treaty in 1918, which limited the number of ducks that could be shot annually.

The demand for shooting stools dropped dramatically, and the carvers were forced to look elsewhere for buyers. Some realised that as they improved the standard of carving and painting, they could sell their decoys to collectors for far larger sums than they were receiving from the hunters.

As competition in the trade increased, and as the carvers were no longer required to meet the hunter's need for durability and buoyancy, they began to pay more attention to shape and detail and produced what became known subsequently as decorative decoys.

The Ward brothers

It is generally agreed that decorative decoy carving began in Crissfield, Maryland, the home of the Ward brothers, Lem and Steve. Crissfield is a small fishing village on the south-east coast of Chesapeake Bay. Its economy is based solely on trading in seafood, particularly crabs and wildfowl (see Fig 1.4).

The Ward brothers were among the first to recognize the need to change from carving working decoys to producing highly decorative and lifelike carvings (see Figs 1.5, 1.6). Graceful poses, raised wings and exposed feet distinguished their carvings from the conventional hunting decoy. In doing so, they are credited with having created a new art form, and accordingly were awarded honorary doctorates by Salisbury State College, Maryland and, amongst many other honours, were presented to the president of the United States.

Although they became famous as wildfowl carving artists, the Ward brothers actually made their living very humbly as barbers for most of their lives. Large earnings from their carvings only came very late in their lives, and it was only then that they became full-time carvers. Steve died in 1976, Lem in 1984, and in their lifetime they had carved over 25,000 decoys between them.

The Great Depression

During the 1920s and 1930s, increased demand for decoys came from two quite different quarters. The depression in America brought a steep rise in the level of unemployment, and, with little or no money coming in, hunting ducks became a cheap way to feed the family. As a consequence more shooting stools were needed (see Fig 1.7).

At the same time, the demand for decorative decoys was also on the increase, but now it was coming from a clientele that included doctors, lawyers, wealthy businessmen and industrialists – all looking for objets d'art. Not surprisingly, as competition for ownership rose, so did the prices (see Fig 1.8).

Fig 1.4 The Ward brothers outside their workshop in Crissfield, Maryland.

MAXWELL HOUSE

Fig 1.5 Lem Ward working in his Crissfield, Maryland workshop.

Folk art

Carvings came to be regarded as a form of wildlife sculpture and widely accepted as folk art. Championing the cause of this new art form was Joel Barber, who, having been a collector of decoys since 1918, published what is still generally considered to be the seminal work on the subject, *Wildfowl Decoys*. In it, he recorded the history of decoys, included profiles of their makers and created in his readers an awareness of the artistic qualities of 'floating sculpture'.

Competitions and the Ward Foundation

National interest in wildfowl carving was fostered by the organization of competitions. However, little or no interest was shown in them until ornithologists, wildlife artists and well-known carvers accepted invitations to join the judging panels.

In 1968, in a tribute to the contribution made by the Ward brothers to the establishment of wildfowl carving as a nationally recognized art form, a group of Maryland businessmen, carvers and decoy collectors founded the Ward Foundation.

Its main purpose was, and continues to be, the promotion of interest in wildfowl carving through exhibitions and competitions. Its foundation coincided with the first Atlantic Flying Wildfowl Carving and Arts Exhibition in 1968, and the event has been held annually ever since.

The Foundation organized the first World Championship Wildfowl Carving Competition in 1971, and over the years it has tended to attract more public interest than the exhibition. It is now the most famous and lucrative competition of its type in the world, attracting thousands of entries, with prize money in 1993 totalling $93,000. The most coveted award carries the title Best in Show (World Champion), the winner receives $20,000 and the winning carving joins the permanent collection in the new Ward Museum.

Fig 1.6 Steve Ward working is his Crissfield, Maryland workshop.

Fig 1.7 A Ward wood duck carving made in 1928, during the Great Depression.

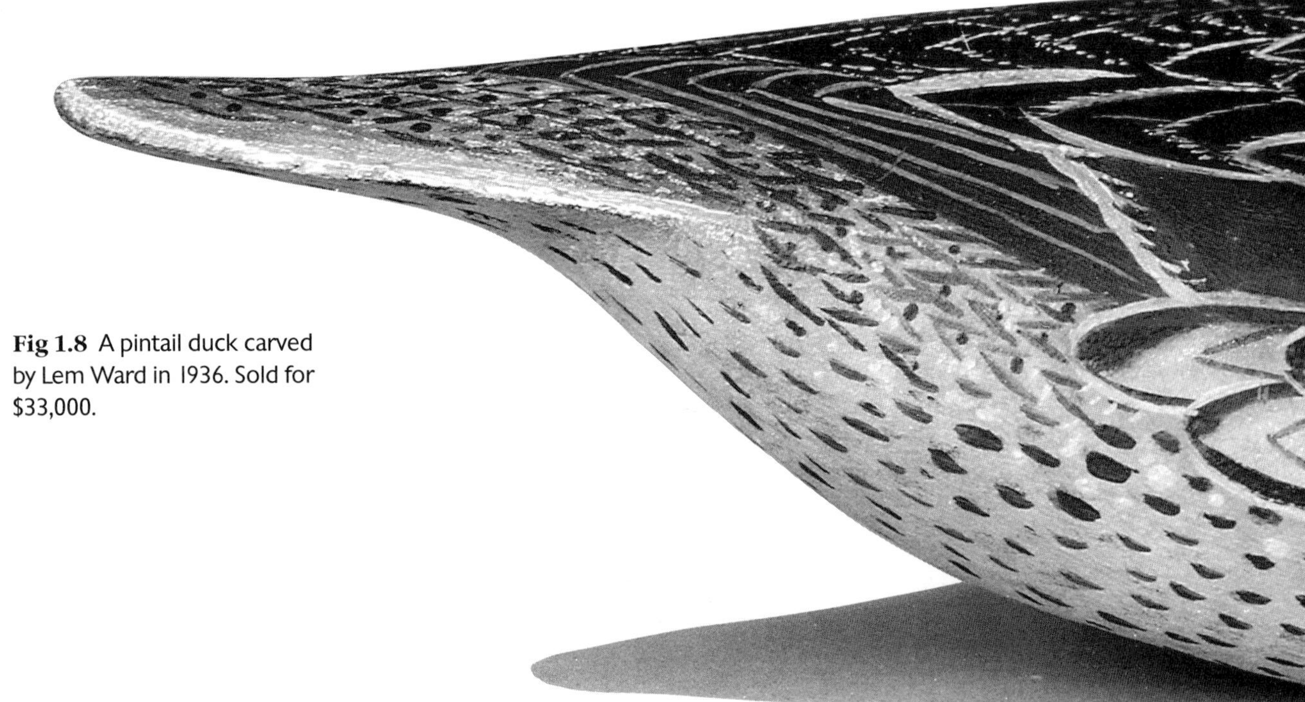

Fig 1.8 A pintail duck carved by Lem Ward in 1936. Sold for $33,000.

Fig 1.9 The new Ward Museum, Salisbury, Maryland, USA.

Fig 1.10 Common mergansers, by Chris Bonner. 1989 Decorative lifesize floating pairs, World Champion.

The Ward Museum

Situated in the centre of the traditional Chesapeake Bay wildfowling region, and named in honour of Steve and Lem Ward, is the new Ward Museum. After 20 years, planning, and at a cost of almost $6 million, the museum opened in April 1992 and is a four-and-a-quarter acre showplace for wildfowl art and wildfowl conservation (see Fig 1.9).

It is the largest museum in the world exclusively devoted to the promotion and perpetuation of wildfowl art. Among its many galleries is one in which the development of the hunting decoy throughout North America is traced, while in another, the decoy is displayed as a work of folk art in its own right. In the Wildfowl Gallery contemporary bird carvings can be seen, with pride of place being given to the winners of the World Championship Wildfowl Carving Competition from Novice to World Class (see Fig 1.10).

Ultimate realism

The move towards greater realism was given a major boost in 1970, when the Reverend Jack Drake, a carver from New Mexico, hit upon the idea of creating feathers on a wooden surface with an electrically heated burning tool. Hitherto, feathers had been carved into the surface of the wood or represented by painting.

The technique soon became very popular amongst the world's best carvers, and in the drive for greater realism, better equipment was developed to produce finer, more lifelike feathers. Texturing now plays a major role in the craft of wildfowl carving.

Wildfowl Carving in the UK

Professional hunters

In the United Kingdom, before World War I, the wildfowl of the fens and marshes were hunted by professional wildfowlers and fishermen.

They caught thousands of birds in Essex, Suffolk, Lincolnshire, Yorkshire and Norfolk, using spring-loaded nets, tide nets, rocket nets and decoys (such as the tunnel net decoy described earlier) and shipped them to Smithfield Market in London.

Huge punt guns were used that could kill up to 20–30 ducks with one blast. All these hunting methods created a demand for working decoys but not on such a large scale as that generated by the market hunters of North America.

Hunting declined after 1918, as many of the wildfowlers did not return from the war. Netting was banned in 1930 and more protection for the birds was being demanded by the public, which resulted in the Wild Bird Protection Act 1953–54.

Fig 1.11 The Gallery of Decoy Art in Chewton Mendip, Somerset, England.

Fig 1.12 Bob Ridges in full flow in the classroom at Faringdon Gurney, Somerset, England.

Professional wildfowlers became guides for shooting parties and more reliance was placed on plastic decoys. The demand for carved decoys slumped.

Bob Ridges

No book on wildfowl carving (decorative decoy carving) published in the UK could possibly omit a tribute to the work of the late Bob Ridges who died in 1989. Bob, as a merchant seaman, saw decoys being carved in the Mississippi port of New Orleans. He determined to take up the craft himself and introduced it into this country.

On retirement from the merchant navy, Bob went to the States to study decoy carving techniques, and on his return to the UK held his first exhibition in Bath. The success of this exhibition encouraged him to become a full-time carver, and with his wife, Sophie, he opened the Decoy Art Studio in 1982, running courses in wildfowl carving and painting, and publishing a quarterly magazine, *The Decoy Art Review*.

He was anxious to promote a wider public interest in wildfowl and wildfowl art, and to this end Bob opened the first gallery of decoy art in this country, in the Somerset village of Chewton Mendip (see Fig 1.11).

Many UK wildfowl carvers, including the author, owe their interest in the craft to Bob and the courses he ran at Faringdon Gurney and at various other locations throughout the country (see Fig 1.12).

BDWCA

With interest growing in the craft in the UK, and with the number of carvers and collectors increasing, it was decided in 1990 to form the British Decoy and Wildfowl Carvers Association. Its aim has been to bring together those interested in creating wood carvings of wildfowl in any style, be they traditional decoys, decorative wildfowl, or stylized carvings.

Membership, though not large by American standards, is expanding annually, and includes both professional and amateur carvers. It holds a national competition annually, continuing the tradition started by Bob Ridges in 1986 (see Figs 1.13 and 1.14). Members are kept in touch with each other and with any new developments in the craft through the publication of a quarterly newsletter and regional group meetings around the country. The Association is always keen to attract novice carvers and every effort is made to encourage them to improve their skills and enjoy all aspects of the craft.

Courses in the UK

Many courses in wildfowl carving are run in this country, from those specifically designed for the novice with no previous carving experience, to the more specialized courses, where distinguished carvers from the States

Fig 1.13 Competitors and the public at the BDWCA competition held at Crewe, England in November of 1993.

Fig 1.14 *Blue Tits,* by Frank Hayward, awarded a first in the intermediate level 'Other Species' category. BDWCA national competition, Crewe 1993.

conduct seminars covering specific aspects of carving or painting (see Fig 1.15).

In answer to the question: 'could I learn the craft?' I always respond by stressing that above all, wildfowl woodcarving requires patience and a little imagination. Since the teaching on courses is based on breaking down the processes of carving, texturing and painting into progressive and simple stages, the skills needed are soon acquired (see Fig 1.16).

The craft is not a male preserve. In fact, many of the very best carvers in this country and the USA are women. The techniques used in this type of carving do not require strength but depend more on skill, attention to detail, and powers of observation. These qualities are to be found equally distributed between the sexes.

Fig 1.15 The author preparing tufted blanks for students at the WI College, Denham, Oxford, England.

Fig 1.16 The author with a group of students at Missenden Abbey Summer School, Bucks.

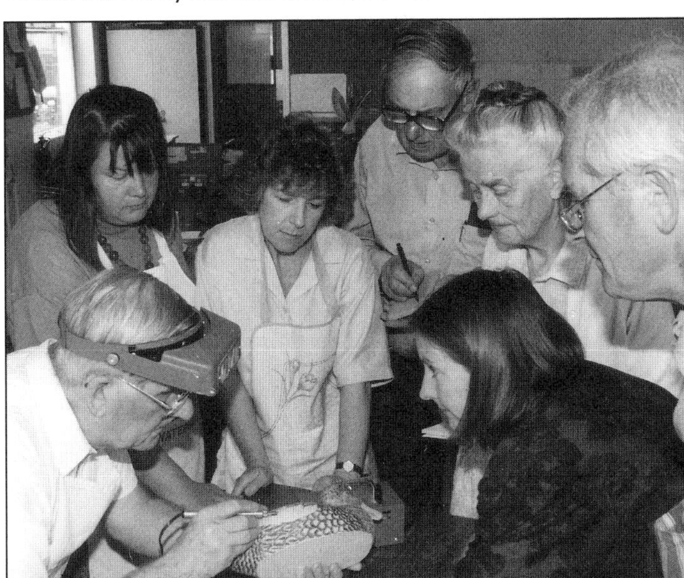

CHAPTER **2**

The Duck

Strictly speaking, only ducks, geese and swans are true wildfowl and of these, ducks are the most numerous, there being some 146 species around the world. There are many other birds classified as waterfowl and from the carver's point of view they can all be created realistically in wood using the techniques covered in this book.

However, to be successful, some knowledge of the anatomy and the topography of the subject is essential. The carver should certainly become familiar with the characteristics of the feather groups, with those parts of the ducks which determine their shape (see Fig 2.1) and with the major differences between types.

Dabblers and Divers

Dabbling ducks

Dabblers, marsh, pond or puddle ducks are primarily surface feeders or 'upenders', and there are some 39 species throughout the world (see Fig 2.2).

Adaptation to their environment includes a longer and thinner body than the diver, to facilitate freer movement amongst the reeds, and much larger and more powerful wings, to enable them to rise more or less vertically from the water when danger looms (see Fig 2.3).

Since they do not depend so much on speed through the water to obtain their food, their feet tend to be smaller than those of the diver. Viewed from the side, their feet are set further forward and more to the side of the body than the diver (see Fig 2.4).

Usually the male and female have quite marked differences in the colour of their plumage, and most have a distinctive iridescence on their secondary and/or head feathers.

Examples of dabblers are: mallard, wigeon, green- and blue-winged teal, wood duck, shoveler and black duck.

Diving ducks

As the name suggests, they dive to search for their food and can remain submerged for some time. There are some 20 species of diving ducks throughout the world.

In the main, they are shorter and heavier in the body than dabblers (see Fig 2.5), and viewed from the side, their legs are set well back towards the tail and give the duck a much more upright stance on dry land (see Fig 2.4).

They have larger feet and more powerful legs to help them swim faster and to assist them in their characteristic way of taking off by 'running' on the surface of the water.

Examples of diving ducks are: common and Barrow's goldeneye, canvasback, greater and lesser scaup.

Anatomy and Topography

The feather

The feather is a very complex structure particularly well suited to fulfilling the triple functions of keeping the bird warm, repelling moisture and helping it to fly.

A single feather consists of a centre shaft, which thickens into a hollow quill and through which nutrients are passed from the body to the barbs (see Fig 2.6). From each side of the shaft are the vanes, which are curved in the shape of a shallow S to create the necessary aerodynamic lift and to provide an efficient seal between the feathers.

Fig 2.1 The topography of the duck.

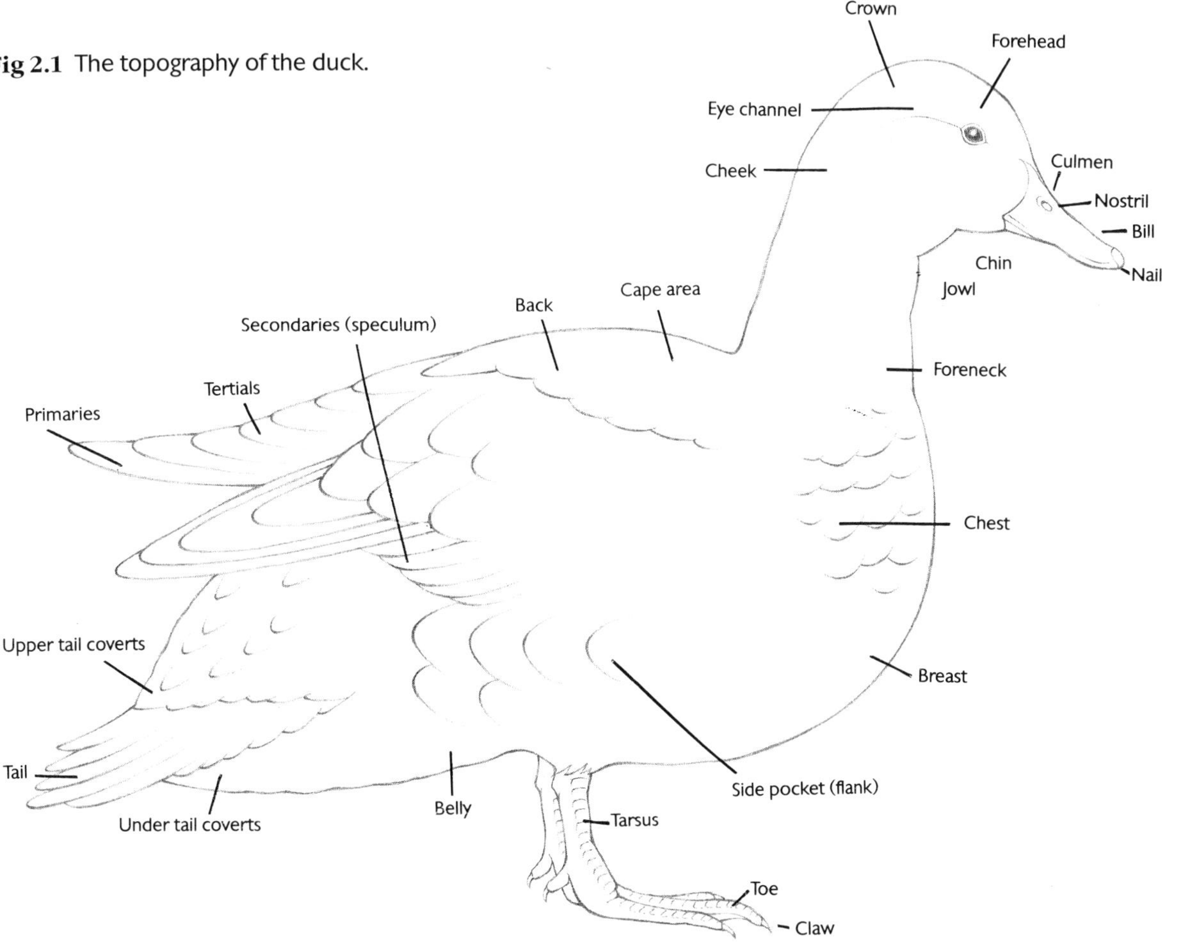

Fig 2.2 The mallard is a dabbler duck and the most familiar duck in the world.

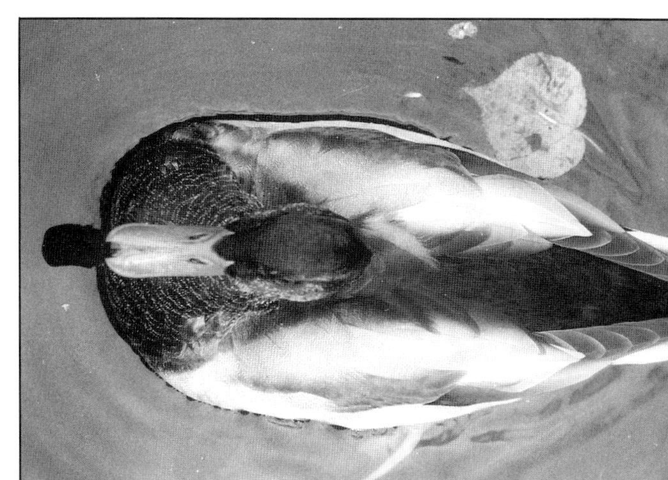

Fig 2.3 Dabblers tend to have thinner and longer bodies than divers. This shape facilitates freer movement amongst the reeds.

Fig 2.4 The diving duck's legs are set well back from the middle of its body *(a)*. The dabbler, or puddleduck *(b)*, has its legs set in the middle of the body.

All feathers are slightly convex shaped, and the overlap between them traps air, ensuring efficient thermal insulation and improved buoyancy. It also allows water to flow freely over the bird's body.

Projecting at an angle from the shaft of the flight and tail feathers are the barbs, along which are barbules and tiny hooklike barbicels, which interlock and hold the barbs together in much the same way as Velcro holds materials together.

Splits in the vane, particularly towards the ends of flight and tail feathers, occur where either the barbicels have separated temporarily or have been damaged. Older birds often have very ragged edges to their flight tail feathers (see Fig 2.7).

Preening realigns the barbs, combing them back into place. It also involves transferring oil from the preen gland to the surface of the feathers to restore the waterproofing and buoyancy.

The lower, thicker part of the shaft is the quill, and it is through this that the feather is supplied with blood during its growth. When fully grown the blood supply ceases and the quill is sealed off.

Functions of feathers

The bird's feathers serve four main functions:

- To provide an insulating layer to retain body heat.
- To create an efficient aerodynamic surface to facilitate flight.
- To provide a waterproof coating and ensure maximum buoyancy.
- The colour of the plumage serves two purposes: (1) to provide camouflage as a protection from predators and (2) to facilitate identity between species and the sexes.

Fig 2.5 In the main, divers are shorter and heavier in the body than dabblers.

Colour and moulting

The basic colours of the plumage, the reds, browns and greens etc., are produced by a combination of pigments, while the very bright iridescent colours are due to microscopic waxlike structures on the feathers which tend to refract light to varying degrees. A good example of this phenomenon is the variations in colour from blue to green of the head of a mallard drake when viewed from different angles.

However, observation over a period of a year shows that the colour of the plumage does not remain constant as birds periodically replace their worn feathers by moulting. During this period the old feathers either fall out or are forced out as the new ones grow.

The usually colourful drake goes into an eclipse moult shortly after the female starts incubating the eggs, and sheds all his flight feathers at once. Fortunately, food can be found in relative safety for, although he retains considerable, if restricted, power of movement during the moult, he remains very vulnerable to predators at this time. The brightly coloured feathers are slowly replaced with a less colourful plumage, similar to that of the female, and throughout this period he takes on a rather drab and scruffy appearance. In time, a second moult takes place and the breeding plumage is restored once more.

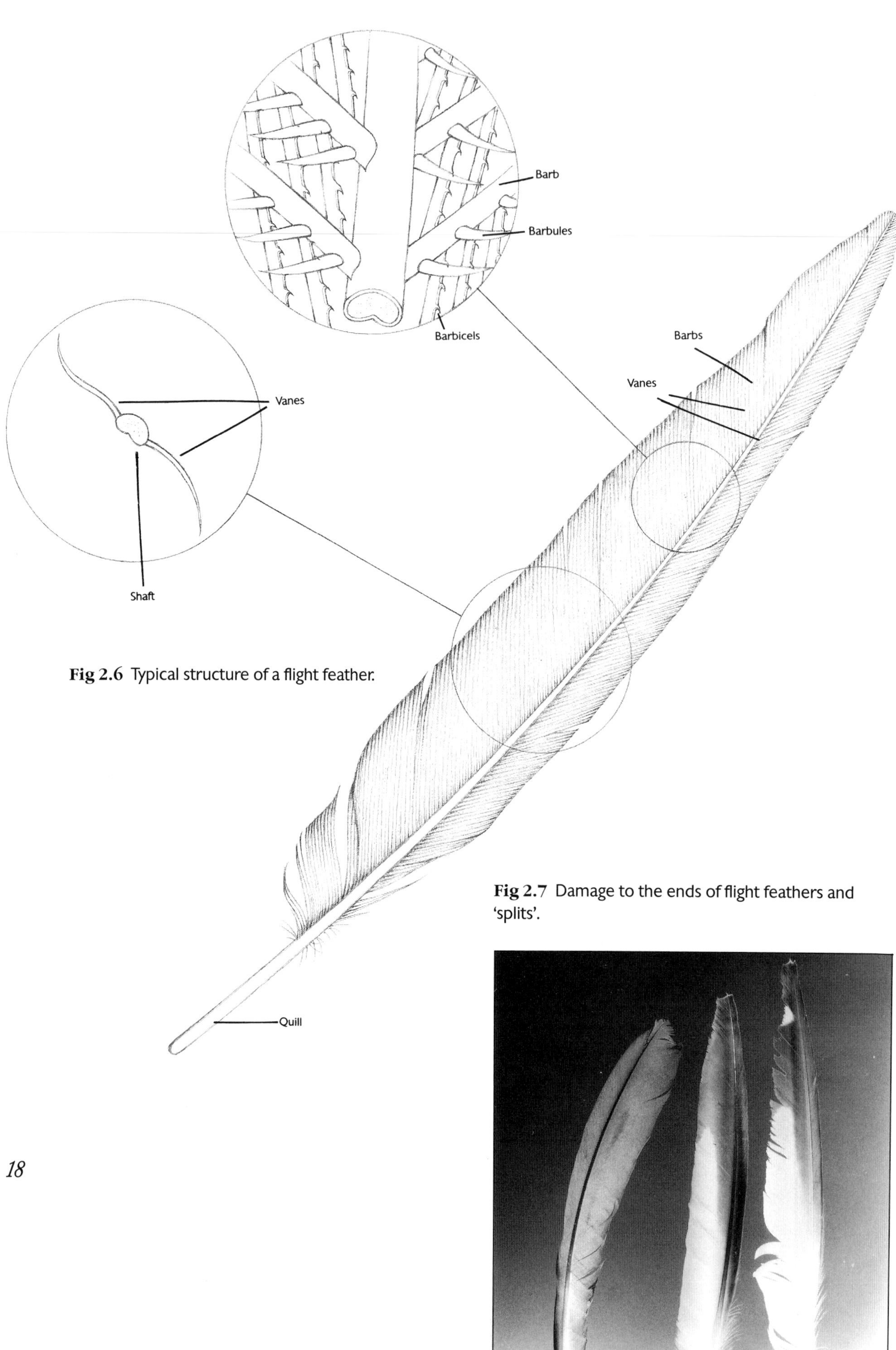

Fig 2.6 Typical structure of a flight feather.

Fig 2.7 Damage to the ends of flight feathers and 'splits'.

Feather groups

The carver's knowledge should also extend to an appreciation of the major feather groups (see Figs 2.8 and 2.9). Wing and body feathers are generally referred to as contour feathers. These include not only the primary and secondary flight feathers and the tail feathers but also the softer, smaller feathers that cover the body and give it its characteristic shape.

Primary feathers

The primary feathers are the larger and stiffer of the contour feathers and are attached to the bones in the hard part of the wing (see Fig 2.10). Their movement is controlled by large flight muscles connected to the heel of the breast bone. Each primary feather can be rotated either independently or in concert with the primary feather of the other wing. The primaries can also be moved as a group with the other feathers of the wing, all of which give the bird considerable manoeuvrability in the air. If the primaries are badly damaged or lost, flight becomes impossible.

Novice carvers will normally work from a blank (see page 45) in which the wings are folded. In this characteristic position, the primaries will appear as two crossed overlaid

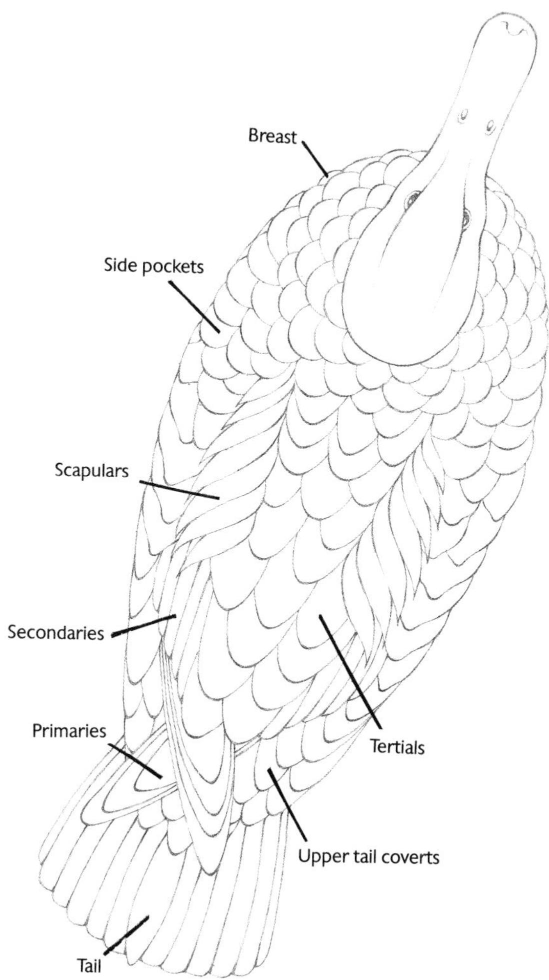

Fig 2.9 Feather groups of the goldeneye.

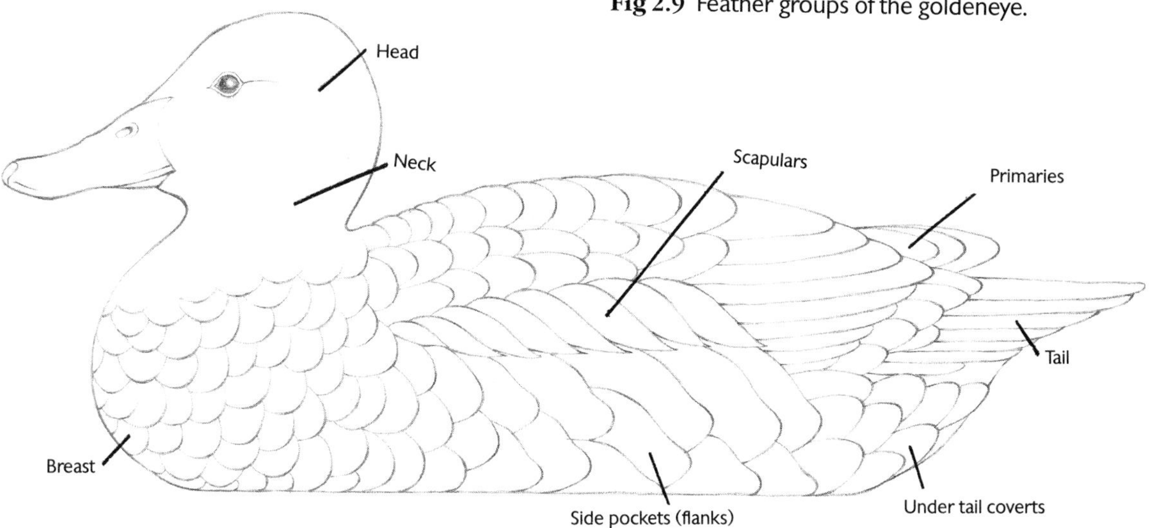

Fig 2.8 Feather groups of the goldeneye.

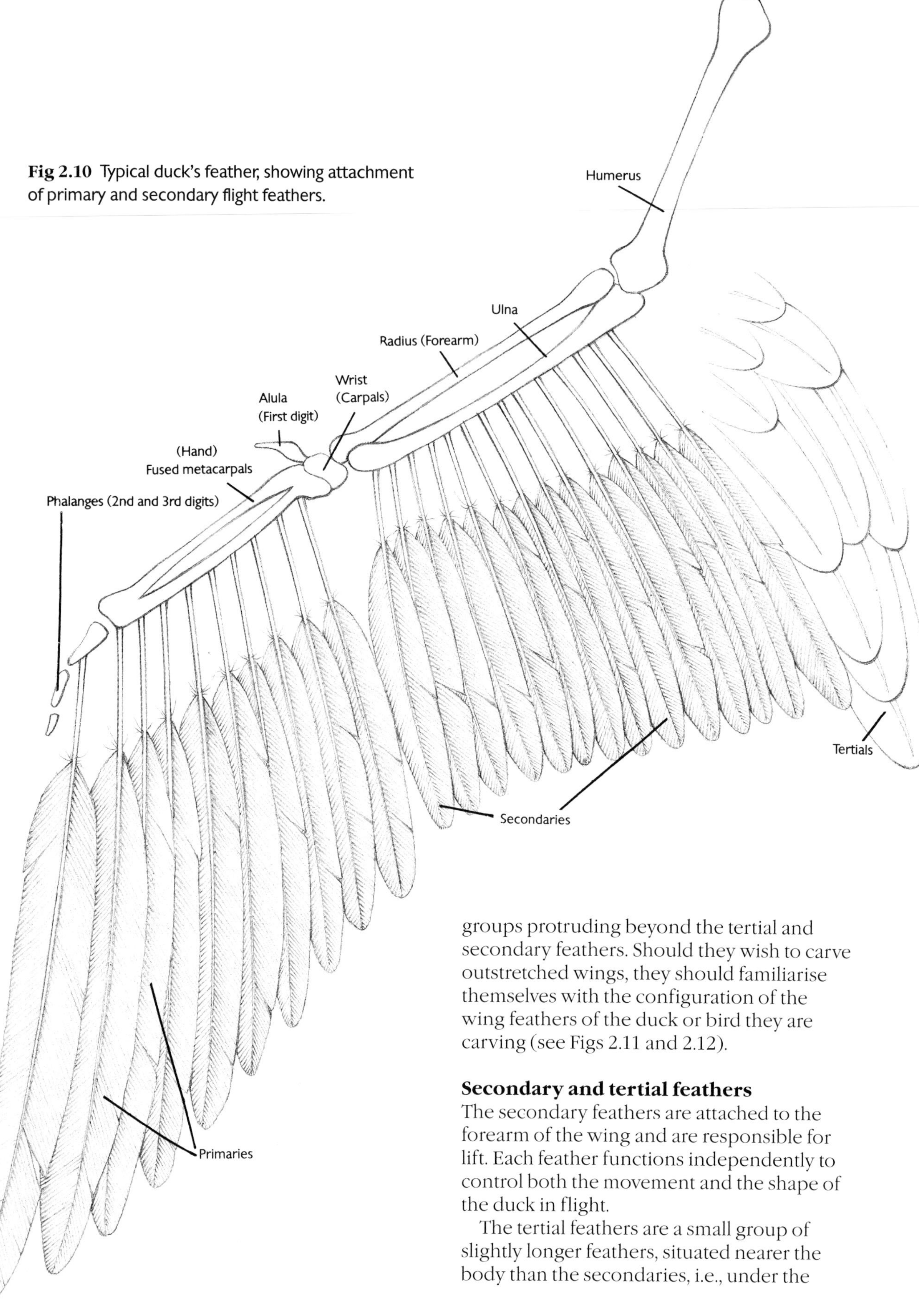

Fig 2.10 Typical duck's feather, showing attachment of primary and secondary flight feathers.

groups protruding beyond the tertial and secondary feathers. Should they wish to carve outstretched wings, they should familiarise themselves with the configuration of the wing feathers of the duck or bird they are carving (see Figs 2.11 and 2.12).

Secondary and tertial feathers

The secondary feathers are attached to the forearm of the wing and are responsible for lift. Each feather functions independently to control both the movement and the shape of the duck in flight.

The tertial feathers are a small group of slightly longer feathers, situated nearer the body than the secondaries, i.e., under the

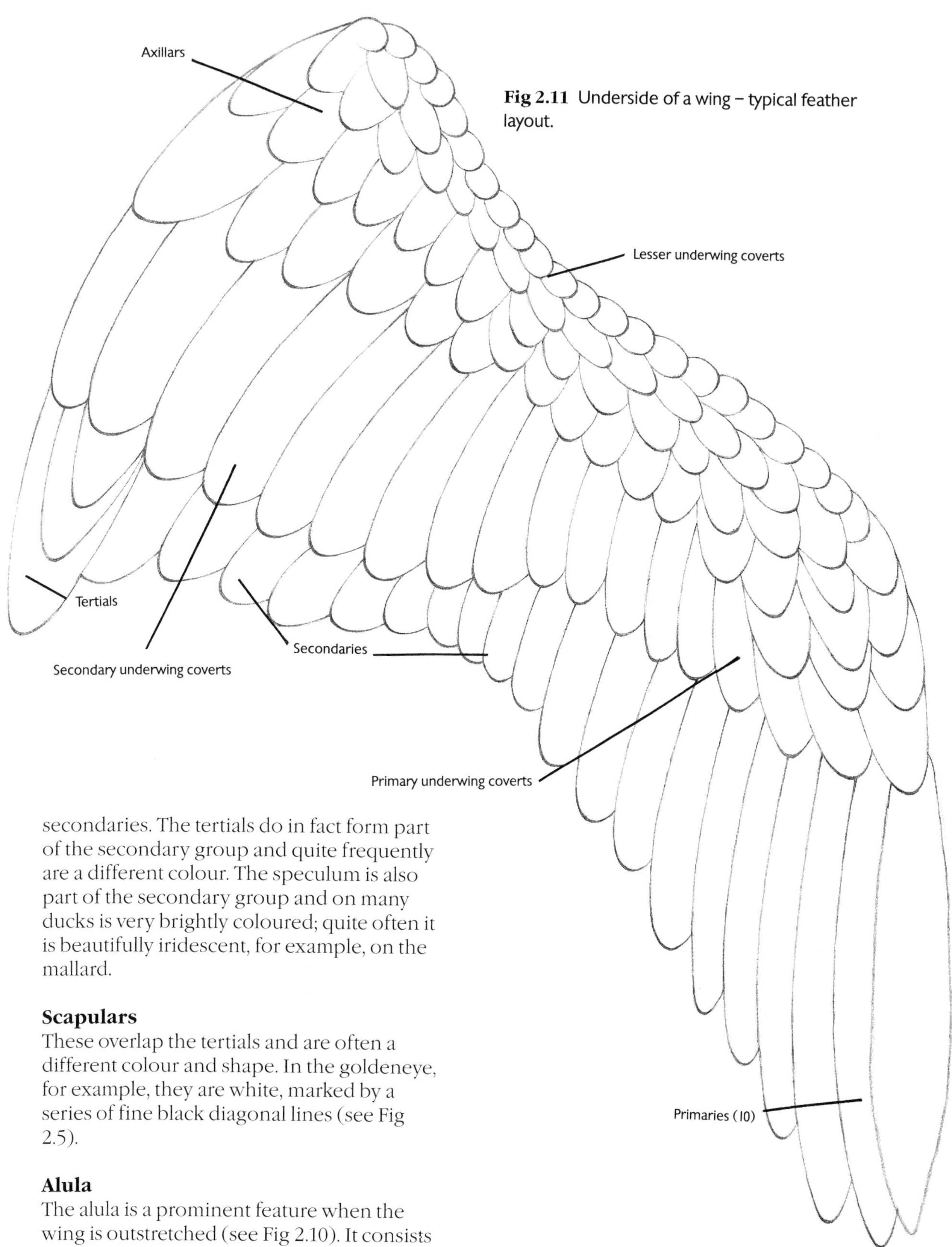

Fig 2.11 Underside of a wing – typical feather layout.

secondaries. The tertials do in fact form part of the secondary group and quite frequently are a different colour. The speculum is also part of the secondary group and on many ducks is very brightly coloured; quite often it is beautifully iridescent, for example, on the mallard.

Scapulars

These overlap the tertials and are often a different colour and shape. In the goldeneye, for example, they are white, marked by a series of fine black diagonal lines (see Fig 2.5).

Alula

The alula is a prominent feature when the wing is outstretched (see Fig 2.10). It consists

Fig 2.12 Upper side of wing.

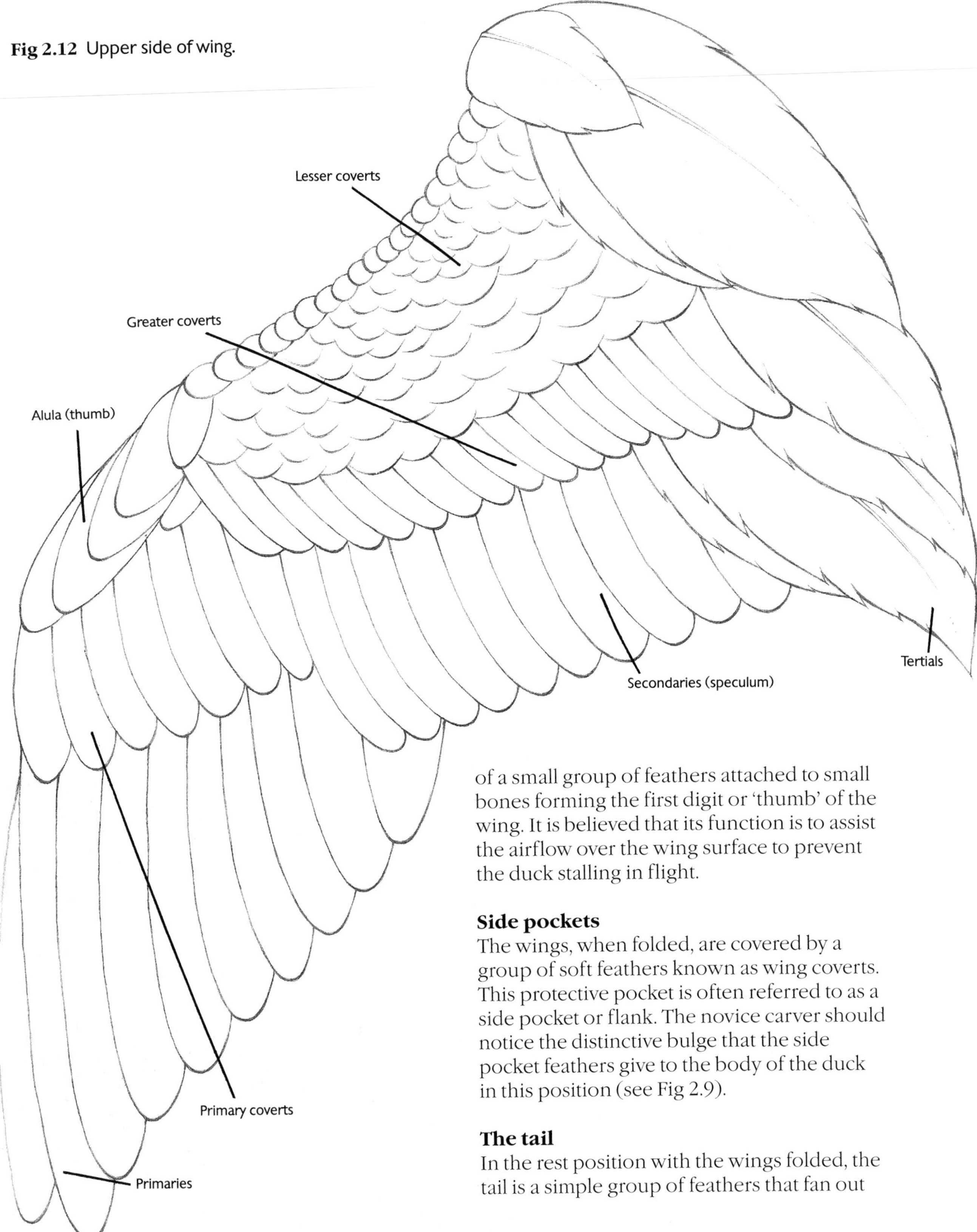

of a small group of feathers attached to small bones forming the first digit or 'thumb' of the wing. It is believed that its function is to assist the airflow over the wing surface to prevent the duck stalling in flight.

Side pockets

The wings, when folded, are covered by a group of soft feathers known as wing coverts. This protective pocket is often referred to as a side pocket or flank. The novice carver should notice the distinctive bulge that the side pocket feathers give to the body of the duck in this position (see Fig 2.9).

The tail

In the rest position with the wings folded, the tail is a simple group of feathers that fan out from the body, with the upper and lower coverts merging with the tail at the point where the body meets the tail. In flight, the upper and lower coverts assist the airflow over the tail (see Figs 2.8, 2.9 and 2.13).

The duck is able to twist and turn in flight by combining wing and tail movements; the tail feathers give stability and act both as a rudder in flight and as an air brake on landing. In fact, any movement the duck makes is reflected in the configuration of the tail. For example, when preening, the tail may be angled and the feathers fanned out to compensate for body movement.

The tail is a single layer of feathers and therefore the edges must be carved as thin as possible. To ensure that both the top and bottom of the carved tail match, the novice is recommended to draw in the centre feather first (see Fig 2.14).

Head and neck feathers

The feathers on the duck's head and neck are very closely packed together and are overlaid to the extent that they appear to merge (see Fig 2.15). The individual feathers are small and narrow and do not have interlocking barbules. They therefore feel much softer than those feathers that do have them.

Since most ducks have the ability to raise and lower the feathers of the neck and head slightly, the surface is gently contoured and the carving should reflect this.

Breast feathers

The breast feathers are also small but become progressively larger nearer and below the water line. Since they perform the important function of insulating and waterproofing, they, too, are very thick and closely packed (see Fig 2.16).

Fig 2.13 Layout of tail feathers.

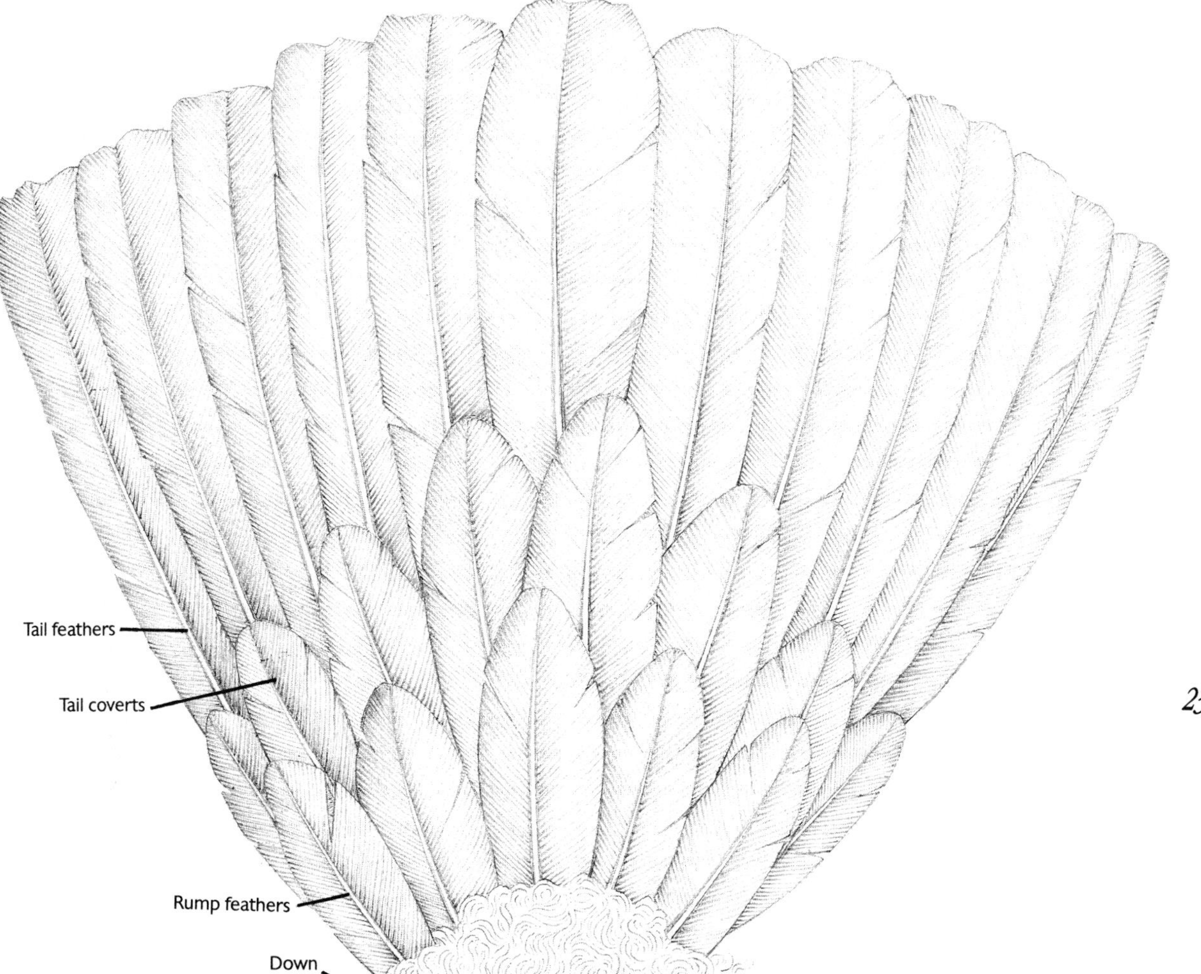

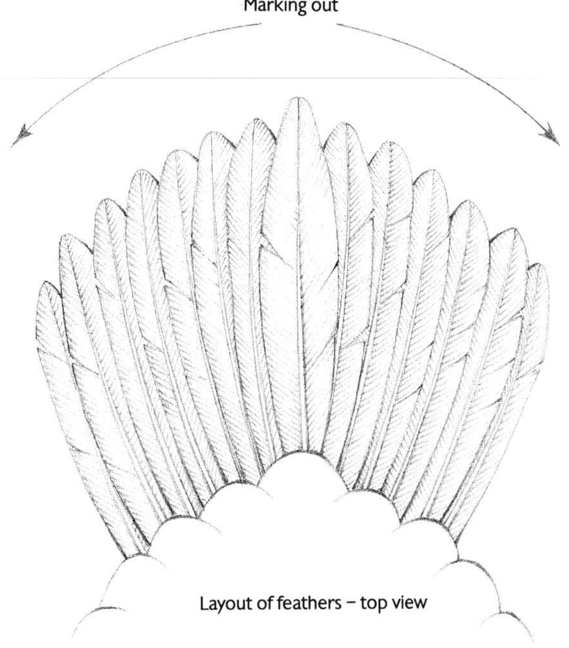

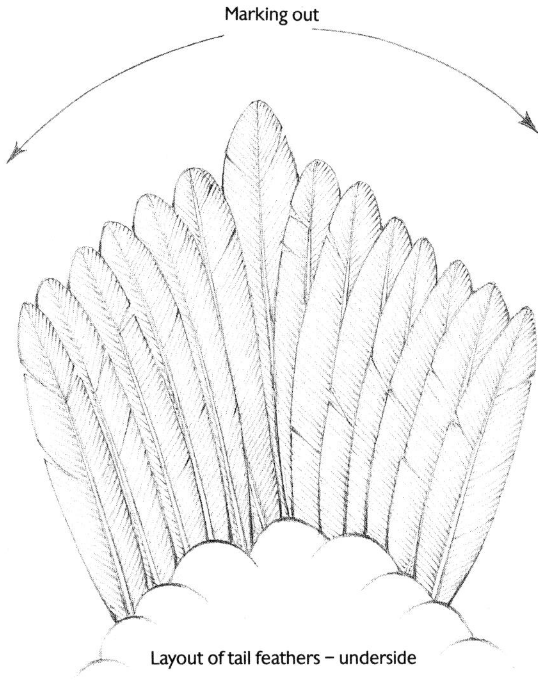

Fig 2.14 Mark out the position of the centre feather first, and work outwards.

Feather numbers

Wildfowl may have anything up to 25,000 feathers and therefore the carver can only really represent this number in a simplified way. The feathers on a live bird merge and may not be discernible as individual feathers or even as identifiable groups. This problem is worse with the feathers of a study skin, as they may well have been badly disturbed or even damaged. In effect, only those feathers which are visible on the surface are carved, and the carver, therefore, in drawing out his feather pattern, must try to create the illusion

Fig 2.15 The small feathers on the head and neck are overlaid and appear to merge.

Fig 2.16 The thick, closely packed breast feathers (mallard drake).

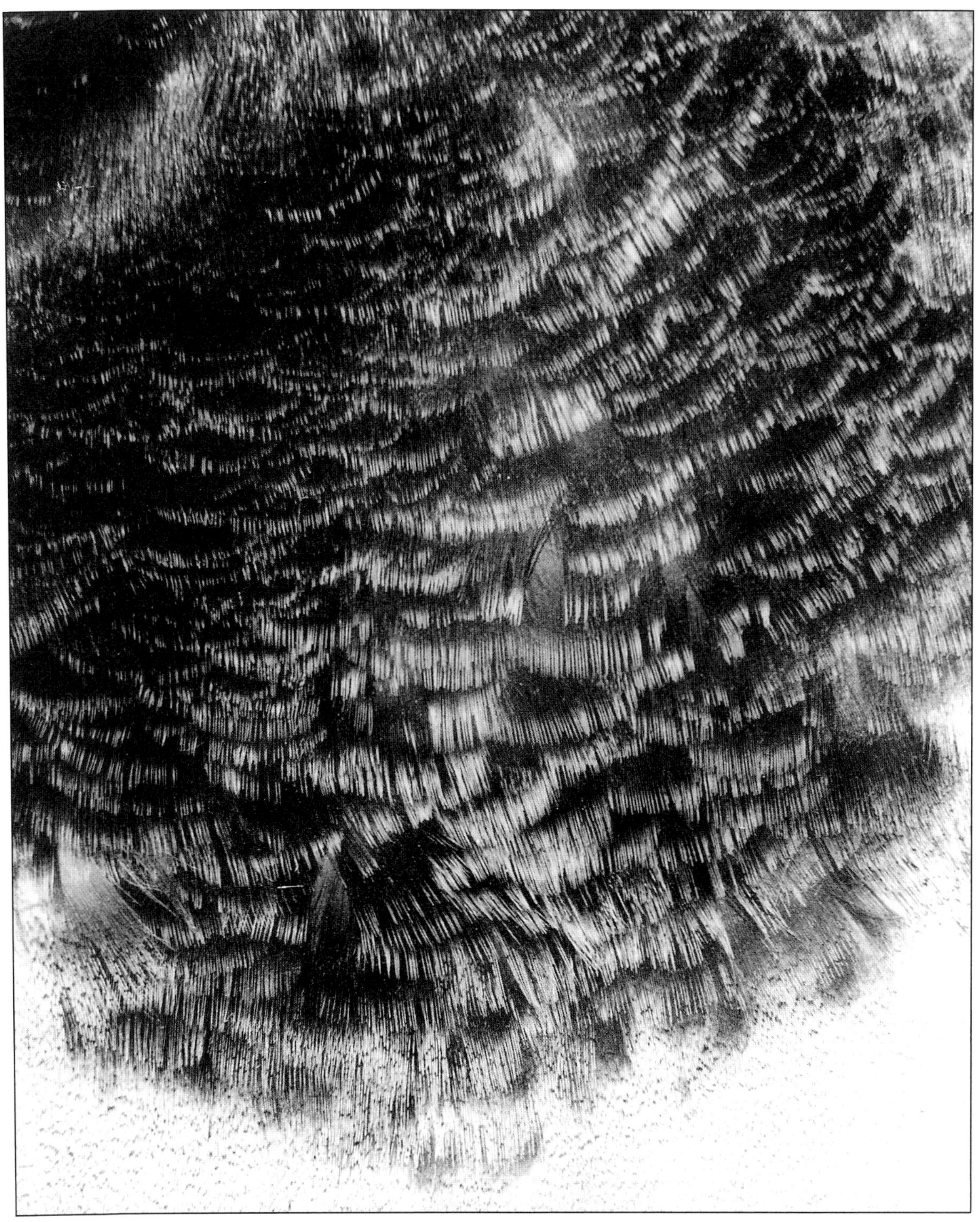

that these feathers are overlaying many others (see Fig 2.17).

On most wildfowl the feather layers are quite deep and soft, and a good carver will create the appearance of depth and softness through contouring, texturing and painting.

The bill

Although plastic in appearance, the bill is not dead and insensitive; it is well endowed with nerve cells and is relatively soft, with a very distinctive hardened tip to both mandibles called the nail. One of the functions of the latter is believed to be to assist the chick to break free of the shell when hatching out.

The bill is subject to wear and tear, and to compensate for this, it grows very slowly throughout the lifetime of the duck. The twin factors of wear and tear and continual growth give rise to noticeably different shapes and sizes of bills within one species.

The general configuration of the bill of any particular species is the outcome of evolutionary changes brought about by the need for efficiency when feeding. A good example of this adaptation is provided by the fish-eating merganser, with its long serrated bill (see Fig 2.18).

Fig 2.17 Creating the illustion of many more feathers than are actually carved.

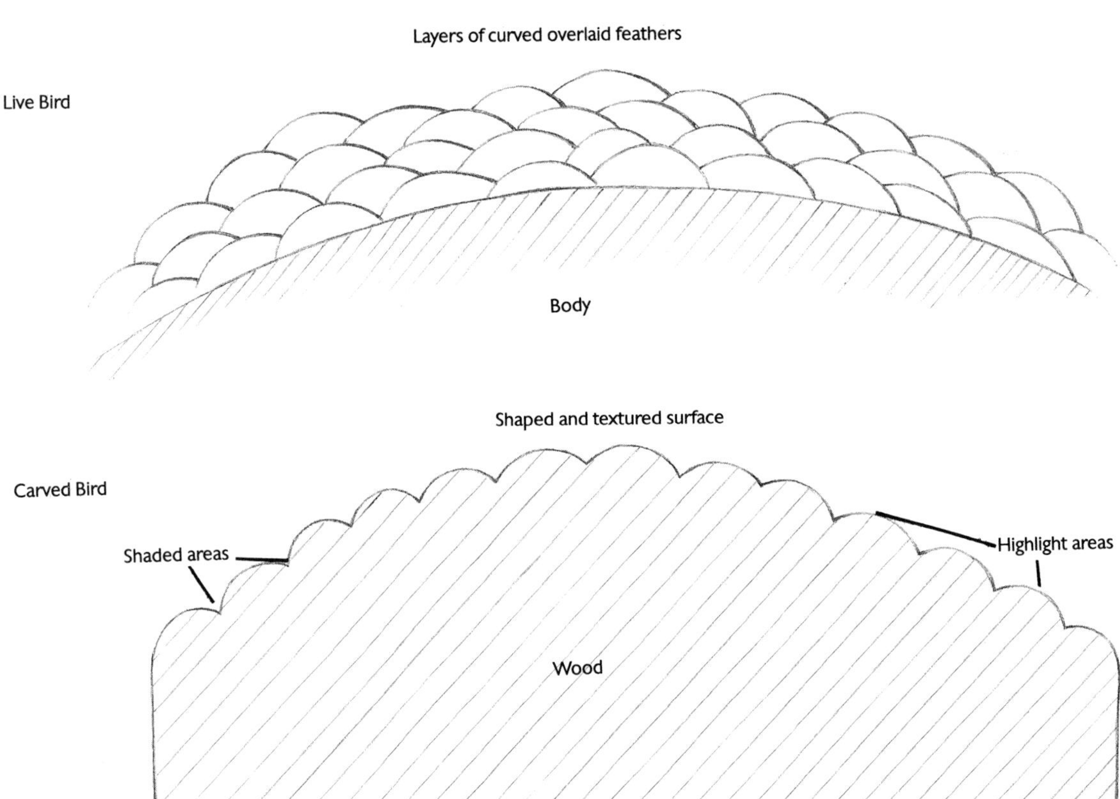

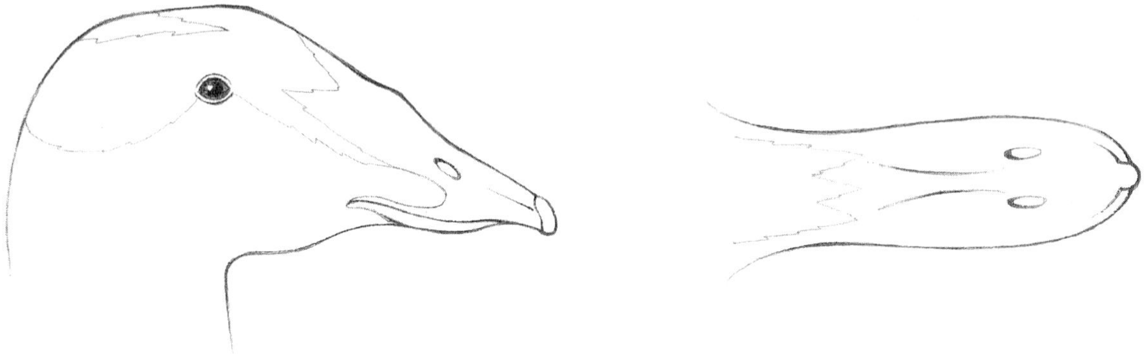

Bottom feeder (eider)

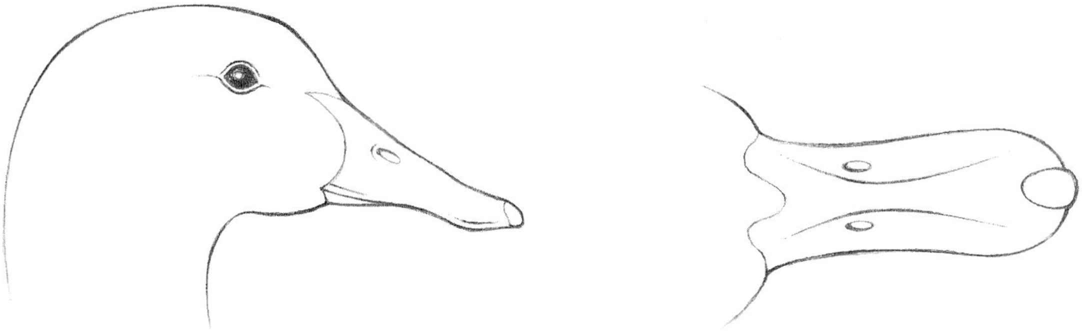

Dabbler (mallard)

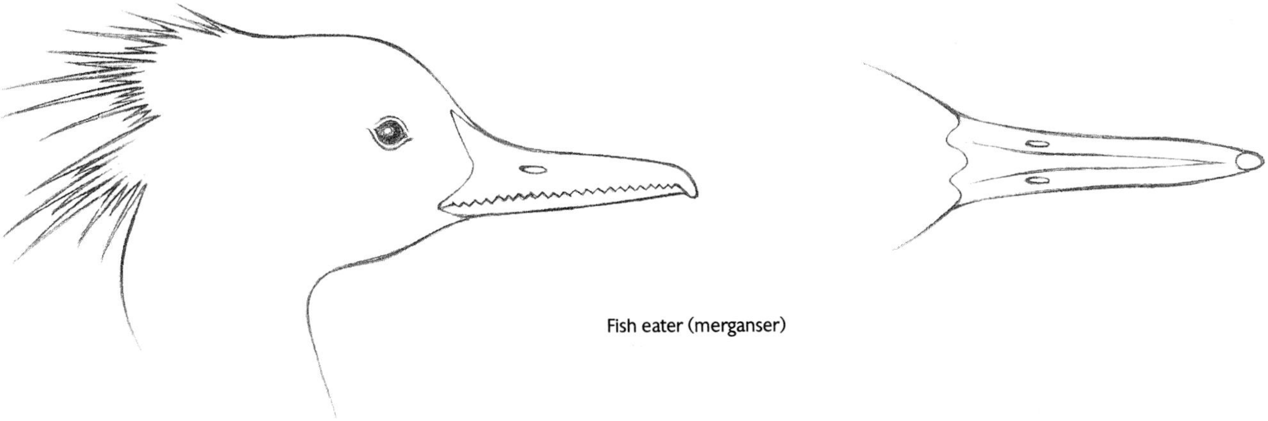

Fish eater (merganser)

Fig 2.18 Evolution has created distinctive bill shapes.

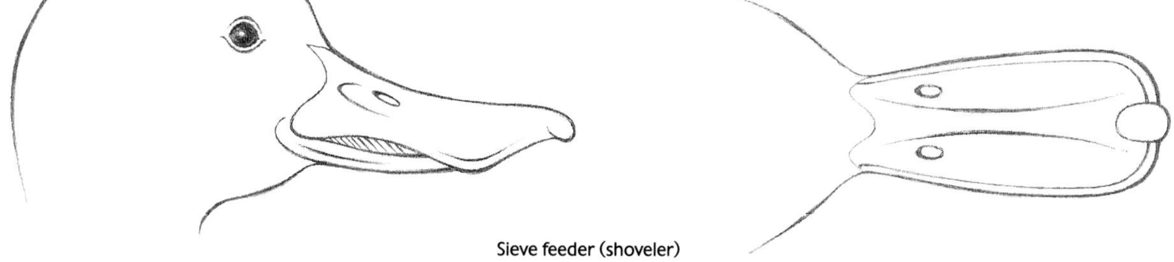

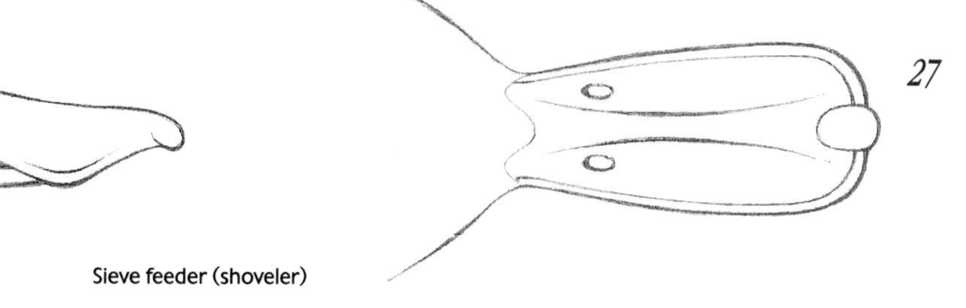

Sieve feeder (shoveler)

Fig 2.19 A study bill of a mallard showing the serrations (lamellae) along the edges of the mandibles.

The carver should note that when the bill opens, it is the lower mandible that hinges downwards while the upper remains fixed in relation to the head. The upper mandible closes over the lower and consequently, for much of its length the lower mandible is not seen.

Both mandibles have serrations or lamellae along their edges, which help to filter food from the water during the feeding process (see Fig 2.19).

Reference Sources

A duck carving of any sort should be regarded as a project requiring a great deal of planning and research. References to shape, dimensions, colour of the plumage, and characteristics or special features that distinguish the particular duck being carved are essential.

Illustrations and photographs

The wildfowl carver should be constantly on the lookout for illustrations and photographs of birds and ducks to build up his reference library. Photographs should be sharply focused and include views of the subject from all angles. Wherever possible, close-ups should be sought, especially of details of those parts of the bird or duck that are not normally visible, or are not usually illustrated.

Skins and mounted specimens

These can be extremely useful for studying feather detail. If they are well-preserved and are undamaged, the plumage will have lost little of its brilliance and the colours can be relied upon as a good reference source (see Fig 2.20). Do not, however, take measurements or create feather patterns from mounted specimens or study skins. Measurements and feather patterns are drastically distorted upon the drying of the skin that occurs after the death of the bird.

Study bills and moulded casts

The best study bills are cast from fresh specimens to avoid the inevitable bill shrinkage that takes place after death. They can be used, therefore, for taking accurate measurements. They show remarkably fine detail and, as part of the head is always included, the location of the eyes can also be determined precisely (see Fig 2.21).

Casts have been made from carvings of some of the best carvers in the USA and Canada. They are excellent for studying body shape, eye placement and feather detail. A moulded bird is also useful to the non-carver and to the beginner as a subject on which to practise painting techniques.

Fig 2.20 Study skins of a male mallard (top) and a goldeneye (bottom).

Reserves and parks

One of the keys to success in wildfowl carving is undoubtedly close observation of the life of the subjects you have to carve. In the UK there are over 90 reserves belonging to the Royal Society for the Protection of Birds and the Wildfowl and Wetlands Trust that are open to the public for observation of birds (see Fig 2.22). For the carver wishing to take photographs, patience and a very long long-focus lens are essential.

On the other hand, as ducks are naturally very friendly and inquisitive creatures, visitors to the seven reserves of the Wildfowl and Wetlands Trust can usually get very close to many of them. They are usually quite happy to feed from the hand, and, therefore, it is possible to obtain really detailed close-ups. As five of the centres have collections of thousands of captive wildfowl from all parts of the world, the carver can build up a library of photographs of some of the most common and the most rare of wildfowl species.

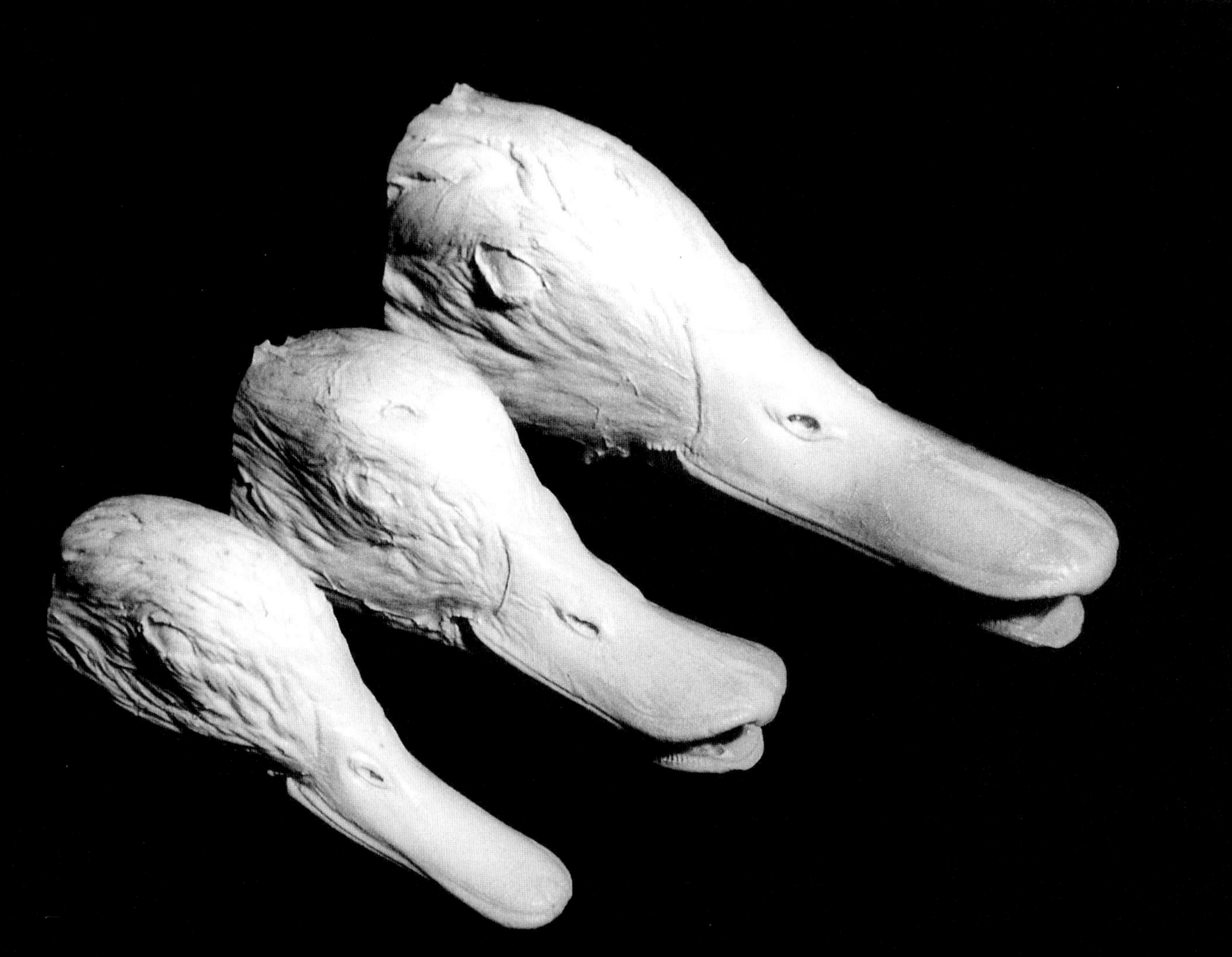

Fig 2.21 Study bills make an excellent reference source. From top to bottom (all are male): mallard, lesser scaup and green-winged teal.

Fig 2.22 The Wildfowl and Wetlands Trust reserve at Slimbridge, Gloucester.

Filing

Accessing reference material when a project is being planned can be very frustrating without a properly organized system of filing.

I maintain two sets of general files, one holds the names, arranged in alphabetical order, of all the ducks and birds about which I have information that would be helpful when carving any of them. The other file details the location of information and illustrations on specific techniques.

At the planning stage of each carving, I open a new file/folder on the subject of the carving. In this will go the patterns and any photographs or illustrations, together with notes covering painting details, eye size and any special features that may require attention. Such a folder proves an enormous help in executing the carving.

CHAPTER 3
Equipment

This book sets out to introduce the reader to the craft of wildfowl carving through the use of relatively inexpensive hand tools, and the application of techniques that might reasonably be expected to be learnt in a very short time.

More expensive powered tools certainly reduce the time spent on various tasks, but arguably, with experience and the acquisition of the appropriate skills, the quality achieved is much the same. Even in the later stages of their working lives the Ward brothers, although they had access to a whole variety of power tools, limited their use to a bandsaw, a belt sander and a drill press, preferring to work directly on the wood with familiar hand tools.

Most newcomers to the craft are astounded by its inherent simplicity. Not only are very few tools required to get started, but it can be practised on any convenient work surface having a nearby electrical supply. In fact, a retired doctor friend of mine carves contentedly by his lounge fire with a dust sheet on the floor and a labrador at his feet. I do not recommend this approach, but it does serve to illustrate the point I am making.

Fig 3.1 shows all the tools a student with no previous knowledge or experience might use on a week's practical course to produce a carved and textured duck. This starter kit includes a blank, a Hot Tool for texturing, a round file, a soft pencil, a craft knife and two sanding strips (one coarse and one fine).

Knives

When buying any hand tools for carving, the soundest advice for the beginner is to buy the best that he can afford. This applies particularly to the choice of knives.

My own preference, and it is shared by many professional carvers in the UK and the USA, is for knives made especially for woodcarving by Alan Knotts, of Knotts Knives of North Carolina. Committed to excellence in

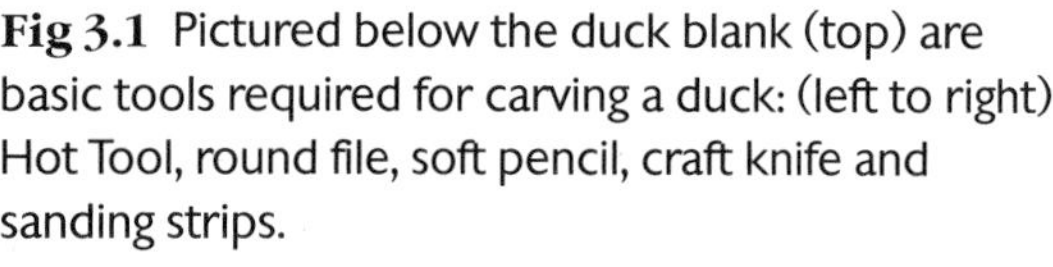

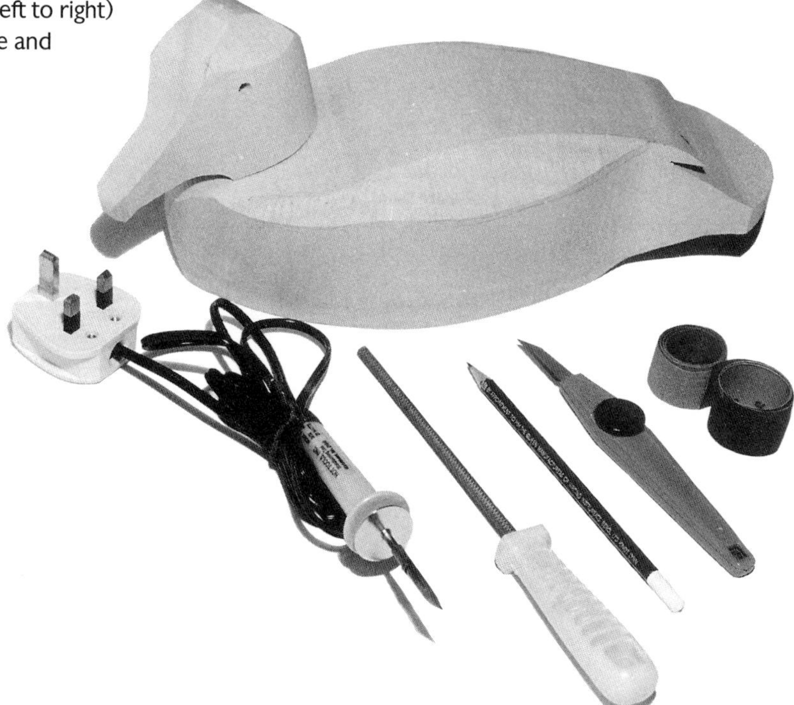

Fig 3.1 Pictured below the duck blank (top) are basic tools required for carving a duck: (left to right) Hot Tool, round file, soft pencil, craft knife and sanding strips.

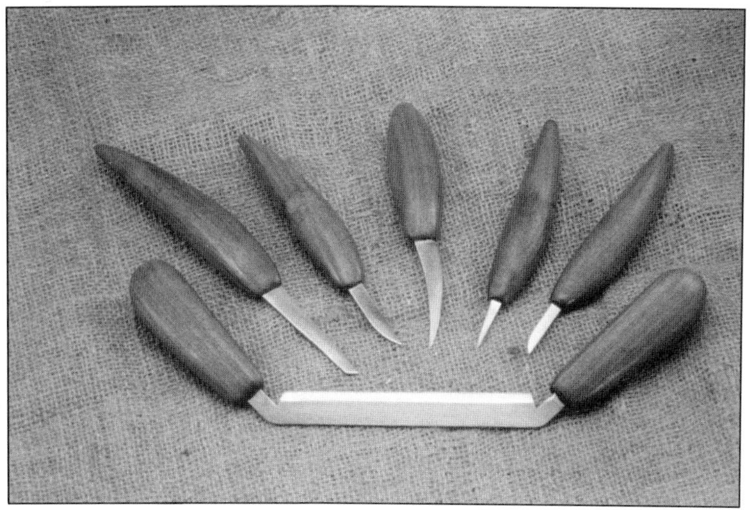

Fig 3.2 Knotts' knives. From left to right, with blade lengths: heavy removal knife – 2 7/8in; general carving knife – 1 7/8in; Cajun-style tupelo knife – 2 3/4in; two detailing knives – 1 1/4in. Below: drawknife – 5/8in wide, 5in long.

craftsmanship, using only the time proven techniques of hand grinding, polishing and sharpening, his name has become a byword for excellence in woodcarving tools (see Fig 3.2).

In the UK, knives of comparable quality and balance in use are those made and sold by David Tippey (see Fig 3.3).

The craft knife

The craft knife shown in the beginner's starter kit (see Fig 3.1), with its interchangeable blades, is a very versatile tool, and an ideal first knife. It is equally at home shaping (see Fig 3.4) as it is relieving feathers (see Fig 3.5) but, although the blades are very sharp, they have a tendency to break on encountering hard wood or if bent too far.

The X-acto knife

The X-acto knife is another relatively inexpensive knife, and is widely used in a number of crafts. It is an extremely useful tool where fine detail is to be cut and where the carver requires close control over the action of the blade.

Fig 3.3 Excellent fixed-blade carving knives by David Tippey.

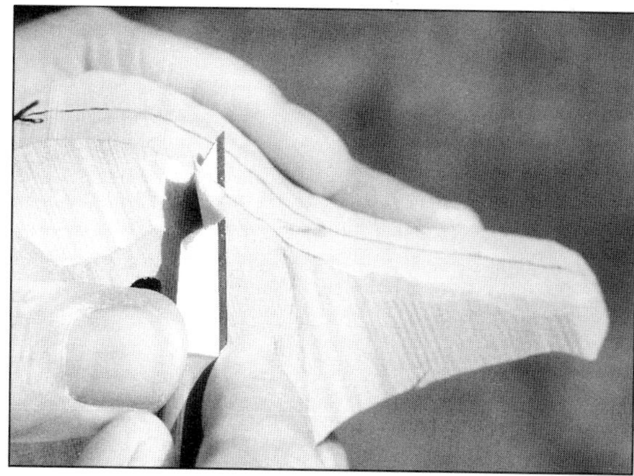

Fig 3.4 The versatile craft knife, here being used to shape the head of a goldeneye duck.

Where feather splits are to be created with a knife, the X-acto, with its narrow, pointed and very sharp blade, is preferable to most fixed-blade knives (see Fig 3.6).

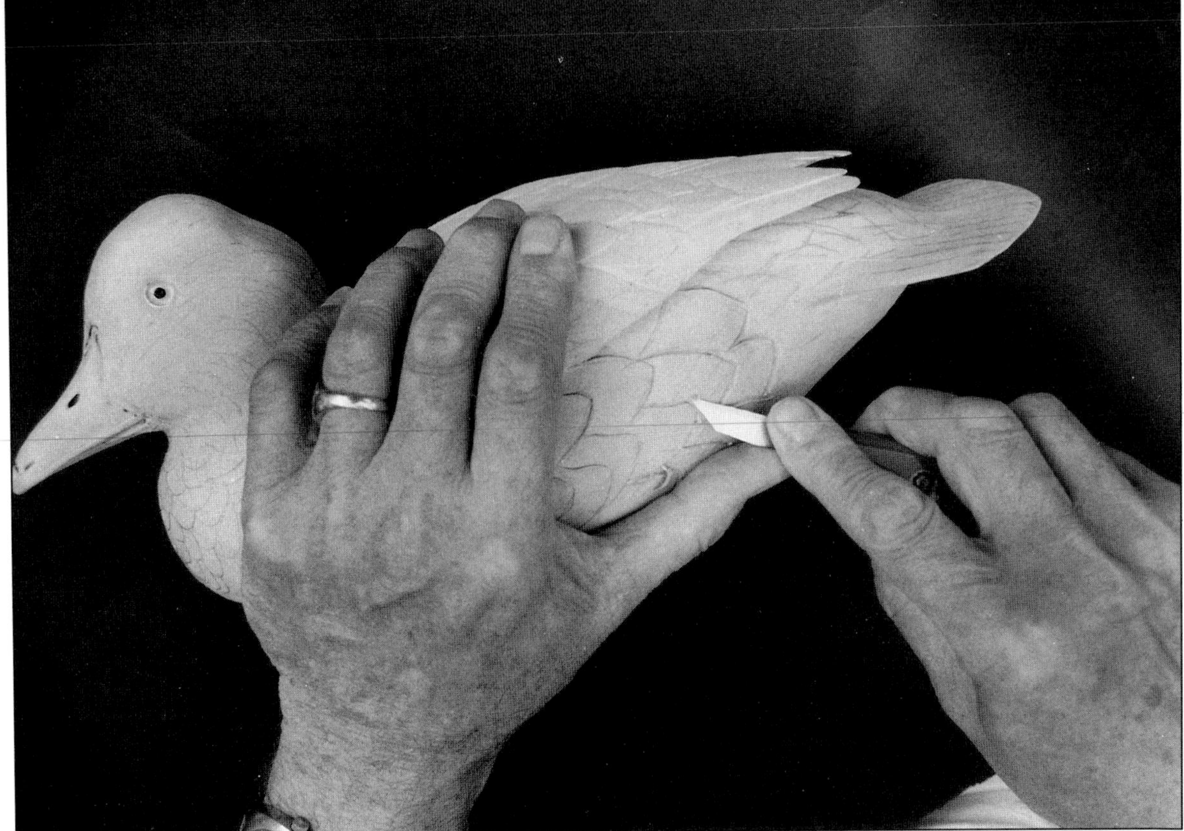

Fig 3.5 A craft knife being used to relieve feathers.

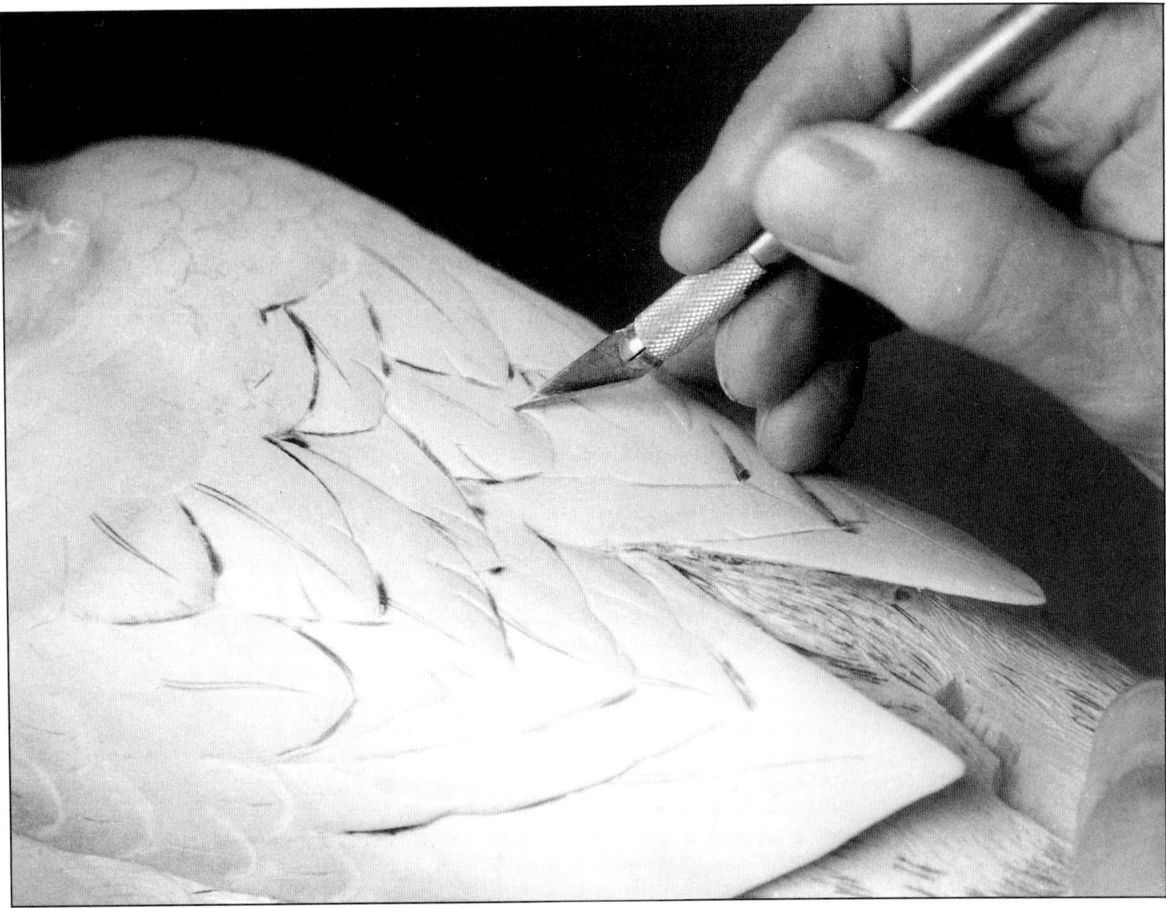

Fig 3.6 The X-acto knife is ideal for carving fine detail such as feather splits.

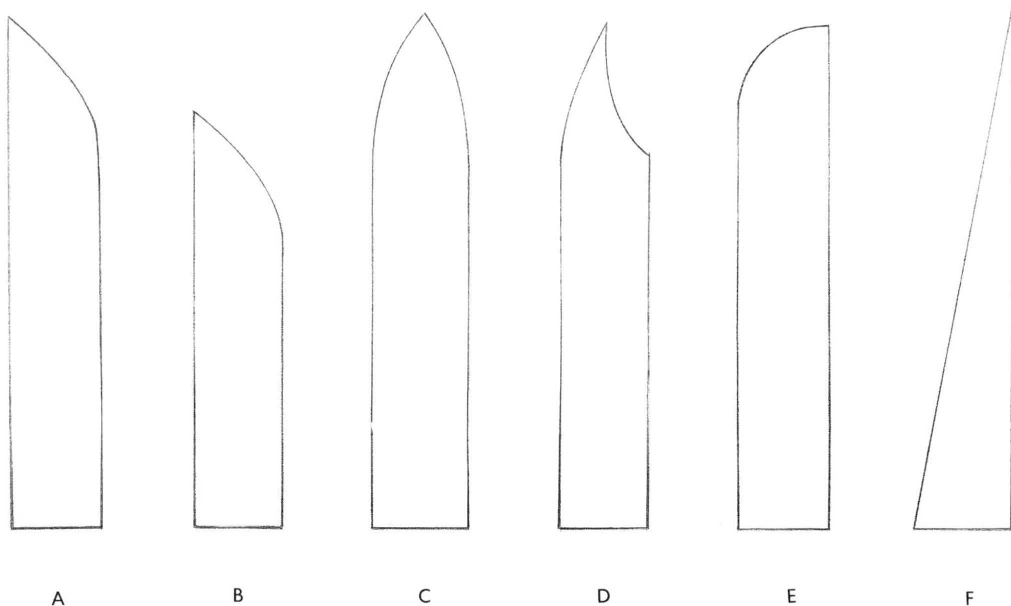

Fig 3.7 General carving knives - typical blade shapes: *(a)* sheepfoot, *(b)* sheepfoot, *(c)* spear, *(d)* sabre clip, *(e)* spey, *(f)* taper.

General carving knives

Although it is possible to carve wood satisfactorily with one good knife, most wildfowl carvers will have a selection of knives. The blade shapes of the most commonly used knives are shown in Fig 3.7.

Blade A sheepfoot. A knife fitted with this type of blade may be used for the bulk of the work on most carvings. It is usually about 1¾in–2in (44–51mm) long, and many carvers use them for everything from roughing out to carving the very finest detail.

Blade B sheepfoot. A shorter version of blade A.

Blade C spear. The arched profile of this blade makes concave carving that much easier.

Blade D sabre clip. This blade has the same cutting edge as A, B, and C but has a relieved back to facilitate undercutting in tight corners.

Blade E spey. Designed to work well in deep concave areas, it is strong enough to be turned on its side and used as a modified chisel.

Blade F taper. Excellent for working in tight radius areas and where a long reach is required when undercutting.

The drawknife

There are larger knives that are designed specifically to 'unlock your carving from a new block'.

The drawknife is just such a knife, and for this type of work a cutting edge of 5–6in (127–152mm) is ideal (see Fig 3.8). It is very useful for rounding off a blank, removing angles and giving the carving its initial shape.

Other heavy removal knives include conventionally bladed knives similar to those recommended for general carving, but having thicker and heavier blades. The beginner, however, is advised to gain more carving experience before deciding which, if any, of these to own.

Another cutting tool favoured by some carvers for shaping is the spokeshave (see Fig 3.9) but like the drawknife, it requires both hands to use it and, therefore, the carving must be held securely in some form of vice.

Fig 3.8 A drawknife is useful for shaping. It removes wood quickly and cleanly.

Fig 3.9 A spokeshave may also be used for shaping.

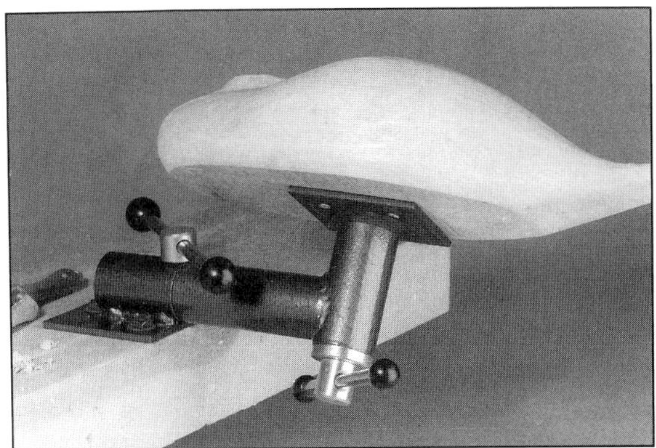

Fig 3.10 A full 360° movement in both vertical and horizontal planes is possible with the 'turtle' workholder.

Fig 3.11 The wide-jaw attachment, fitted to the standard panavise base will hold finished pieces while detailing and painting.

The Vice

A vice is not an essential piece of equipment for beginners, as most jobs that they will tackle should not require its use. Nevertheless, they should be aware of its potential value, and of the features that it should have to satisfactorily meet the carver's requirements. The beginner should also be aware that a good quality, efficient vice is not cheap.

Features of a carving vice

Movement. It should provide adequate movement in both vertical and horizontal planes, ideally a full 360°, possible with the 'turtle' workholder, but 180° will suit most carving operations (see Fig 3.10).

Clamping power. The carving must be held firmly at whatever position it is set. The wide-jaw attachment fitted to a standard PanaVise base will hold finished pieces while detailing or painting (see Fig 3.11).

Access to carving. Good working access to the carving is essential, and can be provided with a universal clamp (see Fig 3.12).

Fixing to Bench. If workbench space is limited a clamp may be preferred to a screwed bench mounting plate, as a clamp allows the vice to be removed from the bench after use (see fig 3.13).

Fig 3.12 All-round access to the carving is usually provided by a universal clamp.

Fig 3.13 Where workspace is limited a clamp allows the vice to be removed from the bench after use.

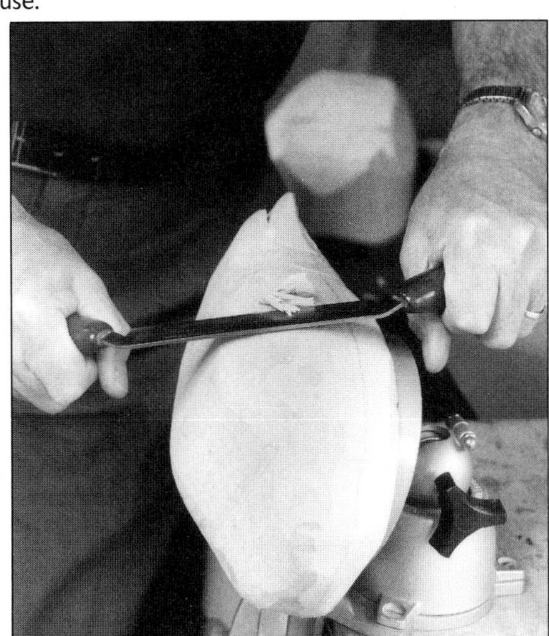

Fig 3.14 A selection of Robert Sorby's new range of 24 popular shapes and sizes of woodcarving tools.

Chisels and Gouges

For the relief carver and, indeed, for most carvers working in the round, the chisel is the tool upon which they rely for most of their work. However, as I demonstrate in this book, for all the carving techniques covered in Volume 1, the novice wildfowl carver need only have recourse to a suitable knife.

Nevertheless, chisels and gouges can be used for the heavy removal of wood and for work on very fine detail. There are literally hundreds of variations, each adapted to cope with a specific task, and an equally wide variation in price and quality (see Fig 3.14).

Shaping the awkward areas around the neck and below the chin of any bird carving is not easy with a knife, and on occasions it could be tackled more easily with a fishtail or scoop gouge.

If the novice carver is tempted to invest in any chisels or gouges, he is advised to buy a prepared set, and to ensure that the tools are of the best quality he can afford.

As with the drawknife and the spokeshave, when chisels and gouges are used, the carving must be held securely in some form of clamp.

Files

There is a wide range of files that might be used by the wildfowl carver, but for the beginner an Abrafile bendable round file would represent a sound investment. It can easily be bent to a required curve by hand in order to reach poorly accessible areas and is an ideal tool for boring out eye sockets to the correct size (see Fig 3.15).

The beginner might also consider buying a set of small riffler files, as they can prove invaluable in very awkward areas and, on occasions, can be used to texture curved surfaces.

Fig 3.15 A round bendable Abrafile is ideal for enlarging the eye sockets.

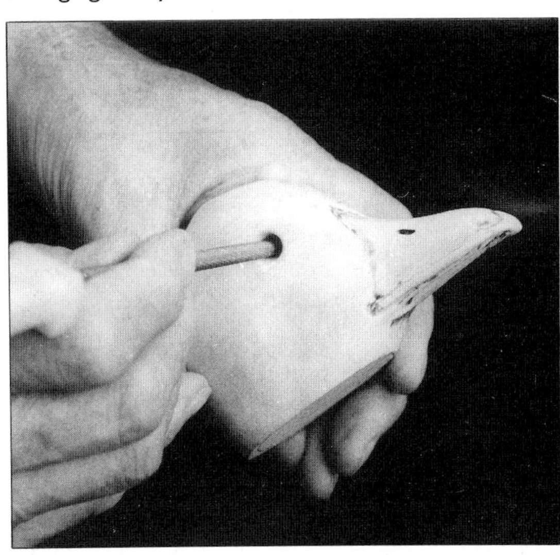

Basic Knife Techniques

Assuming the blade is sharp, the key to good carving is control over the knife throughout any cutting strokes. To remove large pieces of wood requires the same degree of control as cutting away thin slivers from awkward areas. The beginner is strongly advised to practice methods outlined here on spare pieces of wood before tackling carving.

An exercise which is particularly appropriate and one that incorporates the techniques involved is the carving of an egg (see Fig 3.16). Achieving the required smoothness also gives the carver practice in the correct use of sandpaper.

Fig 3.16 Carving and sanding a wooden egg will give the novice excellent practice in the use of the knife and sanding strips.

Fig 3.17 'Pencil sharpening'.

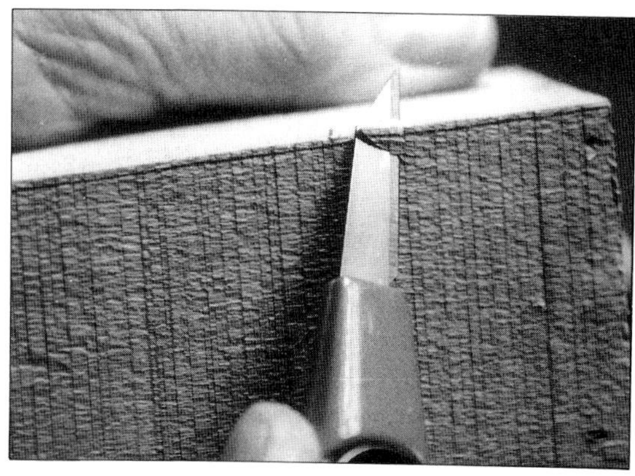

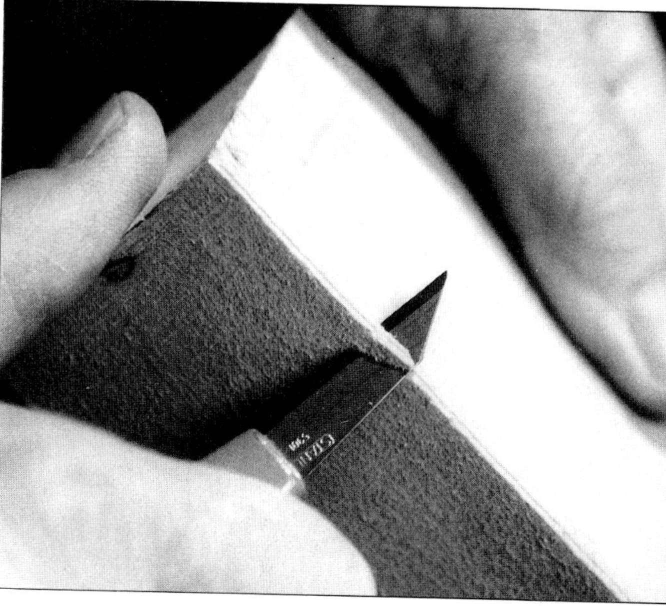

Fig 3.18 'Potato peeling'.

Basic cutting strokes

Method 1: 'pencil sharpening'

With this method the wood is held firmly in one hand and the knife held in the other. The wood is carved by sliding the knife away from the body. The action is similar to sharpening a pencil.

This method is only suitable when removing large amounts of wood in the initial stages of shaping as there is little control over the length and depth of the cut (see Fig 3.17).

Method 2: 'potato peeling'

With the wood held in one hand, the other is used to drag the knife towards the body in the manner of peeling a potato. The power comes from the fingers of the hand holding the knife, but control is limited, and for this reason the method is not suitable for carving where control is essential.

Of the three methods described here, this one is the least safe, and for this reason extra care must be exercised when using it (see Fig 3.18).

Method 3: 'lever and fulcrum'

This method ensures maximum control of the knife throughout the length of any cut. It involves

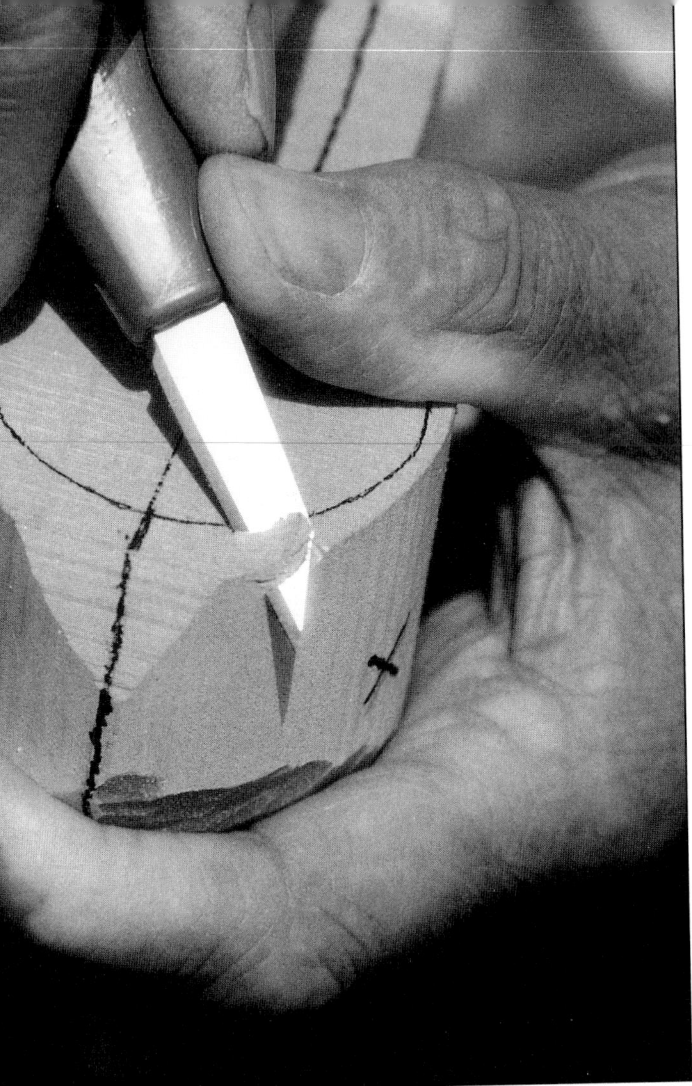

Fig 3.19 'Lever and fulcrum'.

using the thumb of the hand holding the wood as a fulcrum, about which the knife is levered to make each cut. The power and the control comes from the combined use of the fingers of the hand holding the wood and the thumb providing a fulcrum for the leverage. This method can be used at any stage of the carving and is particularly useful where fine detail is required (see Fig 3.19).

Defining and relieving

One technique with which the beginner must become familiar, as it is applied so often, involves using the knife to define a line and throw into relief the area of wood adjacent to that line.

Feathers may be defined and relieved in this way as many are merely raised areas of wood (see Fig 3.20).

1 A cut is made, usually a little over 1/16in (2mm) in depth, at right angles to the surface of the wood. The technique is used, for example, in defining the line separating the feathers of the head from the bill (see Fig 3.21).

2 A second cut is made at a shallow angle to the surface of the wood into the first cut, removing a very thin sliver of wood. More wood may be taken out to deepen the resulting V-section, by repeating the process (see Fig 3.22).

Coping with the grain

The essence of any good carving is cutting the wood cleanly and under control. For a clean cut and to avoid splitting the wood, the knife must be held at a shallow angle to the line of the grain.

The beginner will quickly find that cutting against the grain will not only result in splitting but is, in fact, much more difficult than cutting across or with the grain (see Fig 3.23). He or she will also find that on most carvings there are peaks from which cutting strokes should start moving downhill with the blade (see Fig 3.24).

Sharpening (fixed blade knives)

The makers of woodcarving knives and chisels grind, hone and polish them before they leave the factory to ensure they are ready for immediate use. Nevertheless, if only for peace of mind, it is advisable to hone a new blade to be certain that it has a really keen edge. All cutting tools must be kept sharp for them to be both efficient and safe.

Like so many aspects of woodcarving, there are different schools of thought on the best sharpening methods.

Fig 3.20 Relieving feathers.

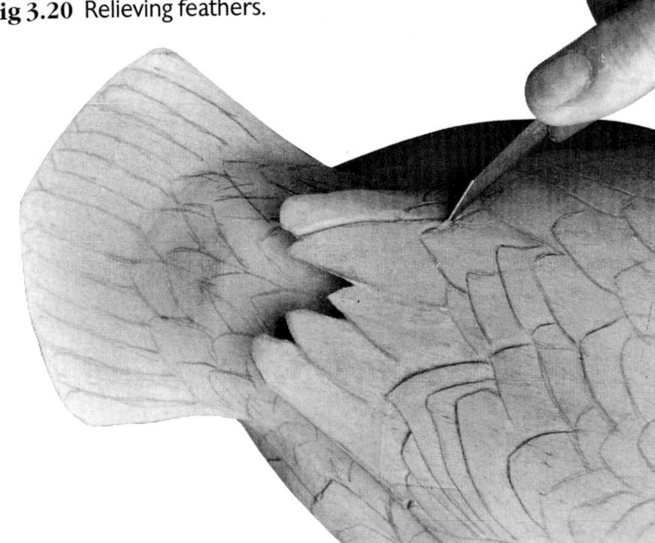

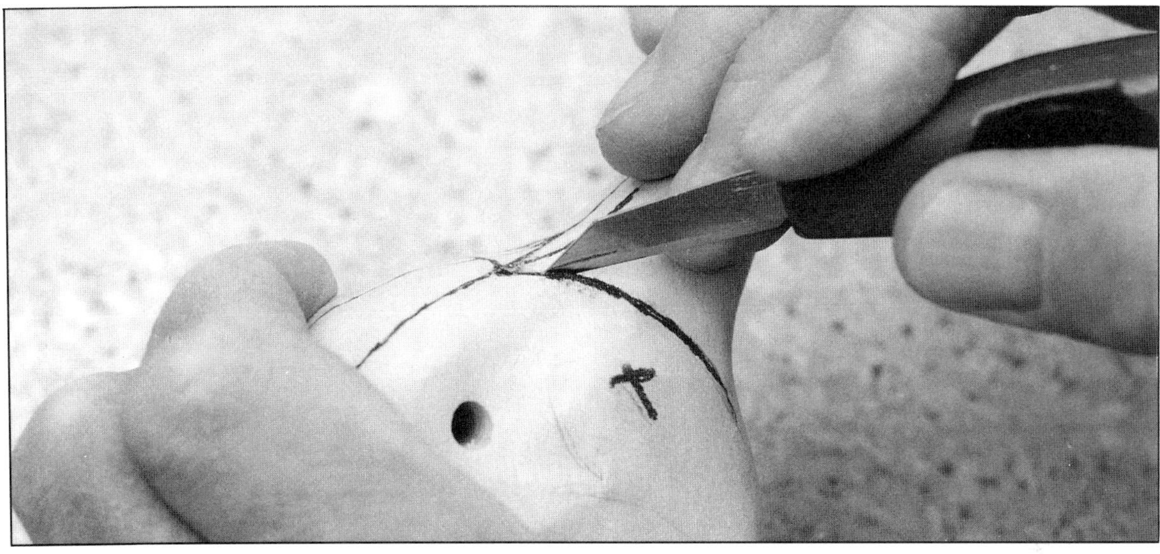

Fig 3.21 The initial cut is made at right angles to the surface of the wood along the defining line.

Fig 3.22 The second cut removes a very thin sliver of wood to raise the area of the head feathers above the surface of the bill.

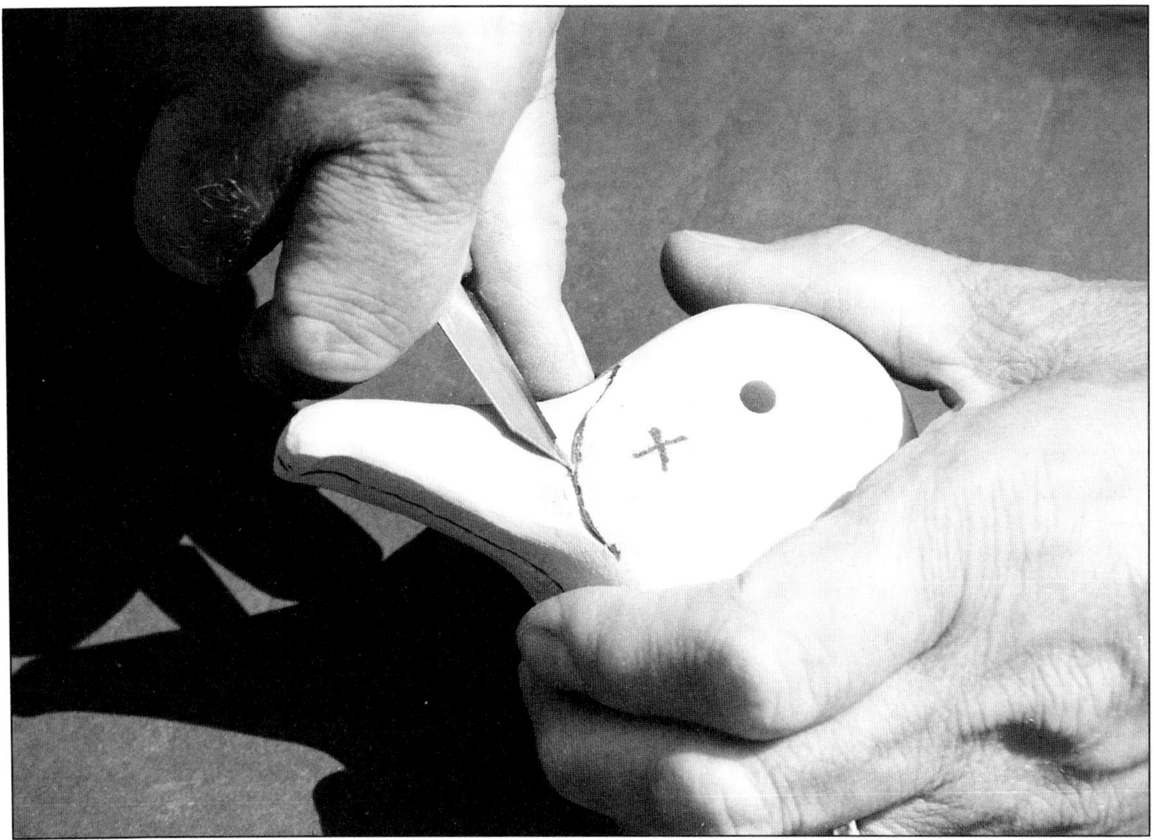

Fig 3.23 The effects of cutting against and with the grain.

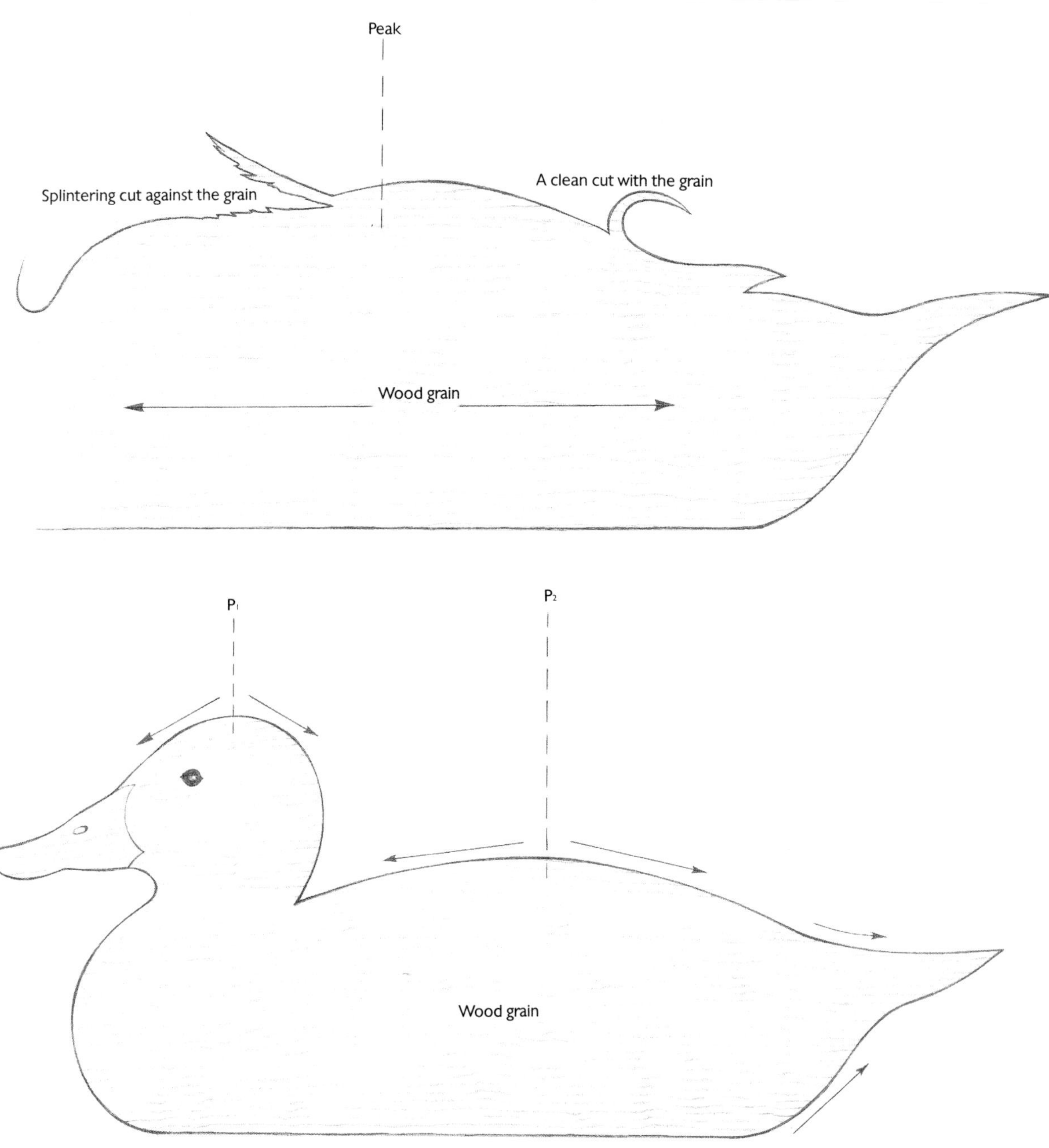

Fig 3.24 Cutting 'downhill', with and across the grain. P1 and P2 represent peaks where the knife cuts start.

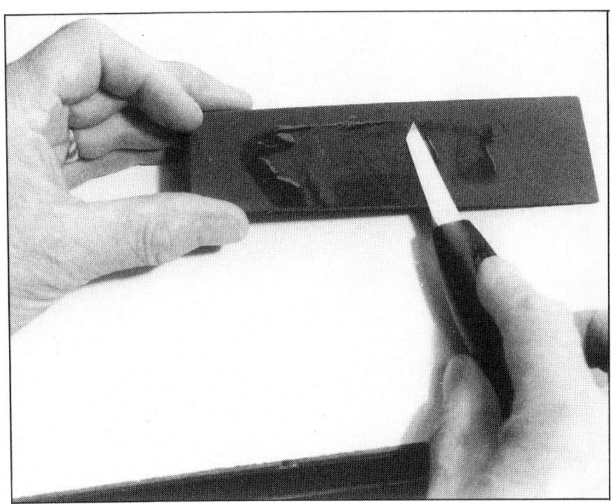

Fig 3.25 Sharpening a fixed-blade knife on a stone. Use plenty of honing oil.

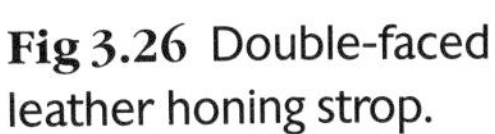

Fig 3.26 Double-faced leather honing strop.

Mechanical clamps

Some prefer to use some form of mechanical clamp that holds the knife securely at a pre-set angle while it is sharpened by pushing a stone along the edge of the blade. The Lansky Sharpening System, used by many carvers in the USA, works on this principle.

Stones

However, I believe that for sharpening single-bevel carving knives, good quality stones are very effective and, with practice, simple to use. They are supplied in medium and fine grades and should be used with plenty of honing oil.

The bevelled blade is held flat on the surface of the stone, working the edge from the tip to the handle, sliding it back and forth over the stone (see Fig 3.25). The stone itself must be kept flat and the blade of the knife held in contact with the stone throughout each stroke.

Japanese water stones give a very fine edge to any cutting tool and are available in grit sizes from 800–8000. In use, a slurry builds up on the stone, and this, together with the actual surface of the stone, acts as a fine abrasive.

Honing

To ensure that the knife slides easily over the wood and cuts as cleanly as possible, the blade of any knife must be honed. Honing not only realigns the cutting edge but also polishes the bevel.

For this, a double-sided leather strop, similar to that used at one time by barbers to sharpen their cut throat (open) razors, is recommended (see Fig 3.26).

These are available from suppliers but can be made quite simply from a strip of wood, 12 x $1^{3}/_{4}$ x $^{3}/_{16}$in (305 x 44 x 5mm) to which are glued two 8 x $1^{3}/_{4}$in (200 x 44mm) leather strips, one rough napped, for honing, and the other, smooth tanned for polishing.

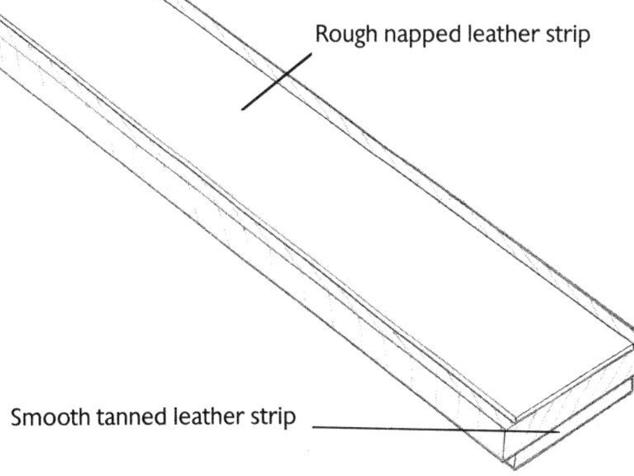

Before using the strop for the first time, the rough side should be dusted lightly with aluminium oxide (400 grit), usually supplied with the strop, or with iron oxide powder or jewellers' rouge. The smooth side should be sprayed with a little light oil (Neatsfoot, 3 in 1, honing oil or WD-40) (see Fig 3.27). After a while the treatment need only be repeated occasionally and not every time the strop is used.

Fig 3.27 Honing using a leather strop treated with WD-40 and aluminium oxide. A small sharpening stone is in the background.

The edge of the knife blade should be dragged along the length of the strop with the bevelled edge flat and in contact with the surface. Care must be taken to ensure that it is kept flat for the entire length of each stroke, exerting only enough downward pressure to keep the blade in contact with the leather.

The stropping action should not be hurried, and eight to ten strokes on both sides of the strap are sufficient to maintain a good edge.

However, to keep that edge while carving, it is advisable to hone every 30–40 minutes. Do not wait until the blade of the knife becomes noticeably dull and difficult to work with. A blunt knife or chisel requires more force to cut through wood, making the risk of slipping that much greater.

When not in use, knives and chisels etc. should be kept in a holder or rack to reduce the risk of damage to the cutting edges and to avoid possible accidents. A home-made holder can easily be made using scraps of wood glued together to form a block (see Fig 3.28).

Fig 3.28 A home-made knife holder constructed from scraps of wood glued together.

CHAPTER 4

Materials

Fig 4.2 The pattern, by Pauline McGowan, used to make the tufted duck blank shown in Fig 4.1.

The Blank

For most beginners, the starting point in wildfowl carving is the blank (see Fig 4.1). A blank is a block of wood cut roughly in the shape of the subject using a carefully drawn pattern as a guide (see Fig 4.2). The cutting is normally done with a bandsaw, although for smaller blanks, it is possible to use a coping saw (see Fig 4.3).

While it is highly recommended that the beginner purchase ready-made blanks for his initial carving attempts, information on how blanks are made is given below. Thus, when the carver is accustomed to the research involved in creating a lifelike carving and has gathered sufficient reference material to draw up accurate patterns, he may wish to make his own blanks, thus increasing his satisfaction in doing the whole of the carving from scratch.

Blanks are sawn on two profiles: from the side and from the top (see Fig 4.4). When the pattern has been transferred to the wood, a cut is made down one side of the top profile of the body. The block is then turned through 180° and another cut made along the other side of the top profile. The three separate pieces of wood are then carefully nailed or glued together again, making sure that the nails or the glue are clear of the drawn lines of the side profile. The block is turned on its side and the side profile cut on the bandsaw.

Fig 4.1 A bandsawn blank of a tufted duck, carved by the author.

Fig 4.3 A coping saw may be used to cut out blanks.

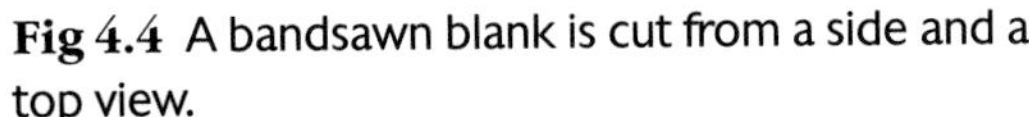

Fig 4.4 A bandsawn blank is cut from a side and a top view.

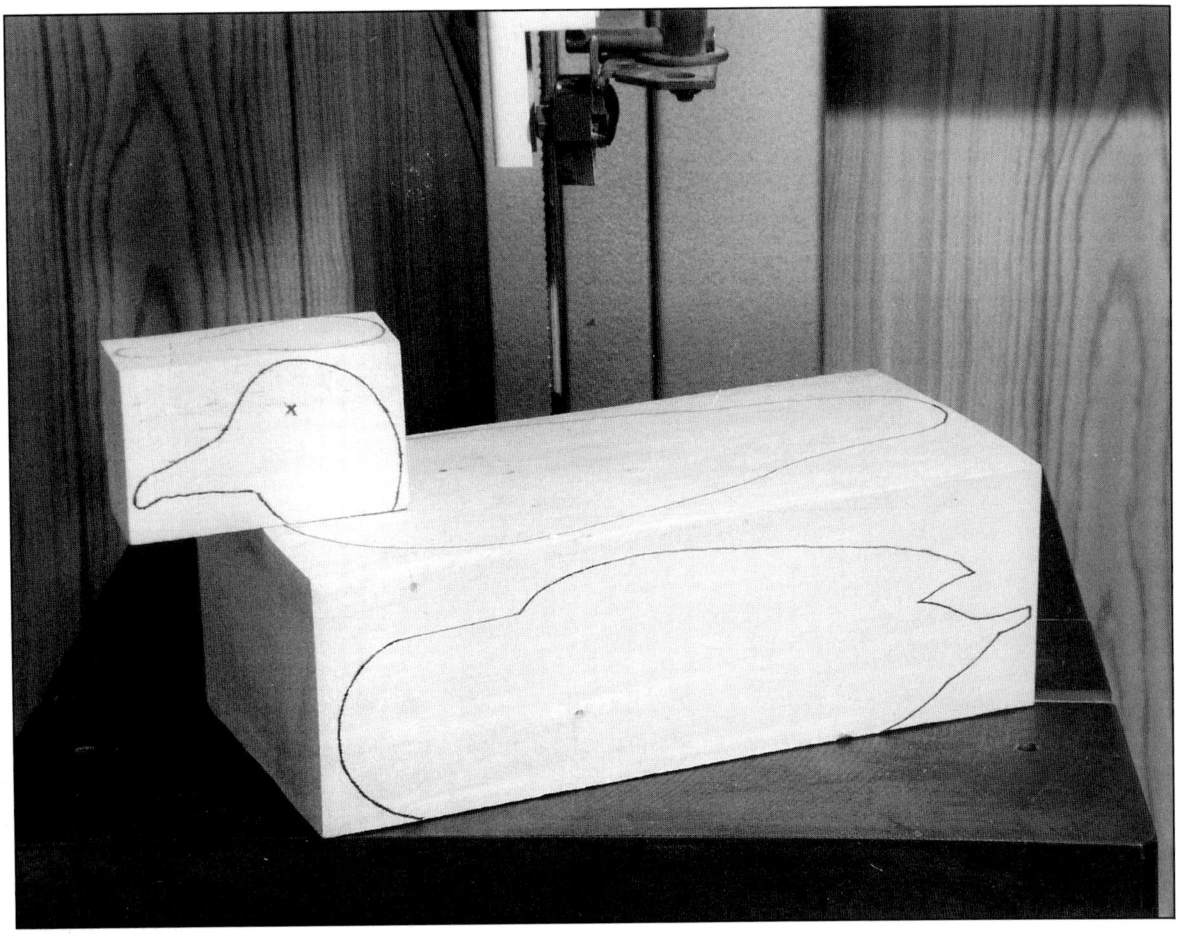

Fig 4.5 The bandsaw table is tilted to 45° in order to trim the blank.

The head is cut using the same procedure, and the eyeholes are drilled.

The bandsaw table may then be tilted to an angle of 45° and some of the edges of the blank removed to save time later at the carving stage (see Fig 4.5).

Availability

Bandsaw blanks are readily available from carving suppliers; their catalogues give full details of those that they supply. Most of the suppliers offer a comprehensive range of subjects covering ducks, shorebirds, birds of prey, songbirds and even fish. The blanks are generally made from jelutong, lime or basswood, with the eyeholes predrilled.

Sizes offered are anything from life size down to miniatures of less than eight inches in length.

Fish carving is fast growing in popularity, and suppliers are now offering a small range of designs of trout and other game fish.

Beginner's blanks and kits

One or two suppliers offer a selection of blanks which have had some of the trickiest details 'designed out' to make them easier to carve. These are ideal for the beginner.

Kits are also offered, and these are an excellent way for a beginner to learn the craft. A typical kit for a duck carving would include the blank with the eyeholes predrilled, a pair of glass eyes on wires, a detailed drawing showing the feather layout and other information designed to help the carver, such as bill details and colours to use when painting. For a songbird, the kit, in addition to the above, would include a pair of cast pewter feet.

After having completed a carving from a kit and enjoyed it, the beginner can then move on to a more ambitious project using a bandsawn blank. The range of bandsawn blanks is so wide, however, that he or she might be well advised to opt at first for one of the more simple 'poses' from the catalogues.

Smooth-bodied blanks

Smooth decorative decoys have always enjoyed a measure of popularity and, in fact, before texturing became so widely accepted as a technique, most carvings were presented in this form, the feather patterns being painted on the surface of the wood.

Smooth machine-made blanks, ready to be painted, are commercially available from many sources. The blanks may vary in character from highly stylized forms to those with remarkably fine feather detail. They are normally sold with eyes set in, and although they are ostensibly ready to paint they always need a great deal of sanding down before the wood surface is smooth enough to accept paint or a stain.

Catalogues list an enormous variety of wildfowl and other birds as 'decorative decoys', and more recently they have included a selection of fish and other wildlife.

Fig 4.6 Stylized snowy owl in spalted birch by Judith Nicoll. The inlaid bill and claws are made of African blackwood. The base is burr elm.

Fig 4.7 Red-necked phalarope in lime by Ted Oxley. Lime will take very fine detail.

Most smooth-bodied blanks are primarily sold to be painted and are supplied in lime, basswood, jelutong or sugar pine. However, where the wood is not to be covered by paint and the grain is to be a feature, blanks are available that have a more attractive grain pattern, e.g. red and white cedar, cherry, walnut etc.

Study birds

The beginner must not confuse blanks with study birds. Study birds are finely detailed castings of carved birds. They are usually made from a blend of resin and wood dust. They are textured and are ready to be painted without any further sanding. As the moulds are taken from the carvings of some of the best carvers in the world and are accurate in every detail, they make excellent reference sources.

To avoid any confusion with blanks, study birds are invariably listed separately in most catalogues.

Carving woods

Probably the first question the carver is asked by those seeing a carved bird (such as that in Fig 4.6) for the first time is 'what wood is it made from?' Indeed, so frequently was this question asked by visitors to his stand at craft shows that a colleague had a printed notice with the information on it displayed by each carving.

For the same reason that carvers need to know about the subjects of their carvings, they should be familiar with the medium in which they are working. A reasonable knowledge of the characteristics of wood is invaluable to help choose a wood that will give the desired finish. For example, if they are looking for fine detail on the finished carving will the chosen wood be suitable? (See Fig 4.7).

Hardwoods and softwoods

The description of hardwood and softwood does not refer to the density or hardness of the wood but to the type of tree from which it came.

Fig 4.8 Three teal in walnut. The carver, Colin May, has made excellent use of the grain characteristics of the wood.

Hardwood refers to wood from broad-leaved deciduous trees, such as the oak, ash, cherry etc.

Softwood timbers, on the other hand, are derived from coniferous trees, which typically bear cones and have evergreen leaves. Softwoods include pines, spruces, firs, yews etc.

Characteristics to consider

Other characteristics of timber with which the carver should be familiar are as follows:

Weight. The weight of a wood is a function of the retained water content and the density of the timber. Tables giving comparative weights are based on figures at a uniform moisture content.

While figures for softwoods may vary over a limited range, hardwoods show a wide variation from balsa (very light) to beech (medium) to rosewood (very heavy).

Grain. The configuration and alignment of the fibres in the wood can be the most important factor in the results the carver may expect to achieve from it.

While the grain is often more or less straight, there are timbers in which it is wavy, and sometimes twisted into spirals running the length of the log (see Fig 4.8).

Fig 4.9 Nuthatch in jelutong by the author.

Fig 4.10 A pair of pintails swimming, carved in yew by Colin May. Colour variations in the wood add interest to the carving.

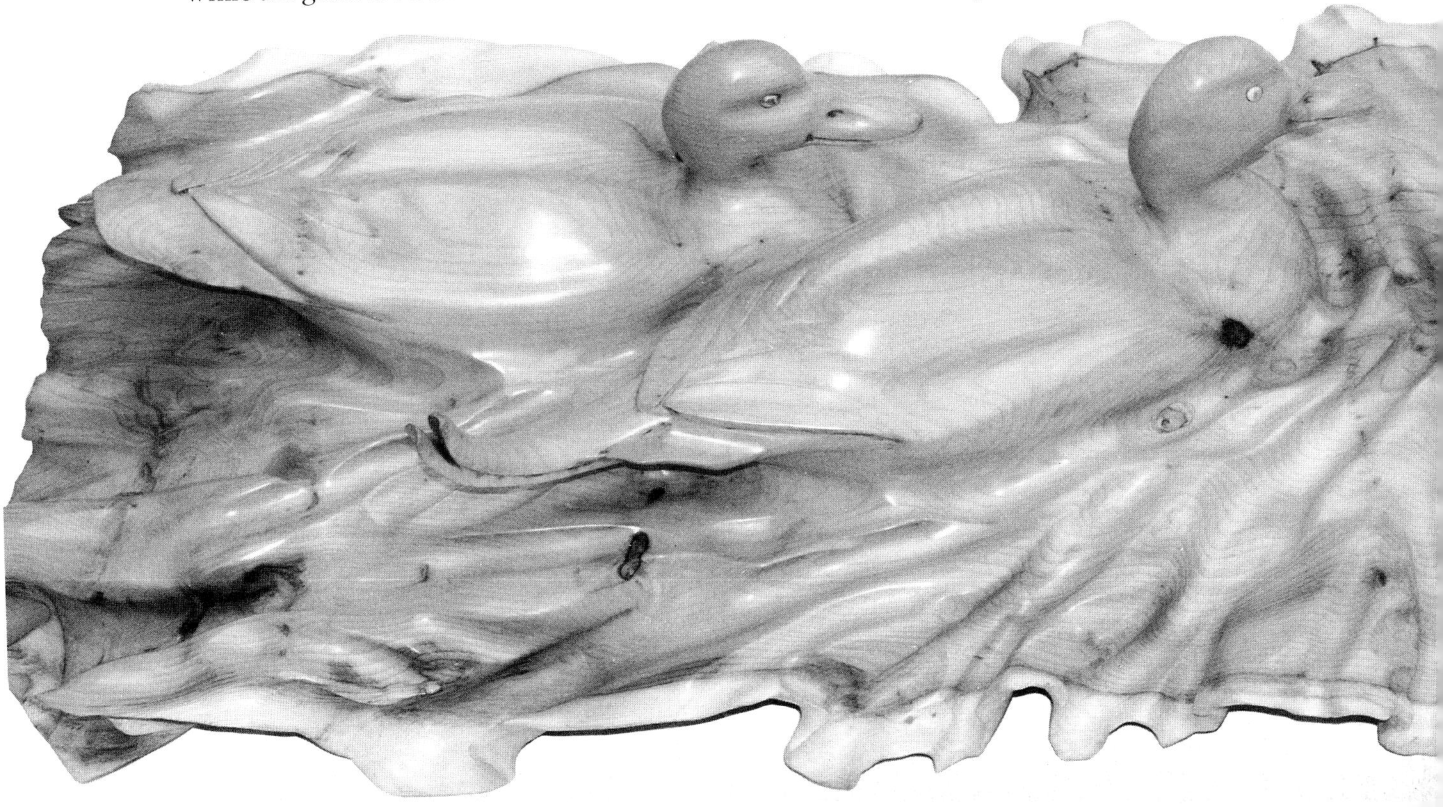

Texture. The texture of hardwoods is determined by the size of the pores in the timber. The main carving woods the wildfowl woodcarver is most interested in are jelutong, basswood, lime and tupelo, and in these the pores are fine and numerous, making them ideal to accept fine texturing (see Fig 4.9).

On the other hand, the texture of many softwoods make them less suitable for fine texturing.

Figure. This is a descriptive term applied to the appearance of a particular wood and refers to its structured features such as growth ring configurations (see Fig 4.10).

Colour. This refers to the colour of the sawn wood, but information on any likely changes due to ageing or subsequent treatment should be borne in mind.

Workability. This is a description of the ease with which the wood may be worked by hand or power tools. The beginner is recommended to take advice on the workability of any particular wood on which he or she chooses to work.

Stability. This is a measure of the wood's dimensional stability, i.e., does it shrink, crack, twist or check, etc.?

Finish. Carvers need to know how well the wood accepts stain or polish if they intend to present the carving in a non-textured form.

Availability. Some timbers, although ideal for particular carving projects, may be very scarce and consequently very expensive.

Popular carving woods

There are four woods that satisfy the criteria for carving involving fine texturing, jelutong, lime, basswood and tupelo gum.

Jelutong *(dyera costulata)*

Jelutong is the most commonly used wood for wildfowl woodcarving in the UK and is also a very popular choice in the USA (see Fig 4.11).

Fig 4.11 Mallard drake in jelutong by the author.

Defined as a hardwood by virtue of its origin, jelutong has a very fine, close grain and is imported from Malaysia and Indonesia. The tree is tapped for a milky latex substance used in the manufacture of chewing gum, hence the name by which the wood is sometimes known, 'chewing gum' wood.

Unfortunately, jelutong is characterized by horizontal cavities that resemble knotholes but which are in fact latex traces (see Fig 4.12). The wood is seldom free from these cavities, but for the carver who intends to texture and paint a carving, these cavities present no problem, as they are easily filled with plastic wood (see 'Masking defects', page 87).

It is a light, soft, fine-textured, straight and close-grained wood that has excellent working properties. Jelutong is not as strong as basswood or lime and must be handled carefully as it may well split and splinter, particularly when the wood is very thin.

It will sand to a very smooth finish with less tendency to fuzz up than basswood. It is available in 6in x 4in (150mm x 100mm) lengths or, by special order, in 12in x 4in (300mm x 100mm) lengths. Its cost is about the same as basswood and lime. Being soft, it cuts and carves easily and is an ideal wood on which the beginner may learn the carving techniques covered in this book (see Fig 4.13).

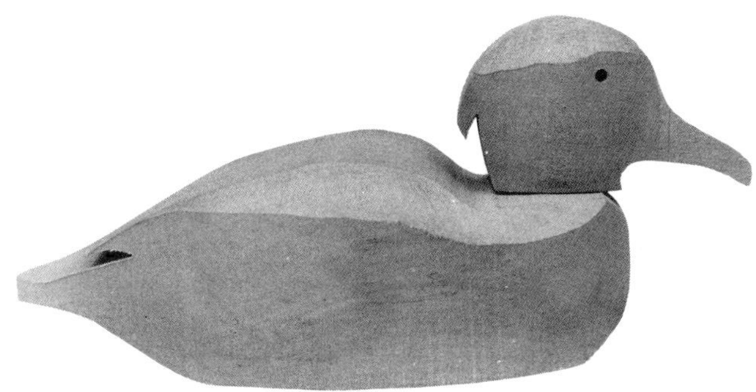

Fig 4.13 A typical jelutong blank from which the beginner may carve his or her first duck.

Lime *(tileu vulgaris/cordata)*

Lime is a pale whitish, yellow wood that has a tendency to darken on exposure to air. It is

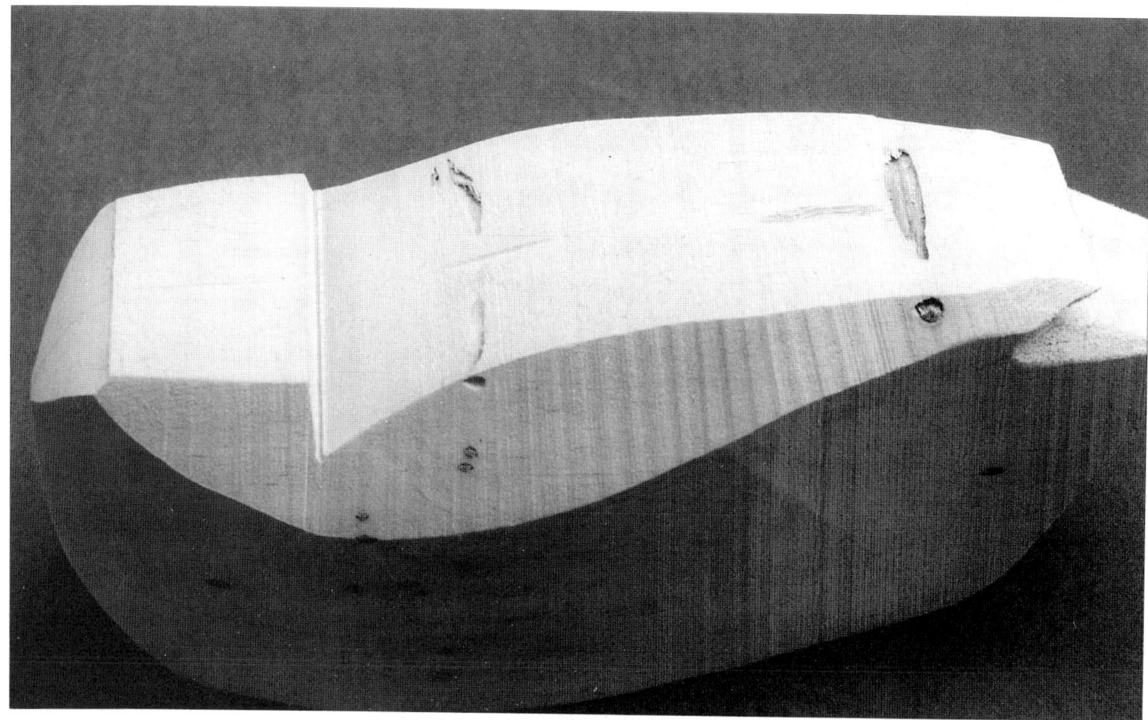

Fig 4.12 Jelutong is seldom free from latex trace cavities. These can be masked by wood filler.

Fig 4.14 Red-breasted goose in lime by Phillip Nelson. Winner, Competitor's Choice, BDWCA championships, 1993.

the classic carving wood and a popular choice of carvers for many years in Europe (see Fig 4.14). It is readily available in the UK, as it comes from trees grown in northern temperate zones. It is similar to American basswood, the most commonly used carving wood in the USA and Canada.

Lime has a straight, close grain and fine, even texture, making it particularly suitable for carving where fine detail is required (see Fig 4.15). It is soft enough to be carved easily using hand tools, and, as it is stronger than jelutong, it is less likely to split when working to feather thickness. It is therefore used quite often for feather and wing inserts (see Fig 4.16).

Basswood *(tila americana)*

Basswood is a creamy coloured wood, the colour varying slightly, depending on the origin of the tree from which it was cut and on the proximity to the centre of the tree, where it is more of a pale brown colour.

Basswood, by virtue of its close grain and fine texture, will accept the finest texturing, but many US carvers complain that it has a tendency to fuzz up. The raised fuzz can be easily brushed off using a stiff brush; a suede leather cleaning brush also works well. To remove the more stubborn residue, some carvers use a propane torch lightly applied to the surface of the wood, but I think that this is a rather drastic measure and not one that I would recommend to carvers of a nervous disposition.

Fig 4.15 Kestrel in lime on branch in jelutong. Carved by Ted Oxley.

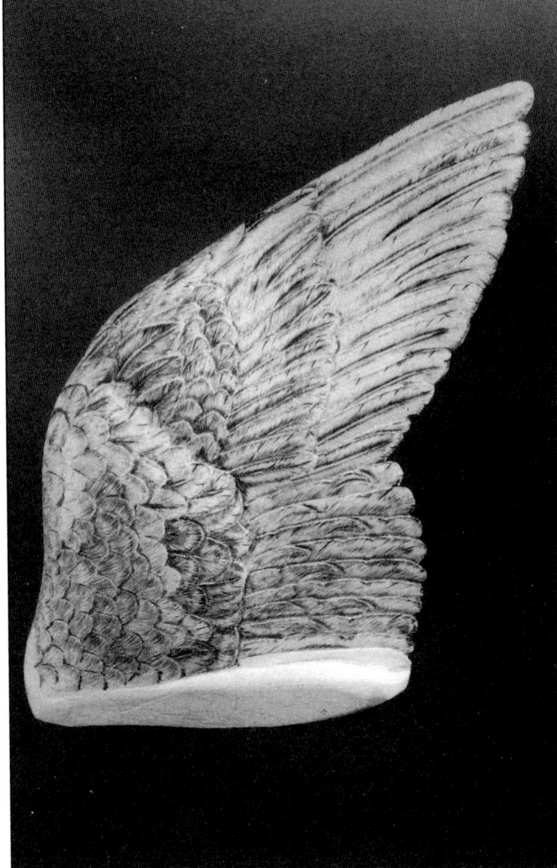

Fig 4.16 Lime is stronger than jelutong and is therefore often used for wing or feather inserts.

After the fuzz has been removed, an application of a lacquer sealant followed by a thin coat of gesso will ensure that it will not reappear.

The main source of basswood in the States is the east coast region, but since there is little demand for it outside of carving and model making, it is not readily available.

I have used both basswood and lime, and, with respect to their carving characteristics, I would have great difficulty in deciding which of the two is the better. They are both excellent woods for wildfowl carving.

Tupelo *(nyssa aquatica and n. sylvatica)*
Tupelo is an American hardwood from the swamps of the south and the east of the United States. It is marketed under several names, tupelo gum, water tupelo, yellow gum, and Cajun wood. The trees from which it comes can grow up to 120ft (30m) high, but only the first 47–59in (120–150cm) of the tree, the so-called bole, is used for carving.

Tupelo can be, and frequently is, carved unseasoned, even wet and straight from the swamps, and in this condition it cuts very easily. However, it becomes harder as it dries and becomes more difficult to carve. Some carvers even take steps to maintain the moisture level in the wood on which they are working. Others have found tupelo to be inconsistent in hardness as it dries out, even in wood from the same tree.

Tupelo is a yellow to pale brown wood having a fine even texture. Whereas with most woods careful consideration must be given to the direction of the grain flow, tupelo can be carved equally well in any direction with little risk of splitting.

It is a relatively light wood but is strong enough to be worked to the finest feather thinness and can be shaped very easily with hand or power tools. Tupelo can sometimes be obtained in thick blocks, and therefore larger carvings are possible without having to laminate several blocks of wood together to get a blank, as is often the case with other woods. Unfortunately Tupelo is not readily available to UK carvers.

Drying/Seasoning Wood

The weight of the moisture content of freshly cut timber can amount to almost twice that of the timber itself. Drying and seasoning is concerned with the methods by which this moisture is removed and the rate at which it takes place.

Stresses and strains can easily be set up within the wood if the drying process is not uniform or is carried out at too high a temperature.

A great deal of timber supplied these days is kiln dried; a process involving passing thermostatically controlled hot air over baulks of timber in a large insulated room. Air drying, on the other hand, relies on exposure to air, and with this method the timber can take a very long time to season properly.

For smaller pieces of timber, the moisture in it may be removed by soaking it in a solution of polyethylene glycol. The process can take from three days to three weeks as the polyethylene forces the moisture out to form a wax. The timber will change colour very slightly.

Yet another method of reducing the moisture content involves the use of the domestic microwave oven. I must confess I have not yet tried this method but a number of woodcarvers I know have done so quite successfully. The principle of heating by high frequency is well known and is simply a method of causing the molecules to generate heat by rapid friction between them. The amount of friction developed and the resulting heat is a property of the medium itself and is called the power factor.

The relatively small pieces of timber used for carving ducks and birds can be dried reasonably well using this method. The microwave action on the water molecules penetrates from the surface to about 3/4–1 1/4in (2–3cm). And the build up of heat by friction is transferred by conductivity to the centre of the medium. This causes a temperature gradient through the mass, which induces vapour pressure differences between the outside and the inside, so helping the transfusion of moisture from the centre, which exudes from the end grain in the form of steam.

Various timbers respond in different ways due to their power factor which should be as high as possible. The oven should be run on low power, as too high a temperature will cause splitting in most hardwoods, whereas the same temperature will be quite satisfactory for softwoods. However, tests have shown that the timbers normally used for duck and bird carving, i.e., basswood, lime, tupelo and jelutong dry well by this method. (I am indebted to Mr W. Flatt of Cambridge for the above information on the microwave oven method of drying timber).

Basic Materials

Sandpaper

Sandpaper is used to smooth down the surface of the wood after it has been carved to shape. It should never be used as a substitute for the knife to remove wood. Sandpaper leaves a fine residue of grit on the surface of the wood that will quickly dull the edge of the knife when carving is resumed.

Sandpaper should be cloth backed, strong and flexible. Swiss sandpaper, although expensive, is by far the best, and is the choice of most carvers in the USA and UK. It will contour around a wide range of curves and is ideal for small areas and intricate corners. It will also cope with large areas of wood without cracking or wearing down too quickly.

Sandpaper is normally sold in 4in (102mm) wide rolls, and for convenience in use is cut into 1in (25mm) wide strips about 1ft (30.5cm) in length. For most tasks, the strip is pulled through the fingers as they press on the surface of the wood (see Fig 4.17). With smaller curved surfaces, the thumb is used to maintain contact with the wood as the strip is pulled across the wood (see Fig 4.18).

Sandpaper is available in a wide range of grades determined by the particle size of the 'sand' or 'grit', which is indicated by a grit number. The finest paper, giving an almost satin finish, is 600 grit, the coarsest is 80 grit. I recommend using strips of 120 grit to smooth down the surface of the wood immediately after carving and, to achieve a surface smooth enough for texturing, a 400 or 600 grit should be used.

Wood filler

A wide range of wood fillers is available to the carver for the purpose of filling holes, cracks or seams. Most products have the following characteristics in common:

- They adhere strongly to wood surfaces.
- They harden on exposure to air to give a surface and body that looks and acts like wood.
- When fully dried they can be nailed, screwed, sanded and textured.

The degree to which they meet these claims varies between products. Most will shrink on

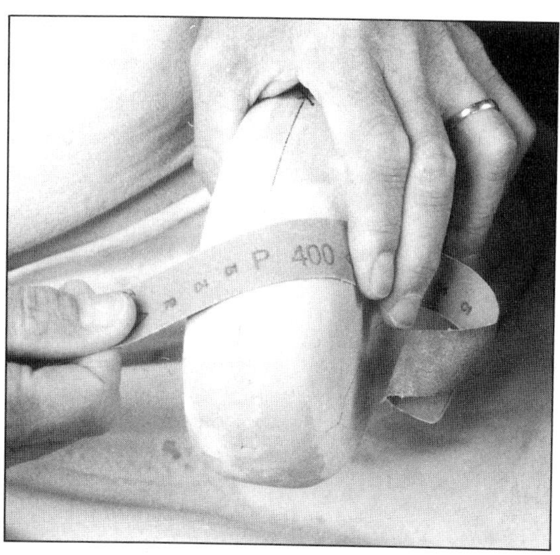

Fig 4.17 A 1in (25mm) wide strip of cloth-backed sandpaper is pulled across the wood, the fingers of one hand pressing the sandpaper to the surface of the wood.

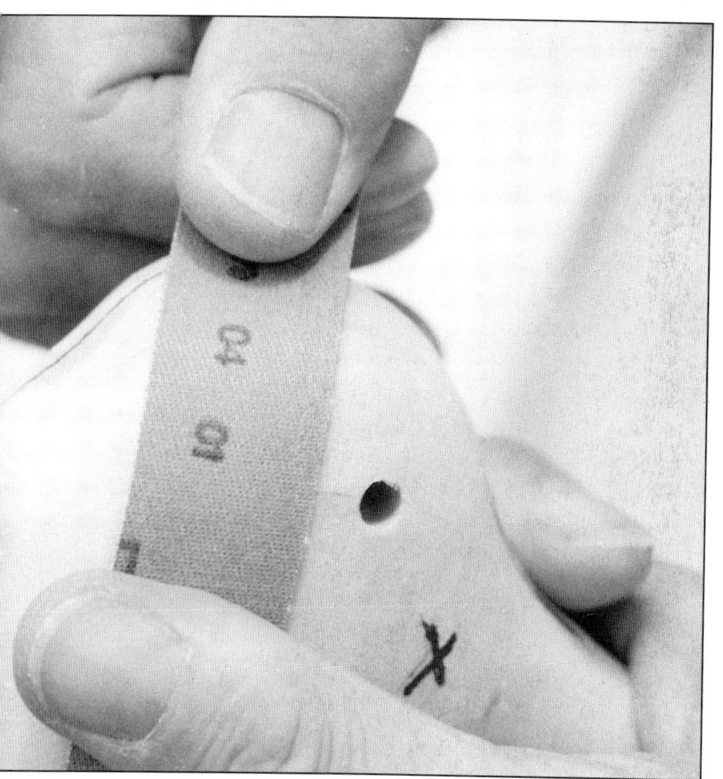

Fig 4.18 For smaller curves, the thumb, or a single finger, is used to maintain contact with the surface of the wood.

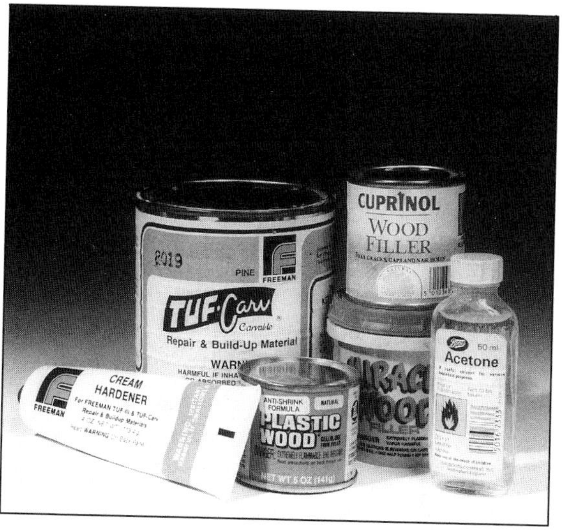

Fig 4.19 Wood filler used with an acetone solvent will fill cracks and seams, and leave a satin-smooth finish.

drying and, consequently, compensation must be made for this when filling larger holes and cracks.

All can be sanded down, but only a few will give a smooth enough finish to allow very fine texturing of the surface.

Used in conjunction with acetone, the smoothness of the finished surface can be considerably enhanced. This technique is explained and illustrated under the heading, 'Masking the joint' on page 86.

Filler products are sold under a variety of names: Tuf-Carv, Miracle Wood, Wood Filler and Plastic Wood, etc. As they are not very expensive, the carver is advised to try various brands until one is found that gives the desired results (see Fig 4.19).

I prefer to use plastic wood, made by Boyle Midway Household Products of New York, or Cuprinol wood filler from Somerset, England. Both give a satin smooth finish and both will accept fine detail texturing.

Epoxy putty

Epoxy putty is a two-part resin compound that can be moulded to any shape and will adhere to, seal or bond wood, plastics, and

Fig 4.20 Two-part epoxy putty, thoroughly mixed, may be used to fill the eye sockets before inserting the eyes.

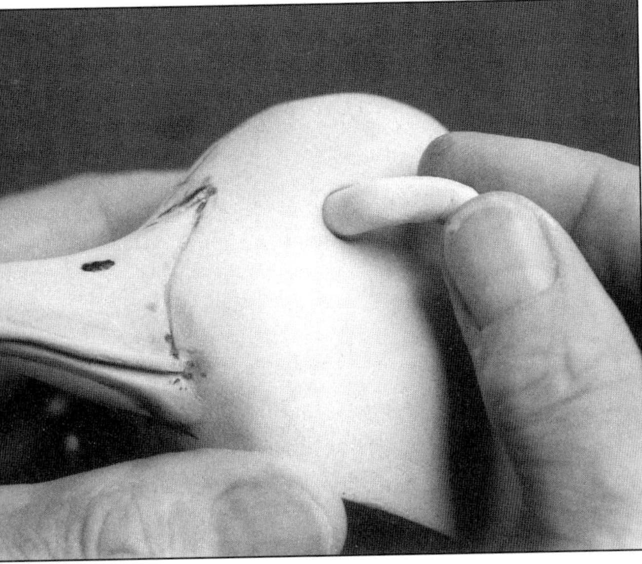

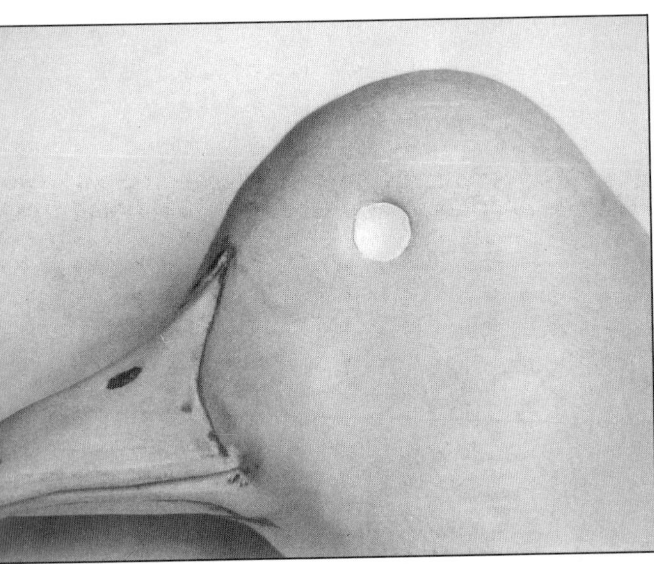

Fig 4.21 The putty is pressed firmly into the eye socket and bonds with the glass eye, holding it securely in place.

metal. These qualities make it particularly useful to the carver. The putty is supplied as two separate compounds, which are combined in equal parts and thoroughly mixed together to be used either as a filler or a moulded shape. As a filler, it is used to fill the eye sockets and hold the glass eyes firmly in place (see Figs 4.20 and 4.21). As a modelling compound, it is sculpted to form legs, feet and claws and to create habitat materials such as rocks and stones etc (see Fig 4.22).

When freshly mixed, epoxy putty is very responsive to water, which can be applied to the surface of the compound which can be brushed or moulded to a very smooth finish. However, when the putty has set hard, it can only be textured using hand tools. It will crumble with the application of heat.

Adhesives

Throughout the book reference will be made to epoxy glue. It is a fast drying (5–10 minutes) two-part glue consisting of a resin compound and a hardener. The chemical reaction between these two cures the mixture and joins surfaces together in a matter of minutes at normal room temperature. While the speed with which it sets makes for convenience in use, there are occasions when a slower drying glue might prove more suitable.

There are so many proprietary brands of wood adhesives on the market that, for any specific tasks, the novice is advised to seek the advice of a local supplier and to read carefully both the information published in the relevant catalogues and the instructions printed on the product label.

Another very useful adhesive, but one that must be used with great care, is superglue. To be effective as an adhesive the wood must be sealed, but superglue has another use: when applied to the thin tips of tail and wing feathers after texturing, it strengthens them and helps protect them from damage (see Fig 4.23).

Stains and polishes

Quite often students on wildfowl woodcarving courses show an interest in how they may present a carving without texturing or painting it. The following very brief summary gives them a little information on the stains and polishes they might use.

French polish. There are many types of French polish, but all are shellac based. The application of the polish is a skilled process involving continuous rubbing with a pad of cotton wool wrapped in a soft cloth. The shine is induced by the gradual build-up of the polish. Unless the carver has had some previous experience he or she should hesitate before trying it on a finished carving.

Teak oil. This is one of the oils based on synthetic resins and is easily applied with a clean soft rag. It dries fairly quickly and will pleasantly darken the wood as it does so.

It is not possible to put paint successfully on wood treated with teak oil.

Danish oil. Although it is also based on synthetic resins, Danish oil has additional ingredients which give the finished surface a lustre. Repeated applications will produce a slight gloss, but should it be necessary this can be reduced by rubbing down with either 600 grit sandpaper or 0000 steel wool.

Polyurethane. Polyurethane produces a very hard and durable matt or gloss finish but will tend to darken with age.

With all these finishes the surface of the wood must be carefully prepared. It must be rubbed down to a very smooth finish, removing all traces of any fuzz. The harder the wood, the better it will accept oil.

Wood filler can be masked, but despite careful finishing it will still tend to darken with age more quickly than the surrounding wood.

Fig 4.22 A selection of stones made from epoxy putty and other lightweight materials to create a realistic looking natural habitat.

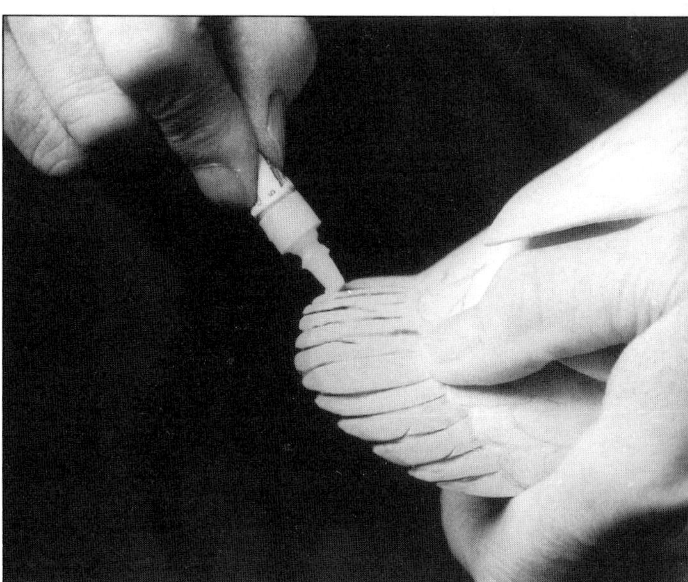

Fig 4.23 Superglue applied to the thin tips of the tail and wing feathers will help protect them from damage.

CHAPTER 5

Carving the Head and Bill

Equipment

Essential

2 pencils (HB and 2B)
Knife (fixed blade or craft)
Round file: – 1/4in (3–4mm)
Hot Tool, with standard and button tip
Hand drill, with 1/16in (1.5mm) and 1/4in (6mm) bits
X-acto knife
Paintbrush (old, size 5 or 6)
Water container
Plastic modelling tool or knife

Optional

Flexible ruler
Small Surform file
Short fixed-blade knife; blade length: 1–1 1/4in (25–30mm)
Countersink bit; maximum width: 5/16–3/8in (8–10mm)
Chisels, straight or skew; blade width: 1/8–1/4in (3–6mm)
Round file; tapering to 1/16in (2mm)

Materials

2 Sanding strips; 80–120 grit and 400–600 grit; 1 1/4 x 1in (30 x 25mm)
1 Pair 11/32in (9mm) glass eyes, clear or lemon yellow
Epoxy putty
Acrylic paint, lemon yellow

Useful reference material/sources

Study bill (goldeneye drake)

The common goldeneye

This book will teach you the basic techniques of carving, texturing and painting wildfowl. The common goldeneye drake, a black-and-white diving duck, has been chosen for the demonstration of these techniques.

The goldeneye drake's black head has an overall green iridescent hue and a distinctive round white patch just below each eye. Its back is black, with white flecked scapulars running diagonally across the body, and the flanks are pure white (see Fig 5.1).

Although originally a North American duck the goldeneye can now be seen widely throughout Europe and Asia. It is usually to be found in small scattered groups on large expanses of freshwater, bays and estuaries.

Separate head carving

With any finished wildfowl carving, it is the head that is always the focus of attention, particularly with judges in competitions. Careful attention to detail, especially the positioning of the eyes, will enable you to create a specific expression and give your carving an element of animation and realism. Conversely, poorly positioned eyes, a badly carved bill or slipshod texturing will ruin an otherwise well carved bird.

Some carvers prefer to carve the body and head in one piece, claiming that it enables them to make the head and neck flow better into the breast, resulting in a more lifelike bird. This was a very popular technique in the past, before power tools were so widely used, but nowadays most carvers work on the head separately. It is far easier to work on the fine detail this way, but the method does involve using techniques to conceal the joint between the body and the head.

Carving the Head

Marking out

The first step in carving the head is to mark with a

Fig 5.1 The European goldeneye.

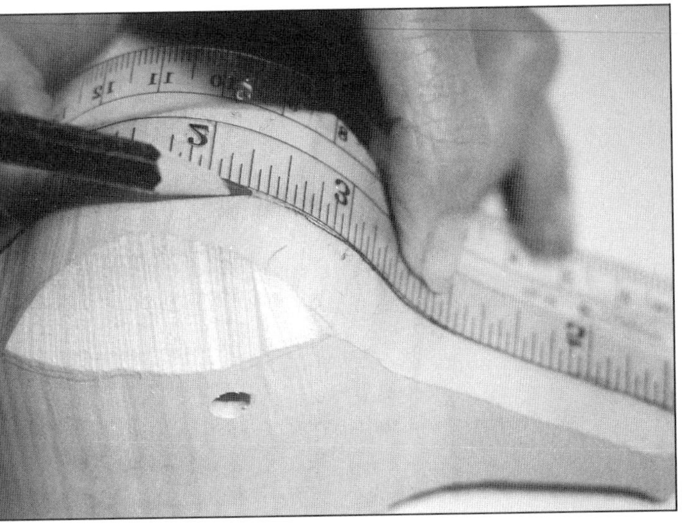

Fig 5.2 A small flexible ruler is very useful when drawing the centre line.

soft pencil, the centre line, the no-go areas and the outline of the neck on the separate head of the blank you have selected.

The centre line

1 Draw a centre line running from the back of the head to the tip of the bill. This can be done freehand, but a small flexible ruler is invaluable for this job, and for much of the measuring and marking that is always required before any carving is started (see Fig 5.2).

2 Continue the line under the bill to the rear of the head (see Fig 5.3).

Fig 5.3 The centre line should continue under the bill to the rear of the head.

No-go areas

Mark the top of the head, the cheeks and the jowls, with a cross. These parts of the head must be left untouched until the final stages of shaping and sanding (see Fig 5.4).

The neck

Draw a circle with the widest possible diameter on the base of the head. This will help you achieve a roundness to the neck when carving off the excess wood in this area. All too often one can see on an otherwise well carved bird an almost square-shaped neck (see Fig 5.5).

Fig 5.4 Clearly mark 'no-go' areas with a pencil or pen.

Carving

In these initial carving steps you are aiming to achieve the shapes that will be required in the finished carving, but in a rougher form. Make sure that you do not take off too much wood or encroach into the no-go areas.

Shaping the head and bill

1 With a knife, chisel or Surform file, round off the edges of the head (see Fig 5.6).

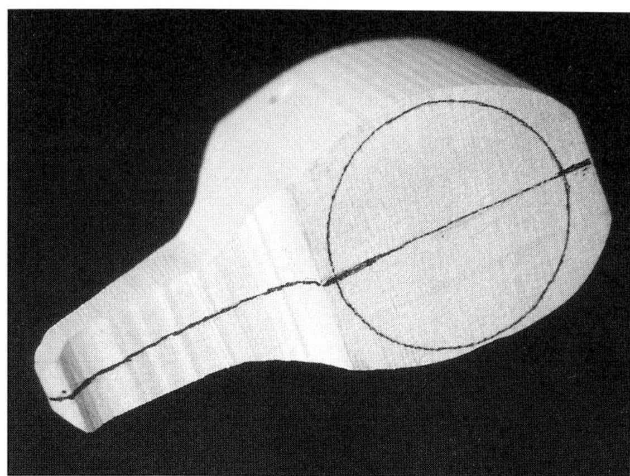

Fig 5.5 Drawing a circle of the base of the head helps to achieve a roundness to the neck.

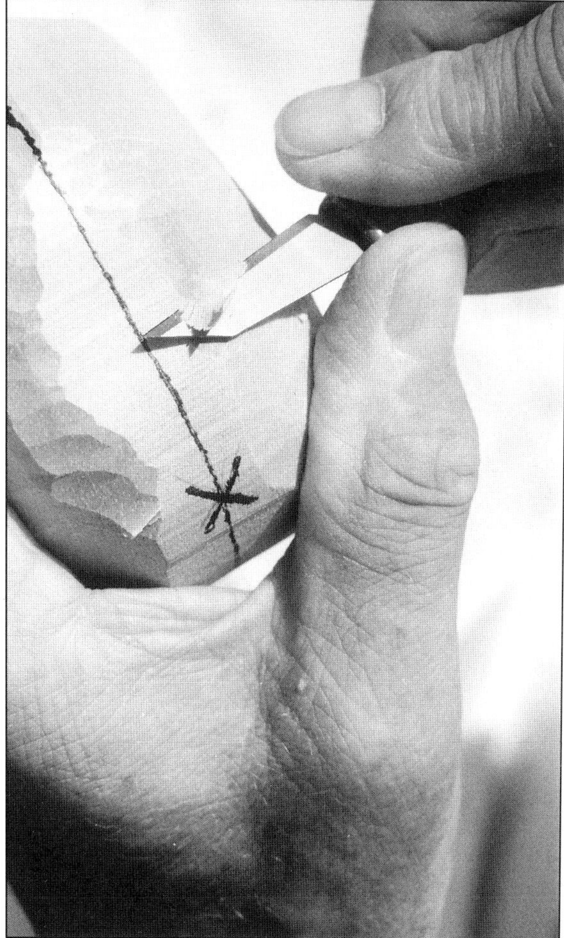

Fig 5.6 Round off the edges of the head.

2 Round off the neck (see Fig 5.7).

3 The bill may then be rounded off as well (see Fig 5.8).

4 Sand down the carved areas. Sanding at this stage will enable you to see more clearly those areas which require further carving. It will also make the job of locating and marking out the other features of the head and bill that much easier (see Fig 5.9).

5 With a soft pencil, shade in those areas from which more wood needs to be removed, indicating by the density of the shading lines the relative amount to be taken off (see Fig 5.10).

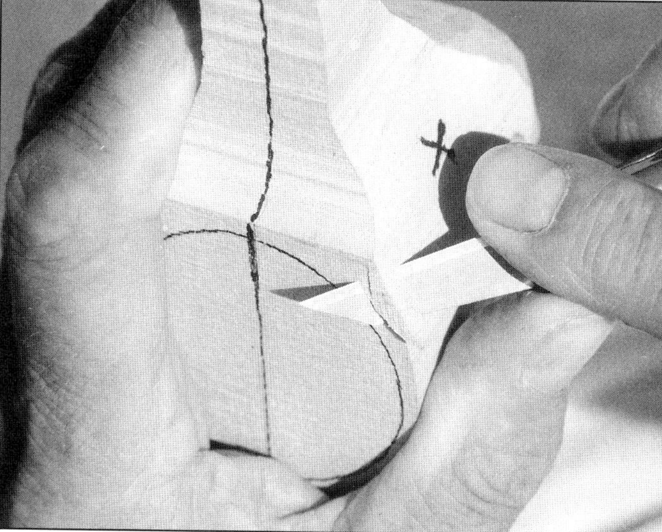

Fig 5.7 Round off the edges around the line of the neck.

The eye channels

1 The eye channels curve from the rear of the head to the back of the bill. When drawing in the guideline for an eye channel, imagine a line running from the centre of the eye to the tip of the bill. Remember that with the live bird, this is his line of vision for feeding (see Fig 5.11).

2 Using a knife, cut along the line of the eye channel keeping the blade of the knife at right angles to the surface of the wood (see Fig 5.12).

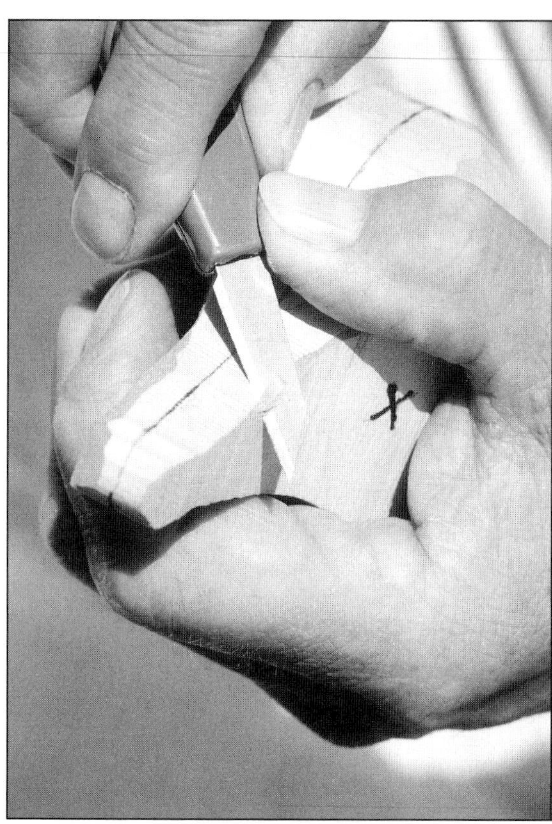

Fig 5.8 Remove the sharp edges along both sides of the bill.

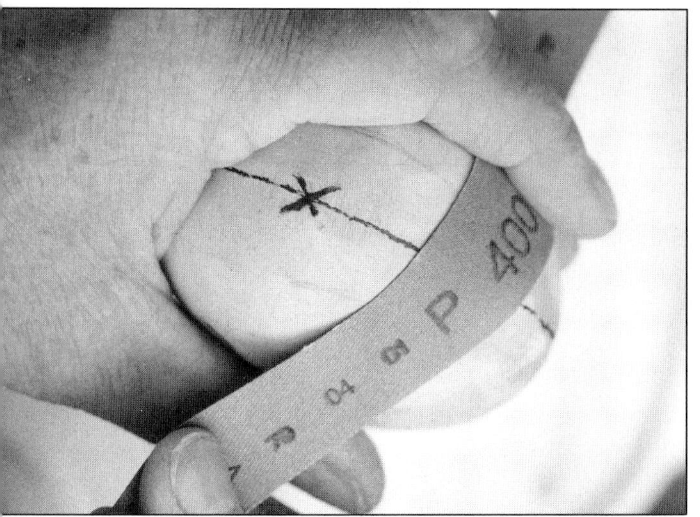

Fig 5.9 Using a sanding strip (400 grit), rub down the carved areas to give a rounded, smoother surface.

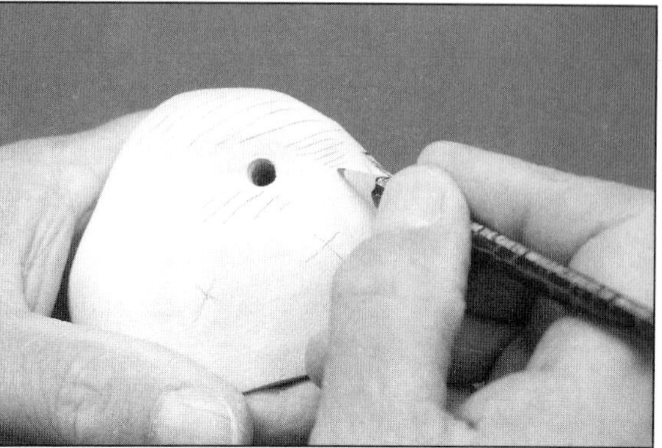

Fig 5.10 Using a soft pencil, shade in the areas from which more wood must be removed. Note that the 'no-go' areas have been pencilled in again after sanding.

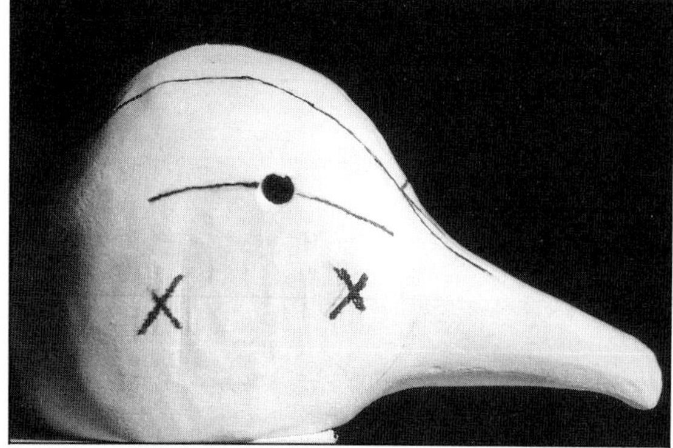

Fig 5.11 The line of the eye channel, if extended forward, should run from the centre of the eye to the tip of the bill.

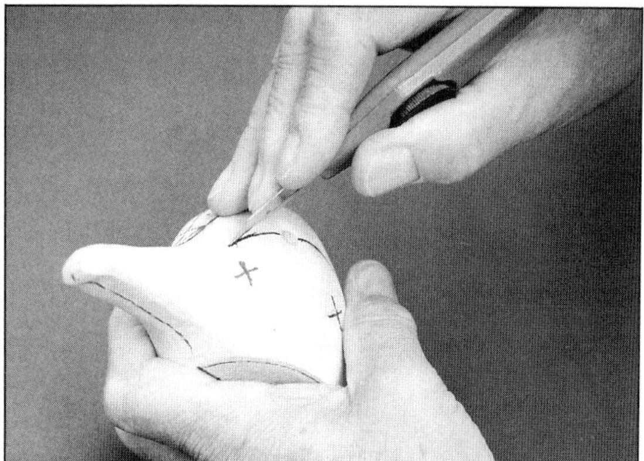

Fig 5.12 Keeping the blade of the knife vertical to the surface of the wod, cut along the centre line of the eye channel.

3 Then cut a groove to form a wide V-section along this line (see Fig 5.13).

4 Widen the groove with a knife or chisel and then rub it down with a sanding strip (400 grit) to give a smooth, curved profile to the channel. Repeat the process for the other eye channel, checking for symmetry between the two channels at each stage (see Fig 5.14).

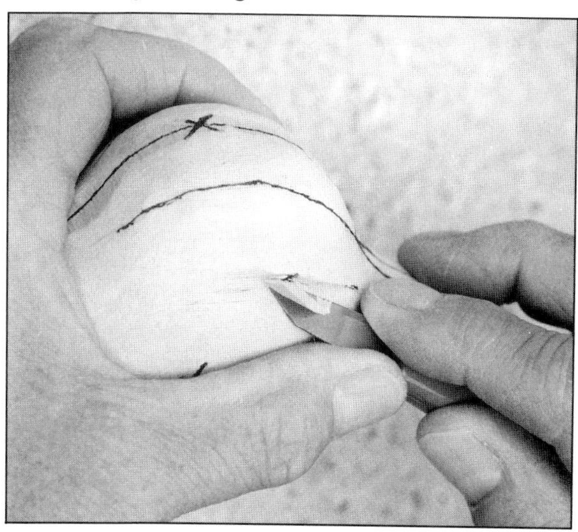

Fig 5.13 Make a wide V-section cut along both sides of the eye channel line.

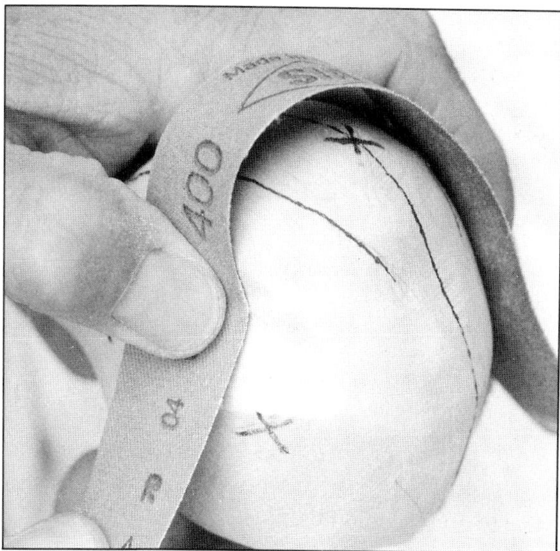

Fig 5.14 Using a fine sanding strip (400 grit), smooth out the eye channel.

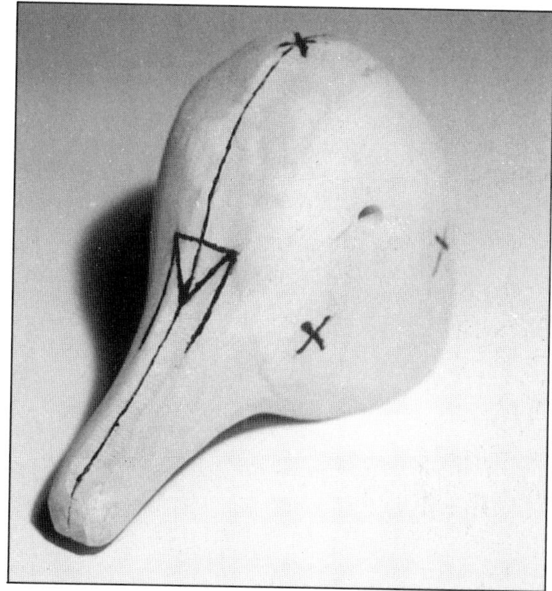

Fig 5.15 Using the centre line as a guide, draw in the triangle of small feathers (the notch) at the top of the bill and extend two parallel lines down the bill.

Fig 5.16 Using the notch as a guide, draw in the crown lines running over the top of the head (see Fig 5.17 for width between these lines).

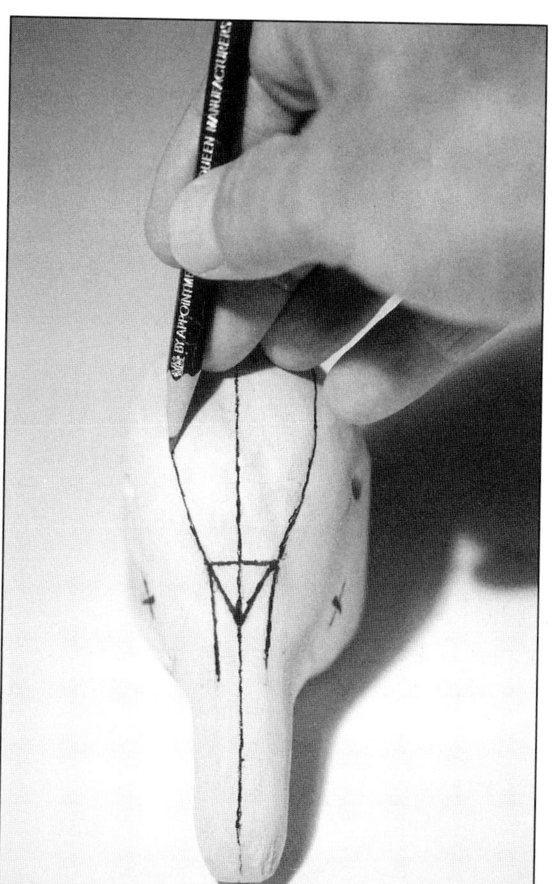

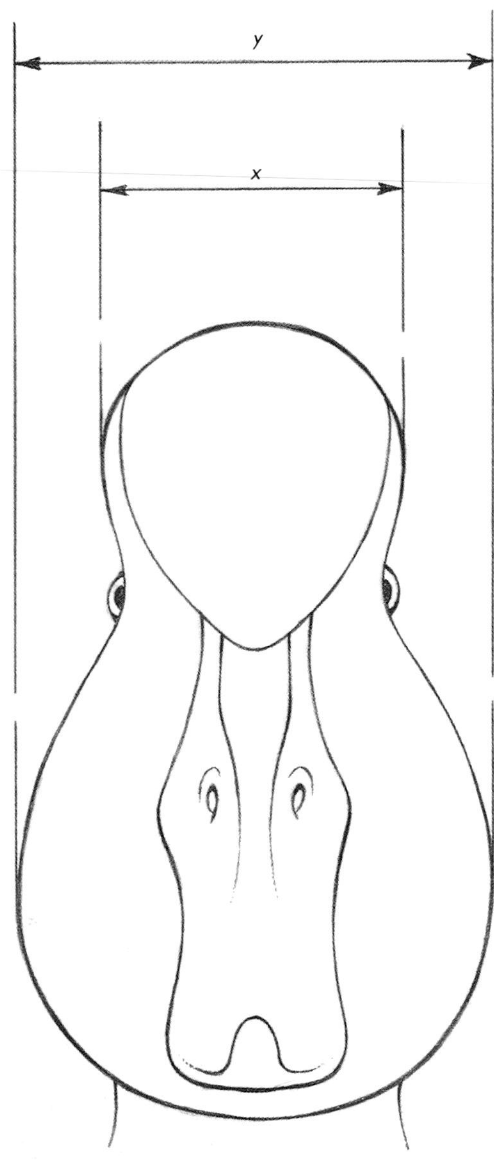

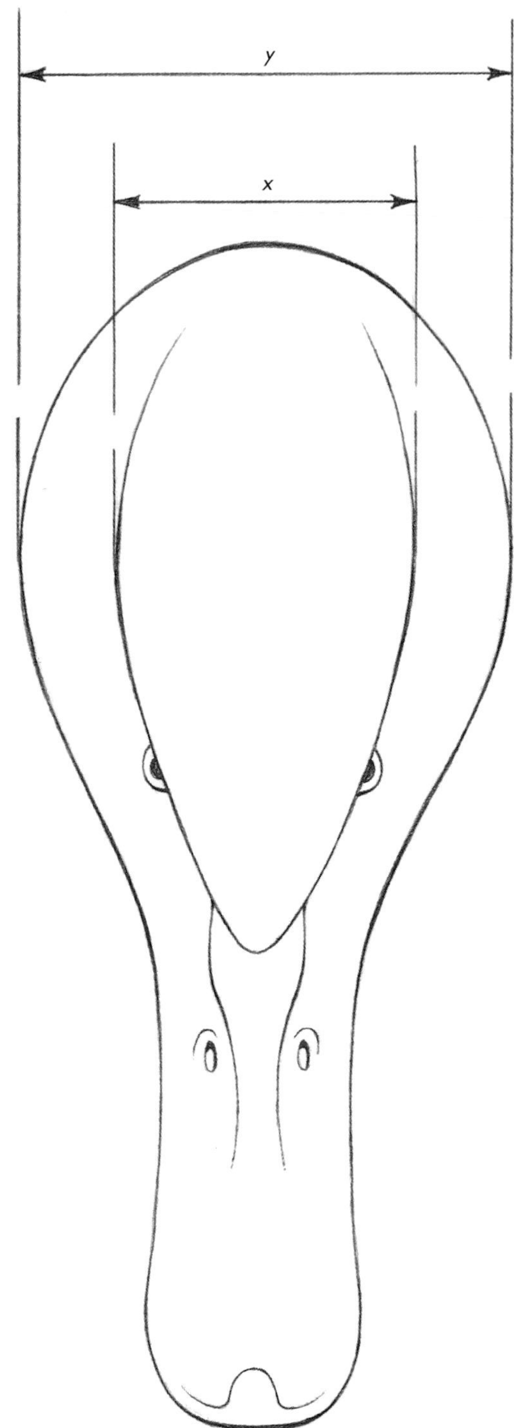

Fig 5.17 The crown width is usually 50–60% of the overall head width.

The lore and the notch

The area of the head between the eyes and the base of the bill is called the lore, and the triangle of small feathers where the lore joins the bill is generally referred to as the notch. Using the centre line as a guide, draw this triangle and then extend two parallel lines from the base of the triangle down the length of the bill (see Fig 5.15).

Crown lines

The width of the base of this triangle should also be used as a guide in drawing the crown lines running over the top and towards the back of the head. The distance between the crown lines at the top of the head should be about a half of the overall head width (see Fig 5.16).

Ducks' heads vary considerably in shape and size, but with most the crown width (*x*) is

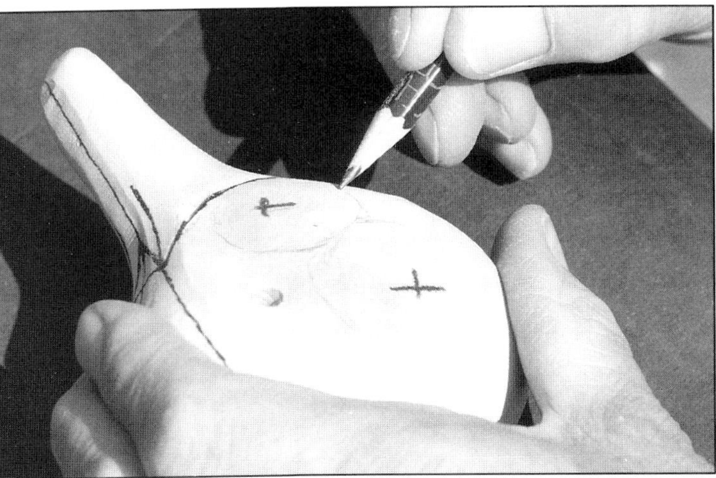

approximately 50–60% of the overall head width (y). With geese this proportion rises to about 70% (see Fig 5.17).

NOTE: Inevitably, lines drawn when marking out are erased during the carving process. Whenever possible, you should redraw these lines immediately.

The cheeks and jowls

1 The face of a well carved duck is characterized by cheeks and jowls (see Fig 5.18) (the two crosses on the sides of the head mark the centres of these no-go areas). Outline these two circular areas with a soft pencil.

2 With a knife remove a small amount of wood from around them (see Fig 5.19). Smooth off the edges with a fine sanding strip, leaving two small humps. The cheek, sited below and slightly behind the eye, is the larger and more pronounced of the humps.

Fig 5.18 Outline the cheek and jowl areas with a soft pencil.

Fig 5.19 Use a knife or file to remove enough wood from around the cheek and jowl area to raise two small humps, the cheek being the larger and more pronounced.

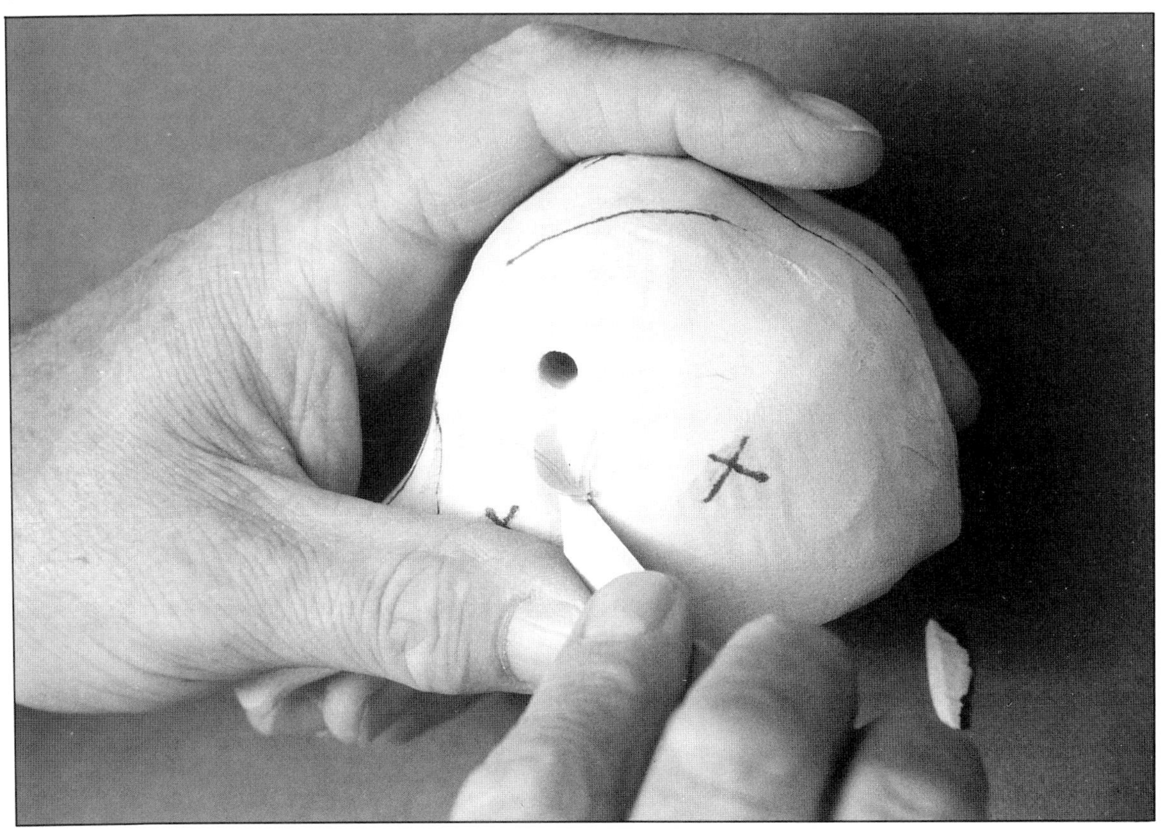

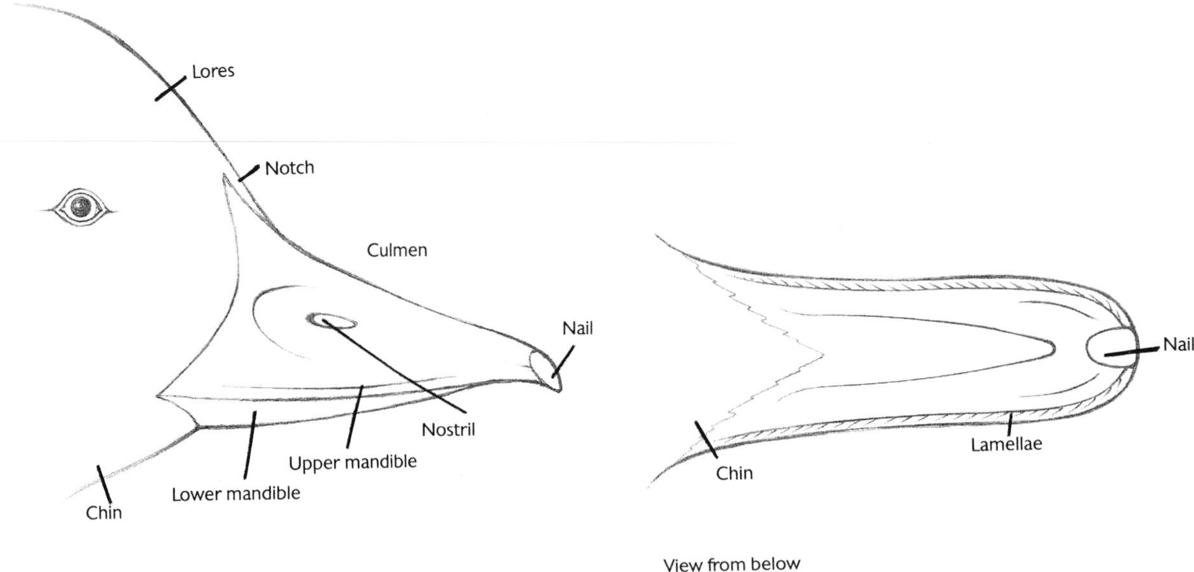

Fig 5.20 Bill details of the goldeneye.

Fig 5.21 A male mallard study bill; the wrinkles and ridges on the underside of the bill of a live duck are seldom seen but must nevertheless be carved.

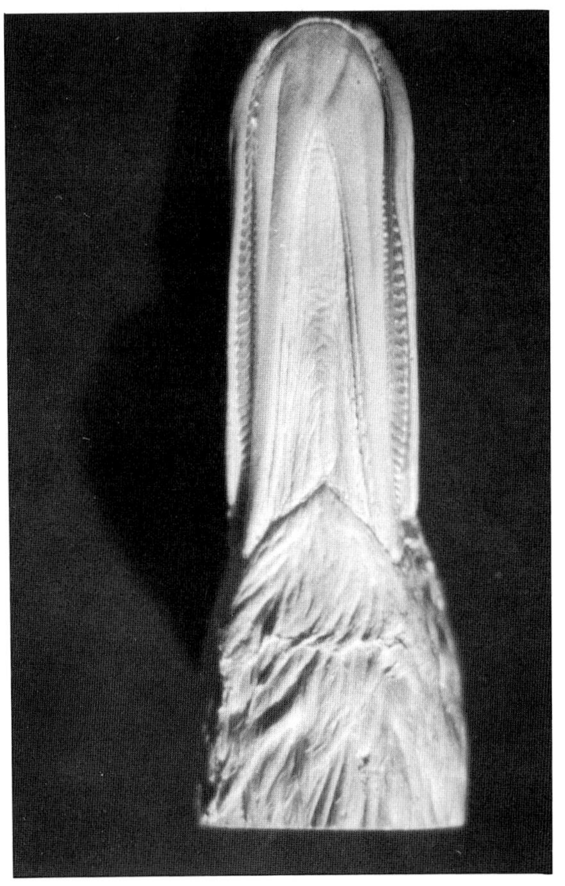

Carving the Bill – the Mandibles

The upper and lower parts of the duck's bill are called mandibles (see Fig 5.20), and they present quite a challenge to the carver. A good carving is characterized by the standard of carving of the details of the bill (see Fig 5.21). Study the details in the drawing carefully before commencing carving.

Study bill

A study bill is an enormously useful aid at this stage. (Fig 5.21 shows a male mallard study bill.)

On the underside of the lower mandible, which one seldom sees on a live duck, are wrinkles and ridges, and on the upper mandible are the nostrils and lips, all of which are carved using specific techniques.

The bill/head division

1 Using for guidance the centre line and the eye channels, draw in the curved line marking the division between the bill and the head. Make a cut with your knife a little over 1/16in (about 2mm) deep at right angles to the surface of the wood along the full length of this line (see Fig 5.22).

2 Then carefully remove a very thin sliver of wood on the bill side of the line to throw the area on the other side into relief. Use your knife to shape the wood on the bill side of the cut (see Fig 5.23).

3 Sand both sides of the line down, leaving one side rounded and the other flat. Use the burning tool to clean up the line of the original cut (see Fig 5.24).

4 Clean off the surplus wood dust with a small brush (see Fig 5.25).

The culmen

1 On the upper mandible cut out the culmen, the flat area at the back of the bill, using a very sharp knife (see Fig 5.26). This will also throw the notch into relief. You might well find that, as this involves cutting across the grain of the wood, it may tend to crumble. Do not worry too much about this, as you will be able to restore the smoothness of the surface with plastic wood later.

2 Use the burning tool in the same way as before to clean up the edges (see Fig 5.27).

The nostril area

Cut out the concave area on the upper mandible where the nostrils are to be drilled later. A knife, file or chisel can be used for this job (see Fig 5.28).

Separating the mandibles

Careful study of your reference sources will indicate where the upper and lower mandible lines should be drawn (see Figs 2.1 and 5.20). You will be very lucky if you can draw these lines accurately the first time, since they are never straight, and on many ducks dip somewhere along their length.

1 Draw in the line of the upper mandible first (see Fig 5.29).

2 Then, with a vertical cut to a depth of a little over 1/16in (approximately 2mm) remove a thin sliver of wood along its full length (see Fig 5.30).

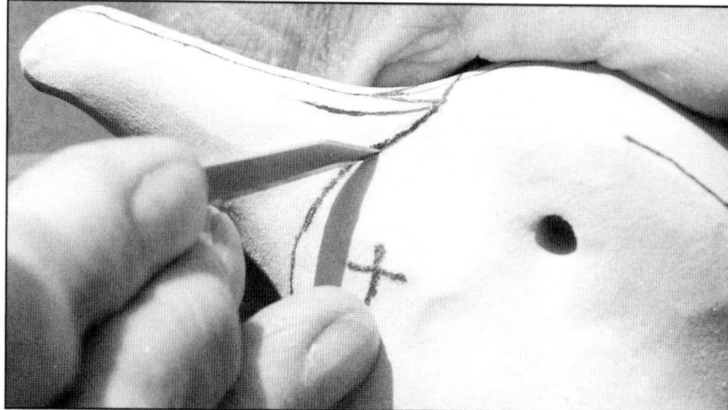

Fig 5.22 Having drawn a line marking the division between the bill and the head, make a cut 2mm deep along the line.

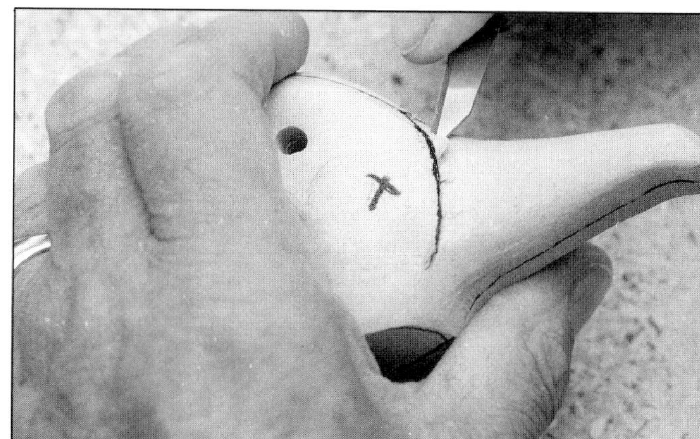

Fig 5.23 Removing a sliver of wood along the cut will throw the head side of the line into relief.

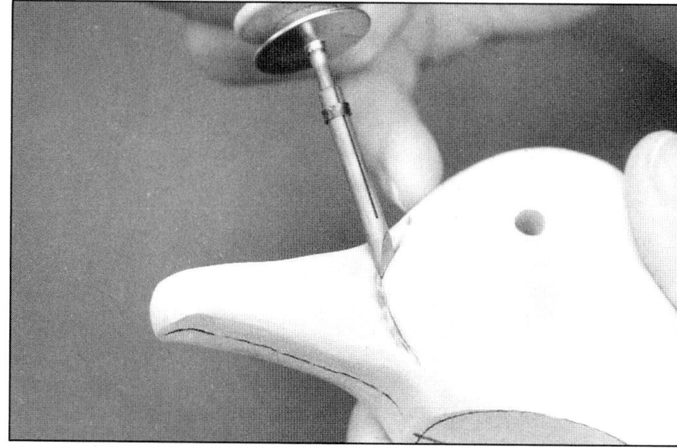

Fig 5.24 Sand both sides of the line and run the Hot Tool along it to give a clean, smooth finish.

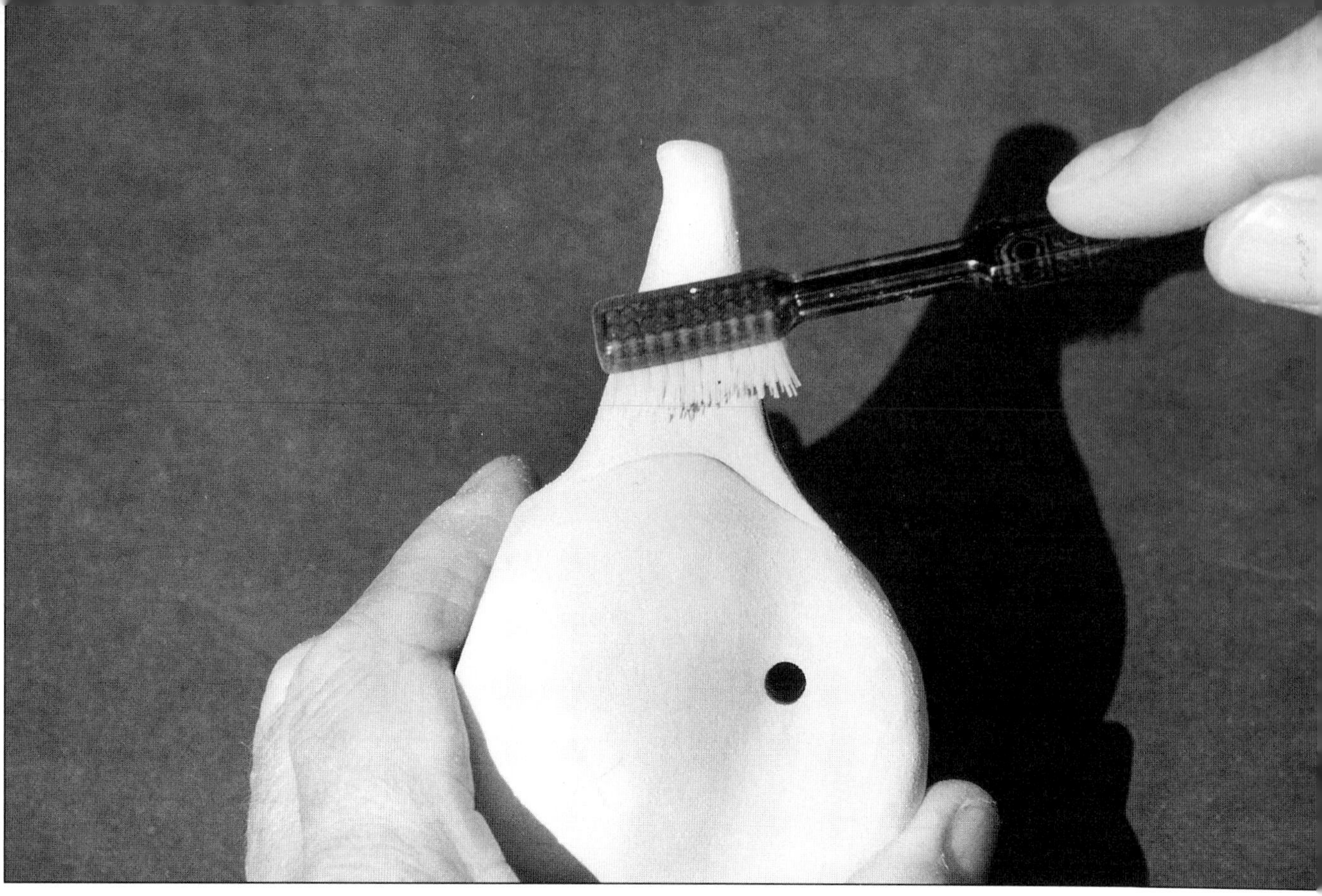

Fig 5.25 A final rub with a small brush removes any remaining wood dust.

Fig 5.26 The culmen, relieved using a very sharp knife.

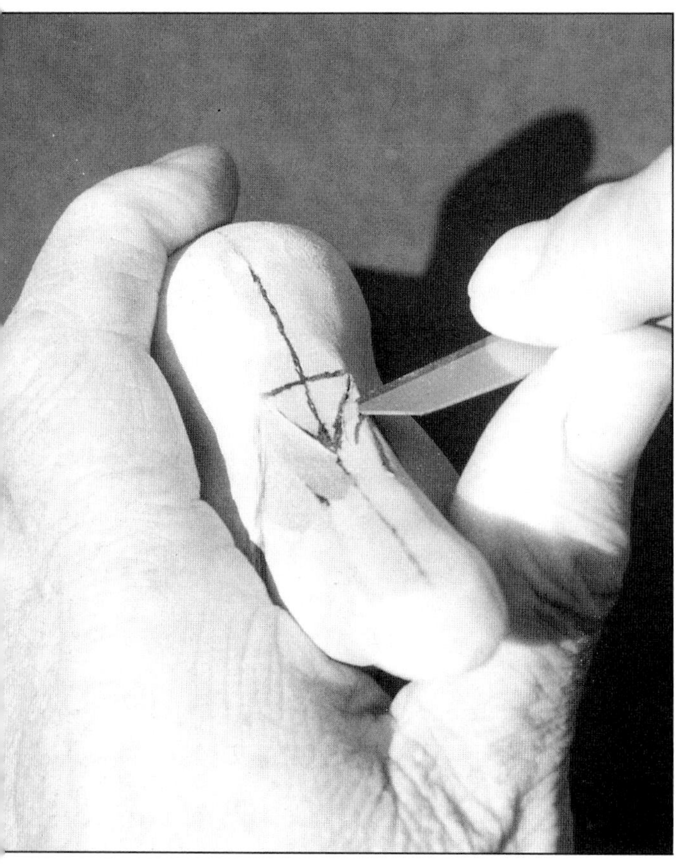

Fig 5.27 The burning tool cleans up the line between the culmen and the notch.

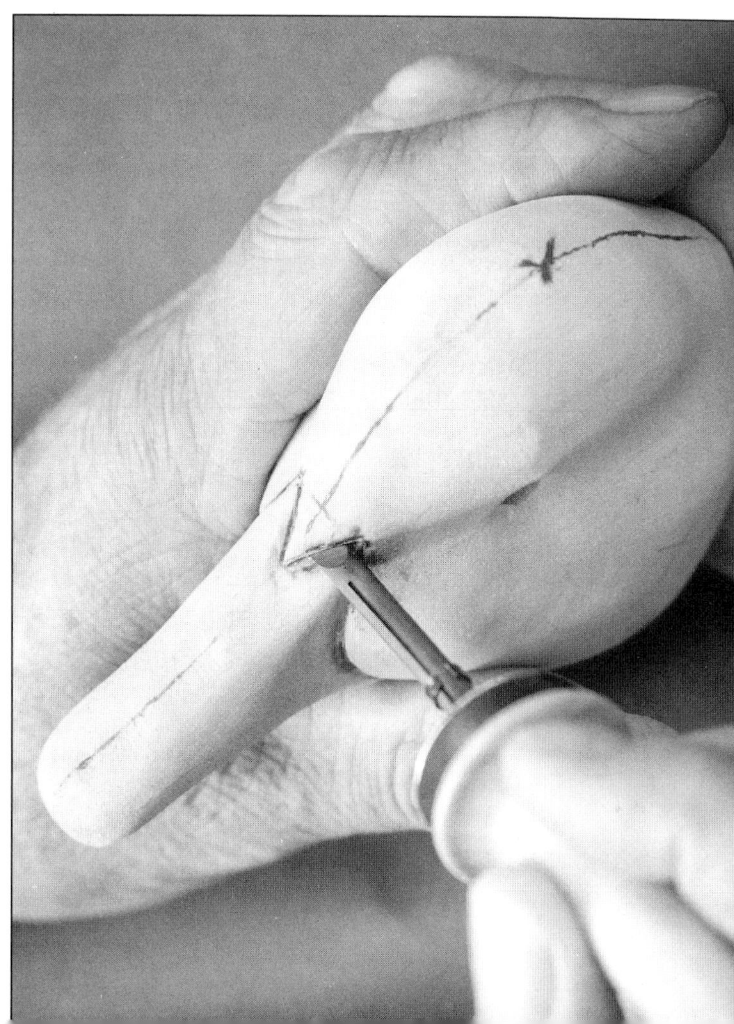

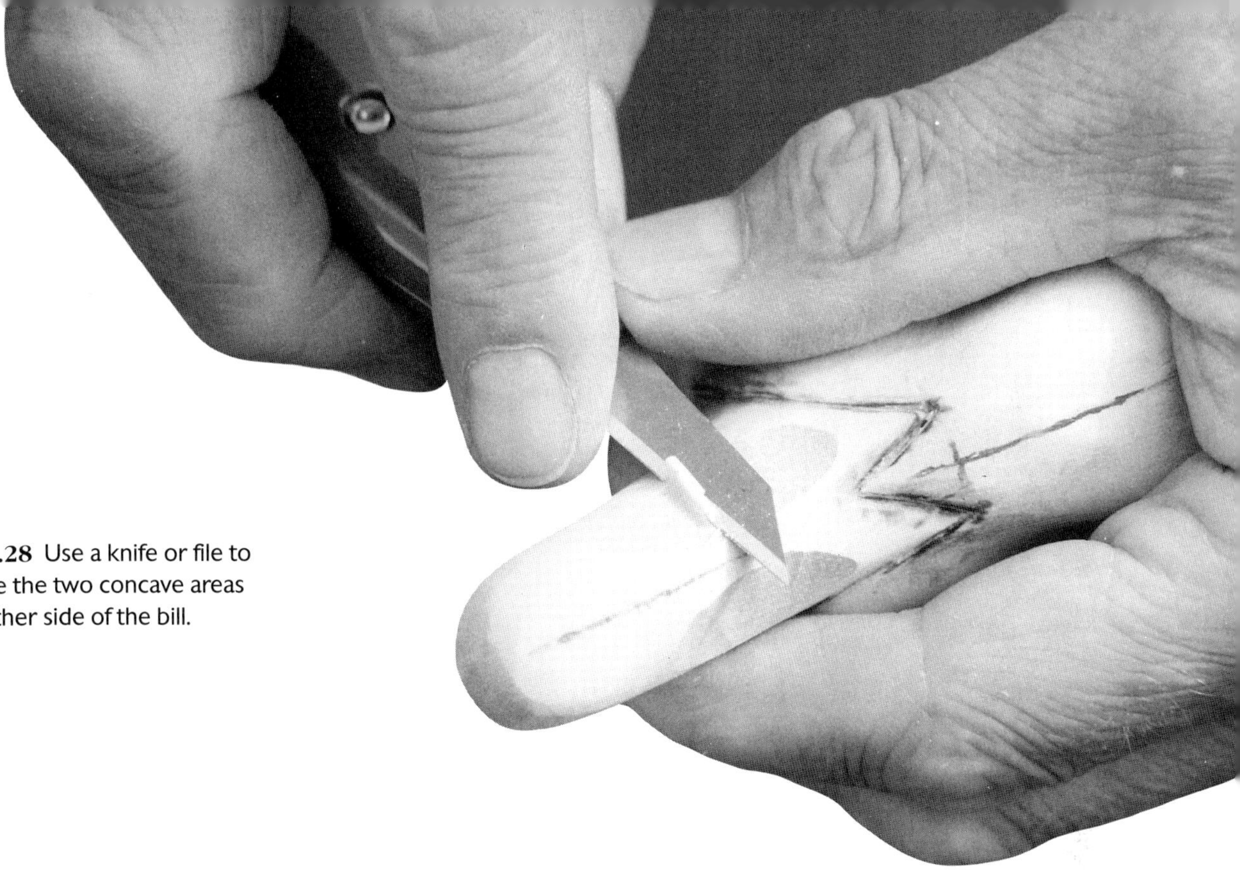

Fig 5.28 Use a knife or file to create the two concave areas on either side of the bill.

Fig 5.29 The lines of the upper mandible may have to be drawn several times to achieve the right line; refer to your reference sources or study bill for guidance here.

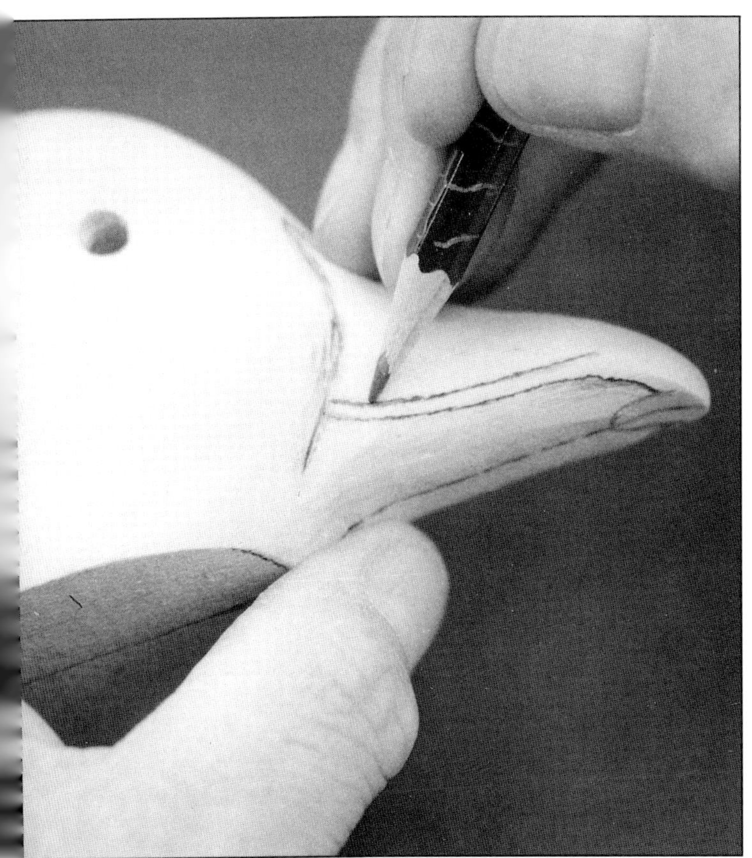

Fig 5.30 If you have made the vertical cut carefully it will not be difficult to remove a thin sliver of wood along the length of the upper mandible.

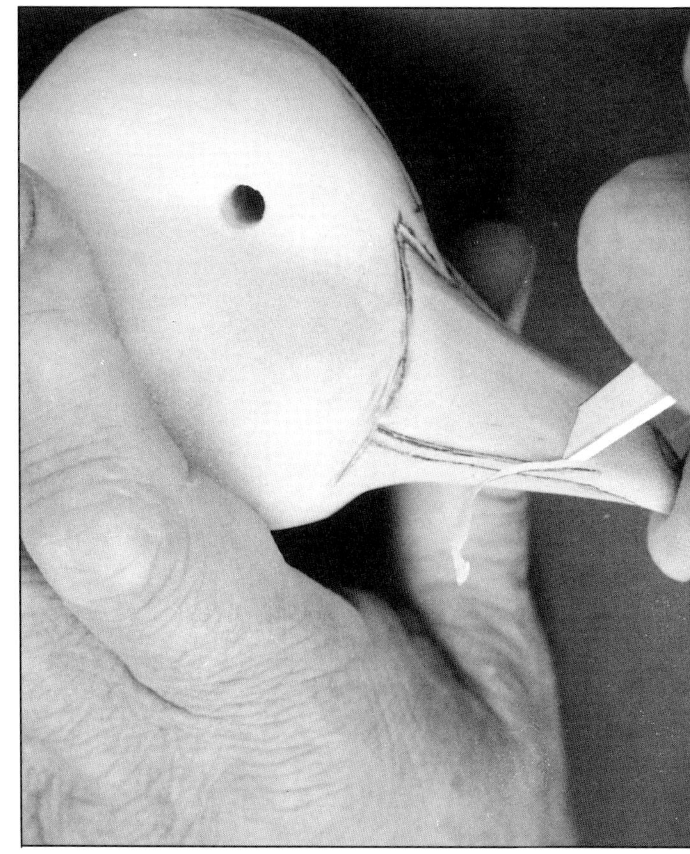

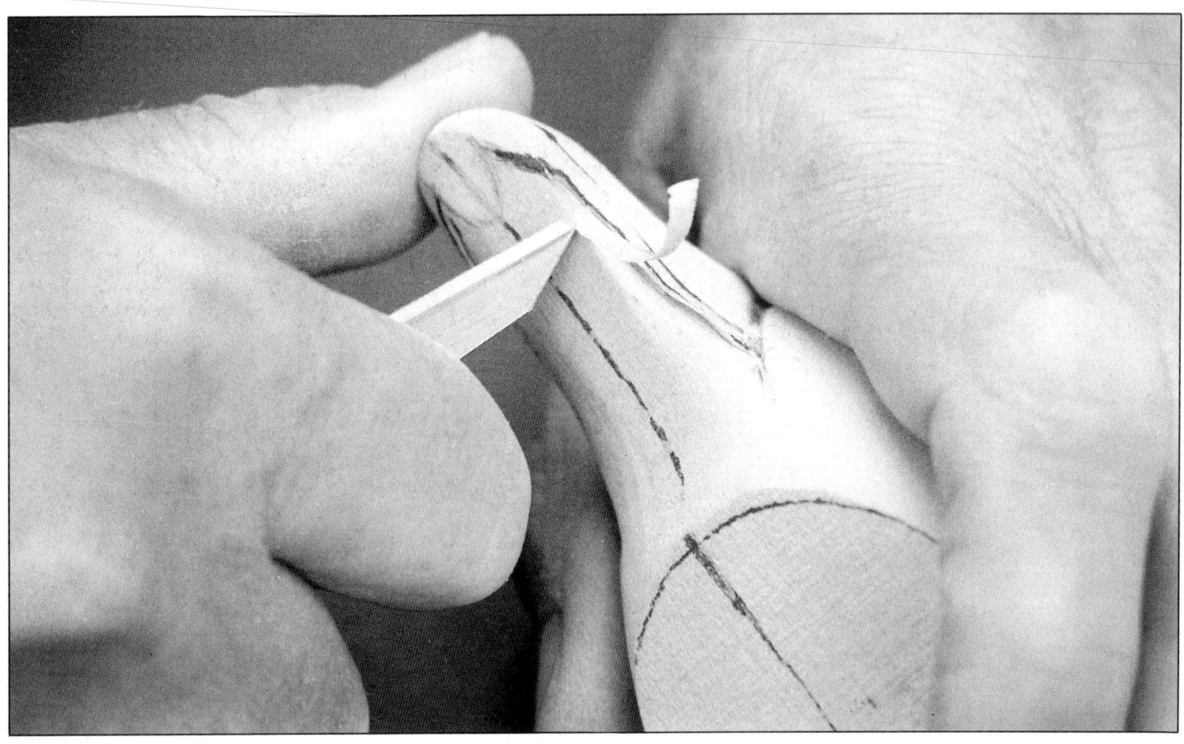

Fig 5.31 Establishing the lower mandible.

Fig 5.32 Hold the head firmly when defining the line of the lower mandible.

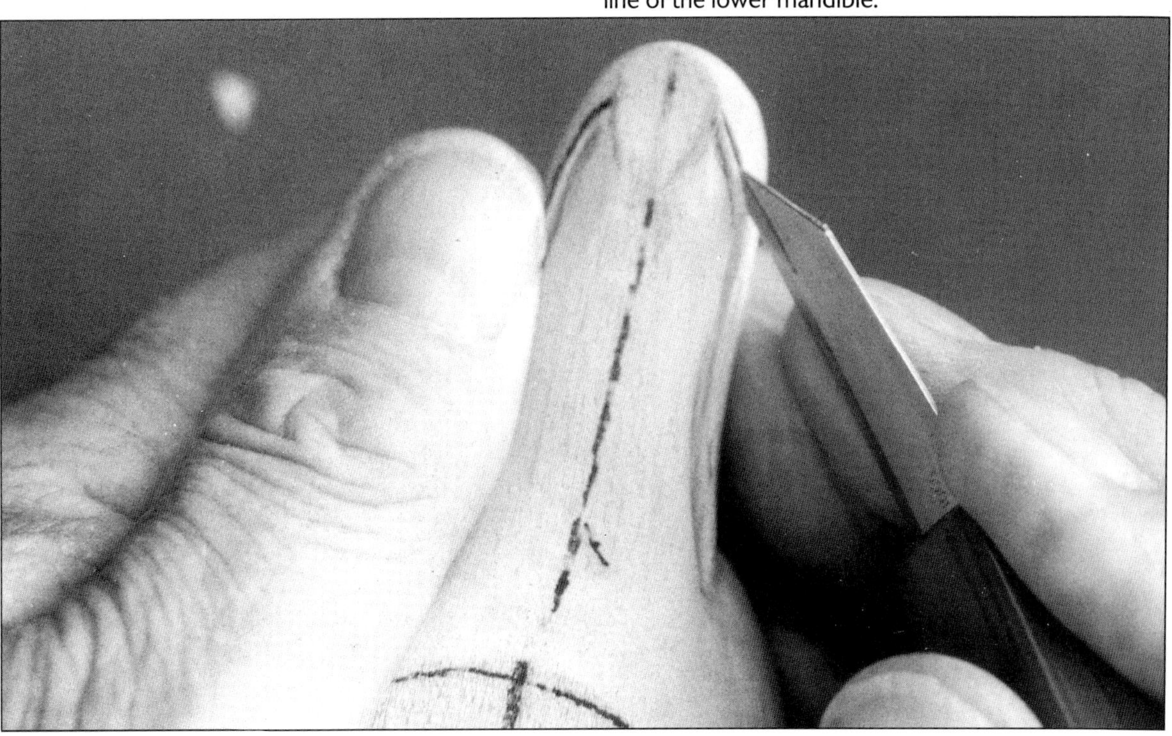

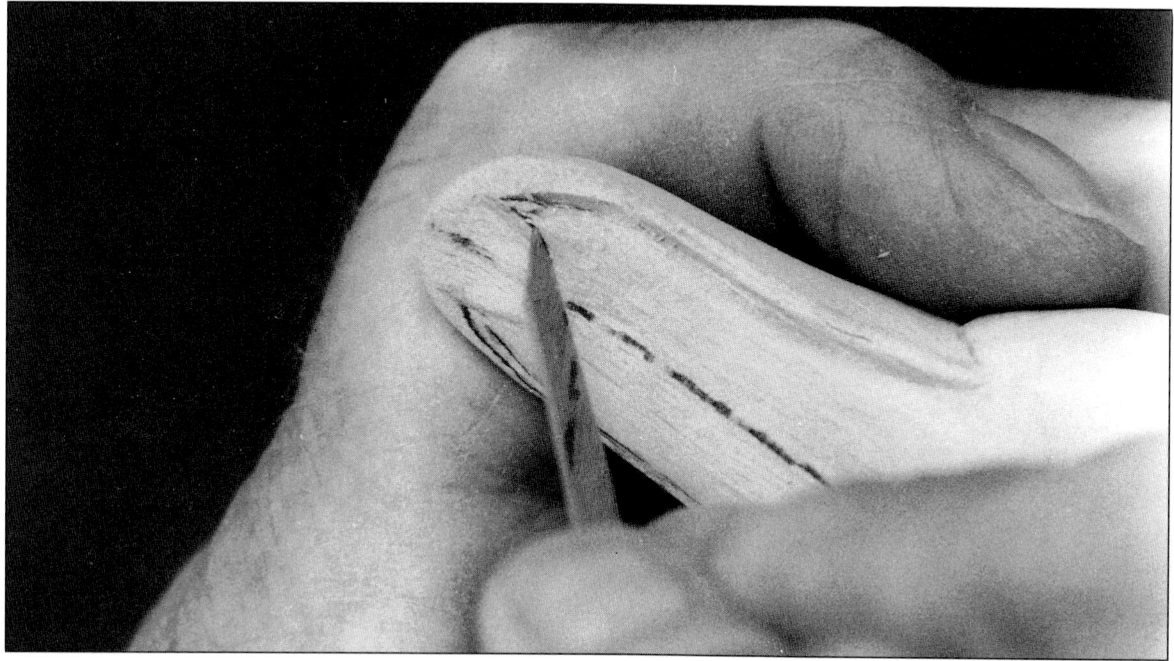

Fig 5.33 The distinctive small, rounded area on the underside of the lower mandible is defined with the knife blade.

3 Repeat this operation to establish the line of the lower mandible (see Fig 5.31).

4 Defining the line of the lower mandible and exposing the underside of the upper mandible requires both a steady hand and that the head is held very firmly (see Fig 5.32).

5 Define the well rounded area at the front of the lower mandible as you do this (see Fig 5.33).

6 To separate the upper from the lower mandible, use a short-bladed knife to remove some of the wood between the two, creating a groove. You may need to use the burning tool again to clean up this groove. Remember that when a duck closes its bill, the upper mandible overlaps the lower, and for much of its length the lower mandible is lost to view (see Fig 5.34).

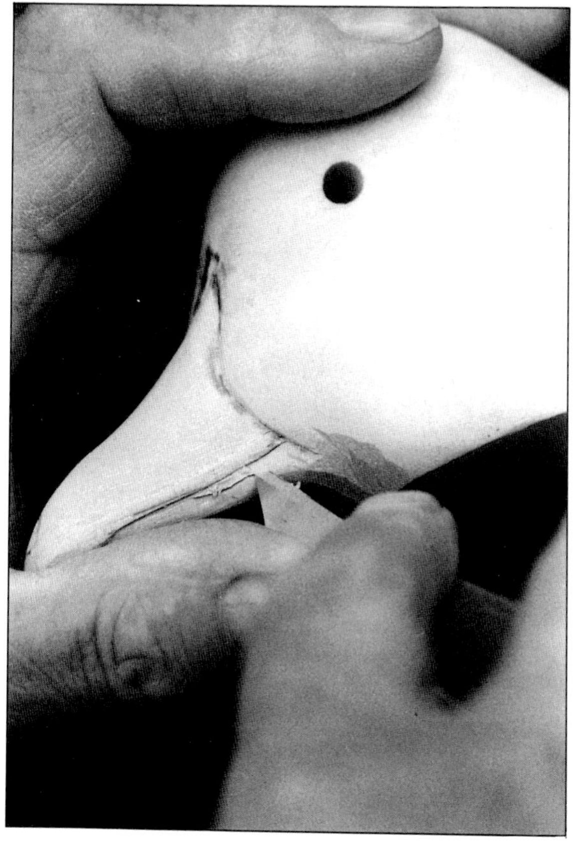

Fig 5.34 Create a groove between the upper and lower mandibles, to be sanded later.

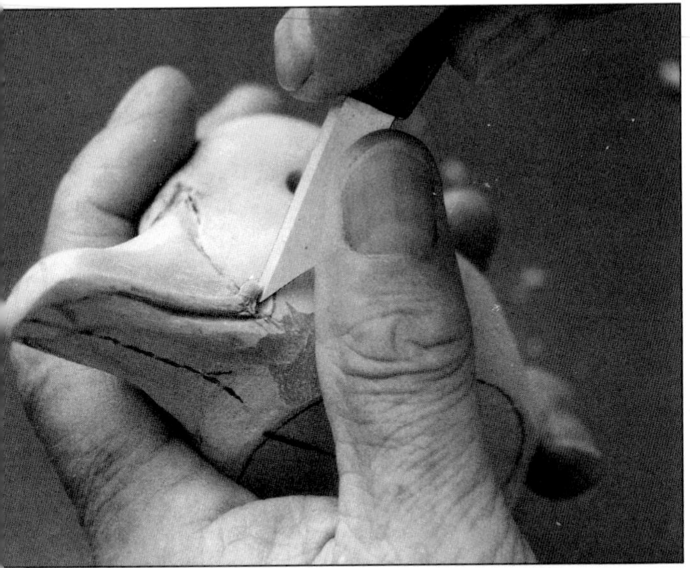

Fig 5.35 Creating the duck's endearing 'smile'.

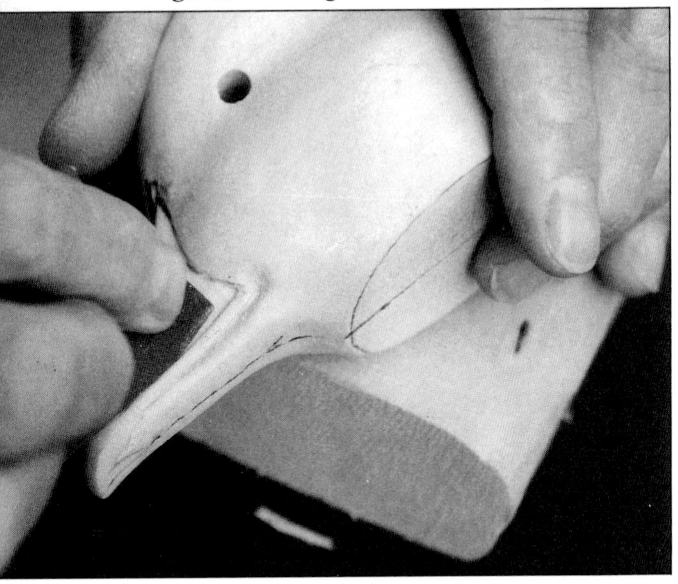

Fig 5.36 Clean up the cuts and round off the edges with folded sanding strip (400 grit).

7 Finally, cut out a small depression in the area where the upper mandible joins the head. This enhances the degree of animation by creating the duck's endearing 'smile' (see Fig 5.35).

8 Soften the edges and smooth out the areas separating the two mandibles using a small folded piece of fine sanding strip (see Fig 5.36).

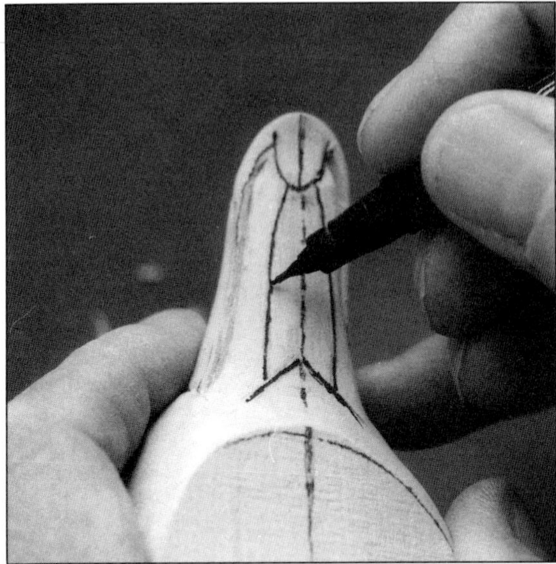

Fig 5.37 Marking out the lower mandible; you will find reference to a study bill very useful here.

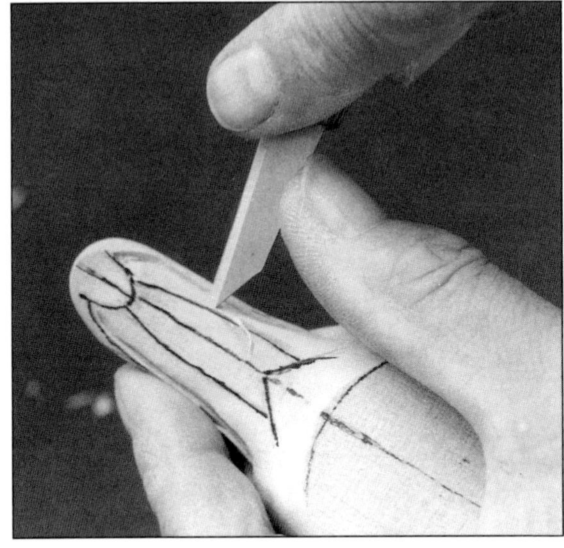

Fig 5.38 Cut only small slivers in this area to prevent the wood splitting.

The lower mandible

1 All duck bills have a characteristic inverted V-shaped area on the underside of the lower mandible. Mark this area out clearly (see Fig 5.37).

2 Be extremely careful when cutting out the wood in this area to form this V shape as it has a tendency to split. With your knife, cut out small

Fig 5.39 Use the Hot Tool to create the lamellae ('teeth').

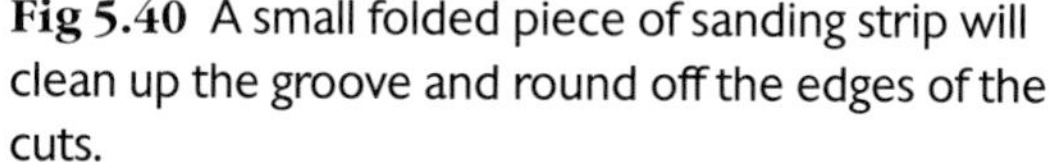

Fig 5.40 A small folded piece of sanding strip will clean up the groove and round off the edges of the cuts.

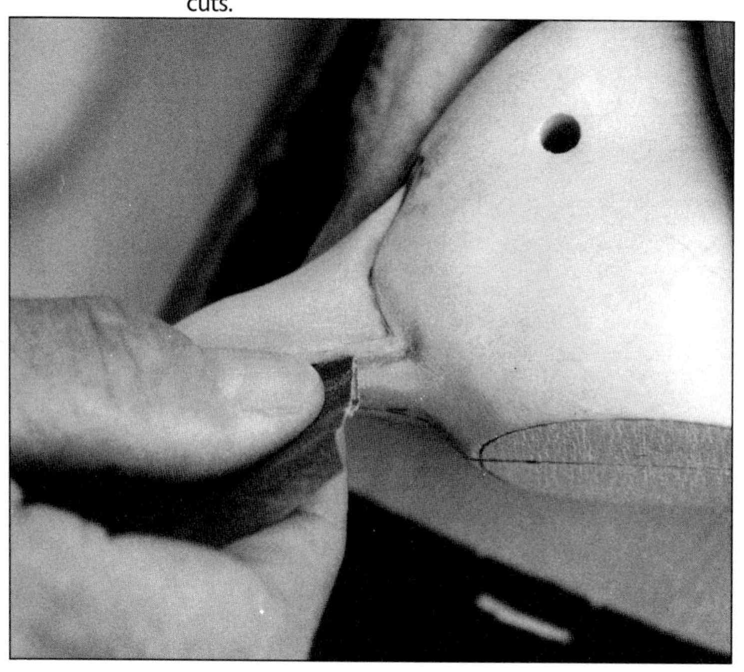

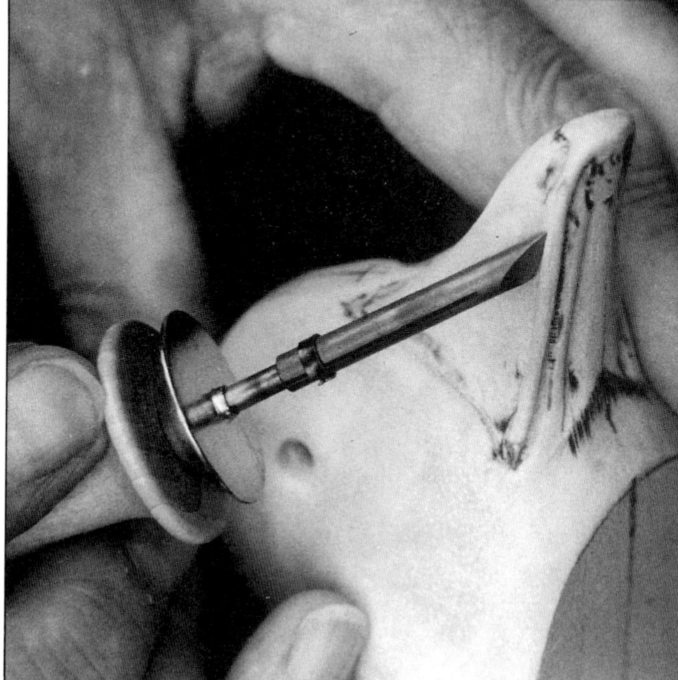

Fig 5.41 Used with care, the burning tool will clean up and define grooves and ridges.

thin sections and then shape the grooves using a sanding strip (see Fig 5.38).

3 The burning tool can now be used to define the final shape of the carved area on the underside of the lower mandible, and to create the small vertical serrations or lamellae on the underside of the upper mandible (see Fig 5.39).

The upper mandible

1 Using the blade of a very sharp knife (an X-acto knife fitted with a new blade is probably the best tool for this job) clearly define the lips of the upper mandible. As always with this technique for removing a thin strip of wood, the initial cut must be made at right angles to the surface of the wood, followed by a V-cut to relieve the wood. Failure to do so may result in sections of the lip splitting off. Sand the groove formed by the two cuts and round off the lip (see Fig 5.40).

2 Use a burning tool to clean up the groove, being very careful not to burn at too high a

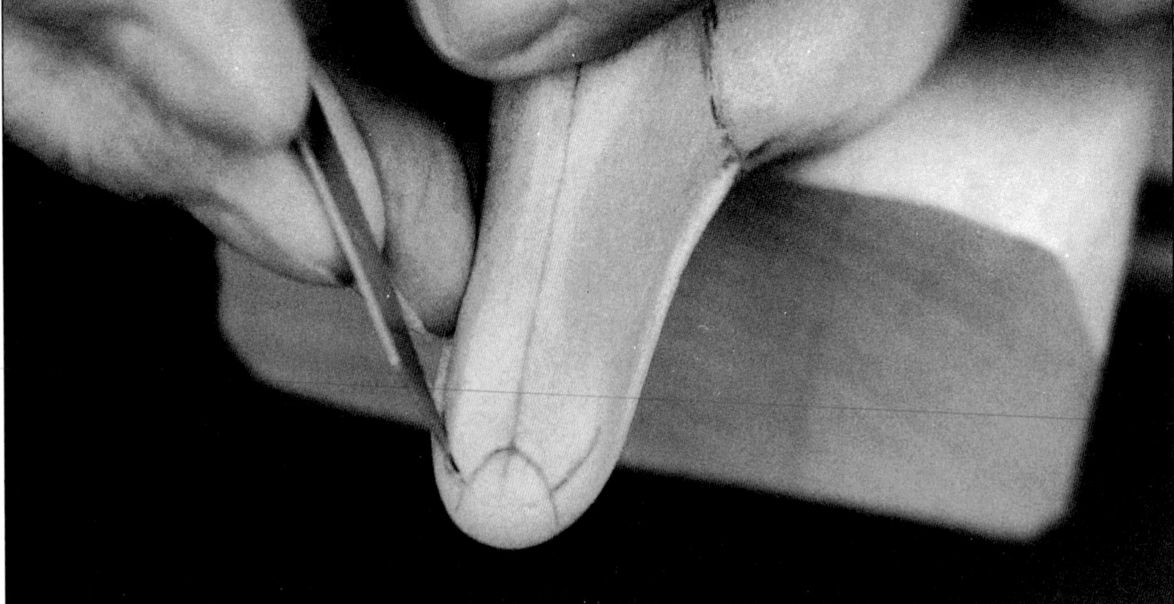

Fig 5.42 Define the nail with a shallow cut and round off with sanding strip.

temperature, otherwise you will have a build-up of carbon in the groove (see Fig 5.41).

The nail

At the tip of the duck's bill is the nail or nub, a hardened pointed area used to assist in cracking open the shell of the hatching egg and subsequently for breaking up food.

Having rounded off the end of the bill, carve the nail using a short-bladed knife and then sand it to a roundness by hand. You need only take off a very thin shaving of wood; I normally use a sanding strip (400-600 grit) to shape the nail and to give it a really smooth finish (see Fig 5.42).

Fig 5.43 Enlarge and shape the nostrils with a small file or the tip of your knife blade.

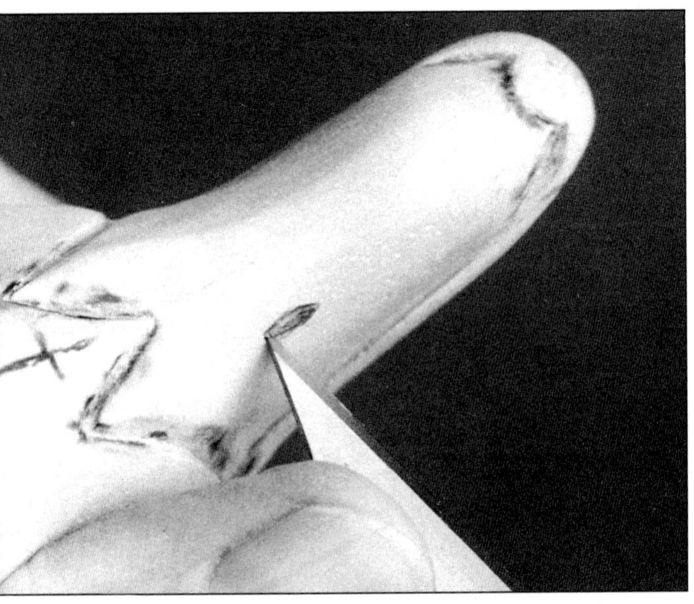

The nostrils

By carefully studying your reference sources, the nostrils can be marked out accurately enough, but be sure to check the position and alignment. Having done so, drill a *very small hole* in the centre of the marked area; a dental drill bit is ideal for this. The nostrils can now be enlarged using either a knife or a small file (see Fig 5.43).

The eye sockets

1 Blanks normally come with pre-drilled eyeholes. These eyeholes may be enlarged using a round file with a diameter less than that of the eye socket (see Fig 5.44).

Fig 5.44 As you enlarge the eye socket with a round file make sure the hole retains its shape.

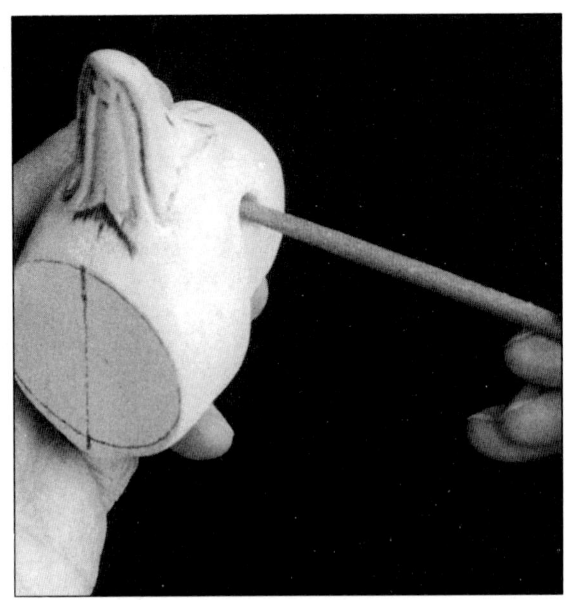

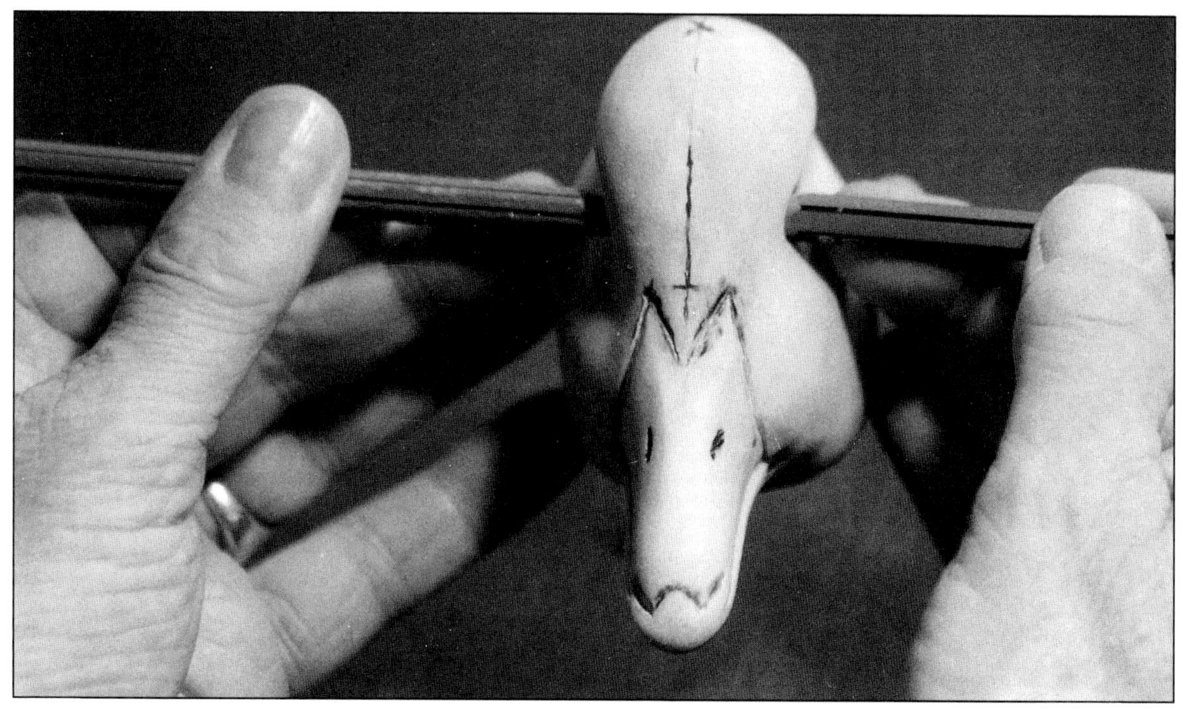

Fig 5.46 Correct eye alignment is very important and should be checked frequently as the sockets are enlarged.

Fig 5.45 The European goldeneye (photo by Joe Blossom, reproduced by kind permission of the Wildfowl and Wetlands Trust).

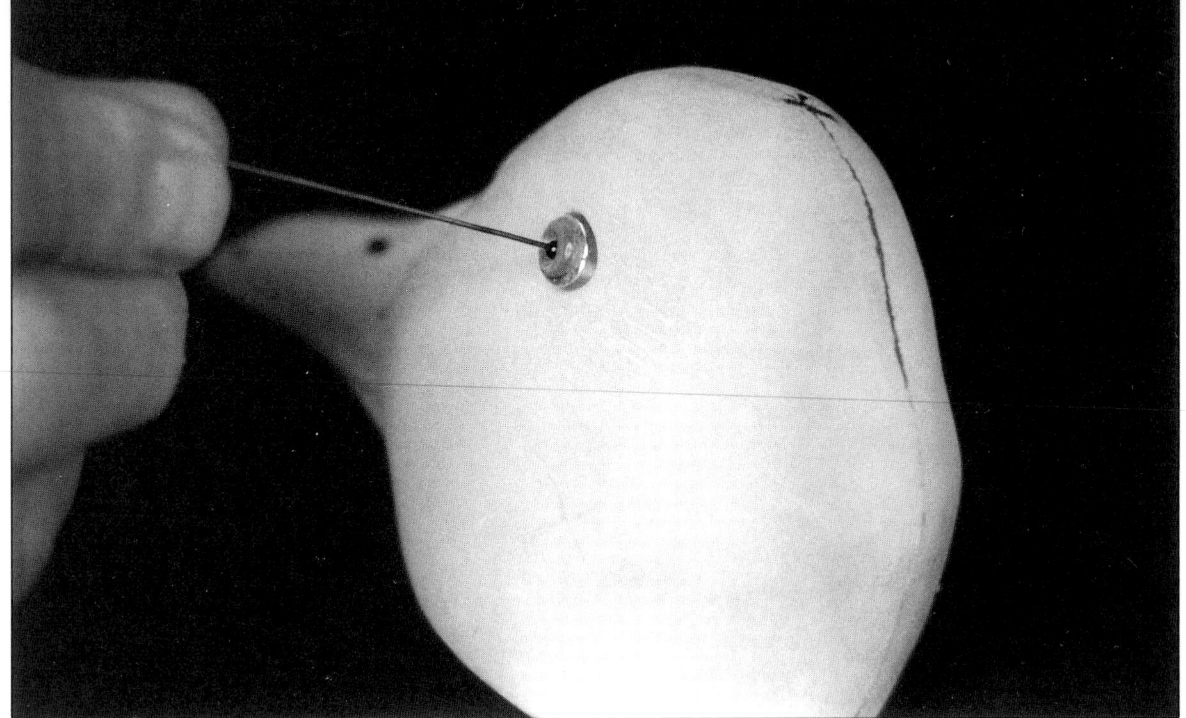

Fig 5.47 As you work, frequently try fitting the eye (reversed) to the hole.

Fig 5.48 Before the epoxy putty dries hard, check the eye alignment from above and from the front.

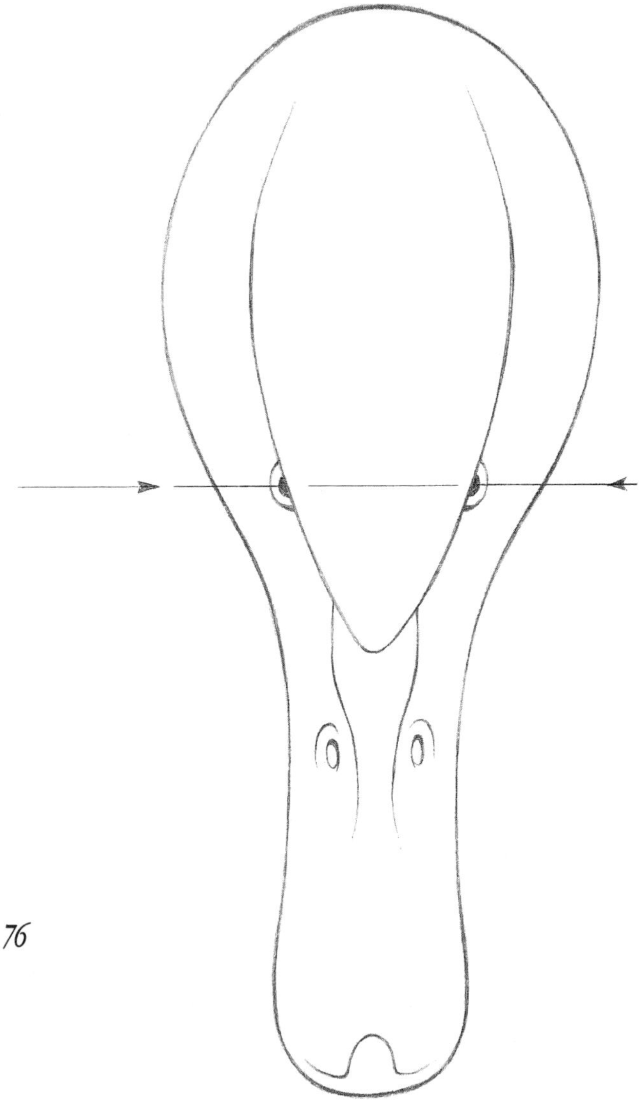

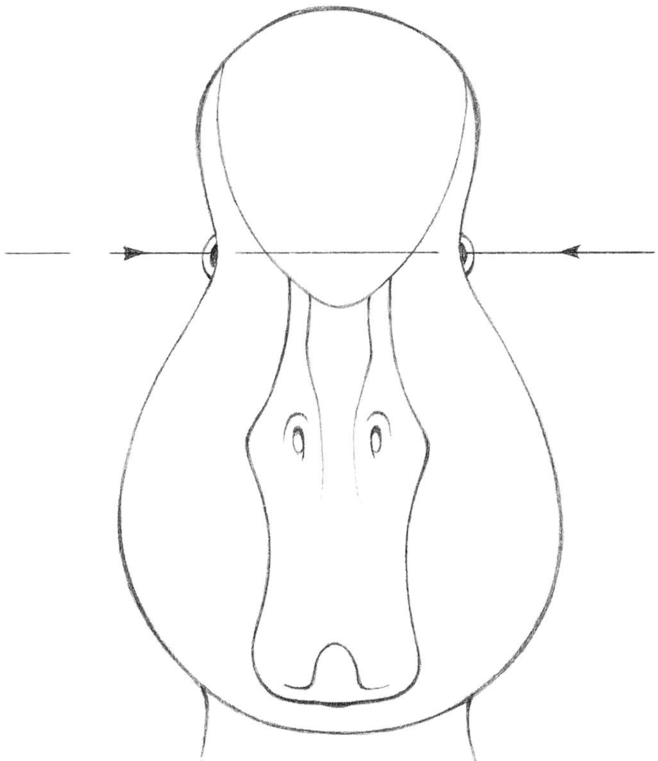

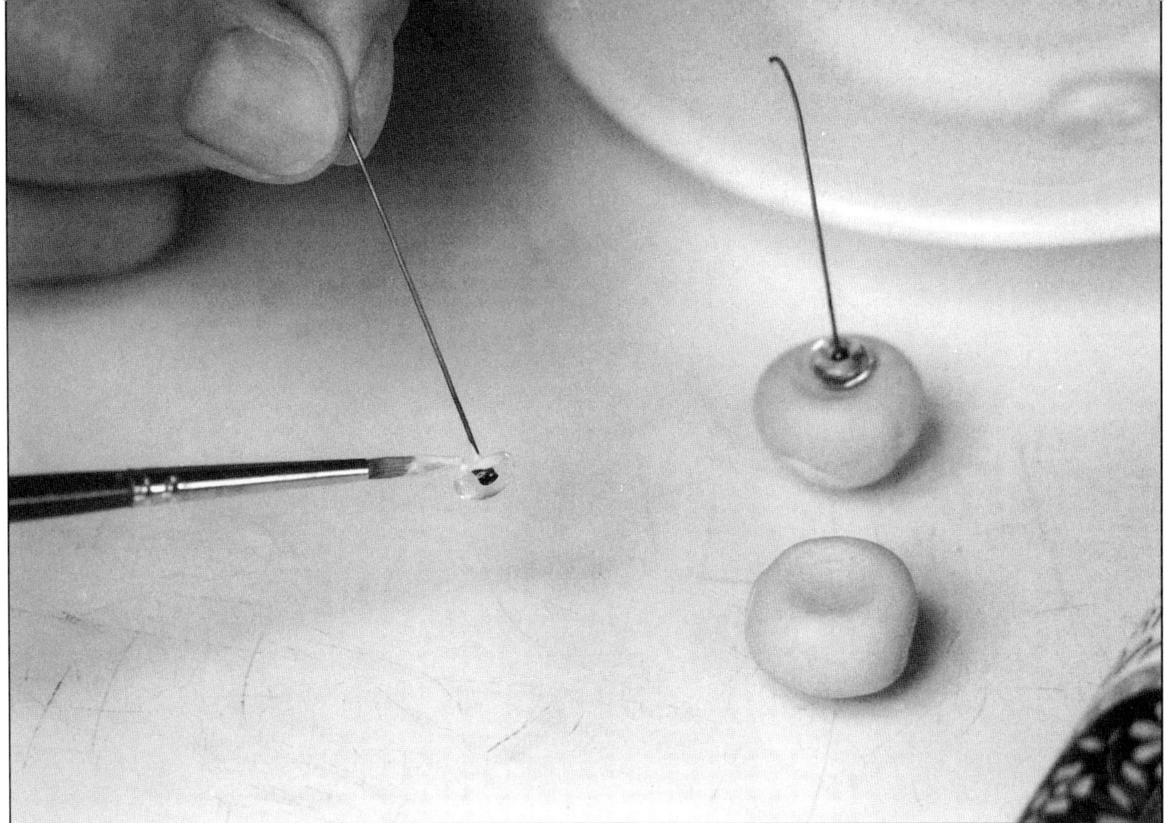

Fig 5.49 With clear glass eyes, apply the required colour mix of paint to the back of the eye and allow to dry on a ball of Blu-Tack.

A countersink bit may also be used to enlarge the eye sockets, but be very careful to avoid tearing the wood. I make the eye sockets slightly angled towards the bill and large enough to allow adjustment in the final positioning of the eyes.

2 As the head is the focal point of the carving, the correct positioning of the eyes is vital. Notice in the photo of the live duck (see Fig 5.45) that both eyes are in perfect alignment. In wildfowl carving, merely by moving the eyes very slightly forward, backward, up or down, the expression of the bird can be significantly altered.

3 To check the alignment of the sockets, use two pencils placed in the eye sockets and view the head from the front and from above (see Fig 5.46).

4 As you enlarge the sockets, make sure that the holes retain their shape and that at frequent intervals you try fitting the eyes into the holes in which you are working. You will probably find it more convenient to offer the front of the eye to the hole (see Fig 5.47).

5 When there is only a small even gap around the eye, and you are satisfied that both eyes fit properly, check the alignment from above and in front of the head (see Fig 5.48).

Choosing and setting the eyes

The eyes you fit must be of the correct size and colour. Appendix A (see page 134) is a table giving the sizes and colours of eyes for life-size carvings. For smaller carvings merely scale the size down proportionately. The common goldeneye has yellow eyes, 9mm in diameter.

There are several grades and shapes of eyes available. They are sold either as coloured eyes, where the colour has been fired in during their manufacture, or as clear glass.

1 Clear glass eyes have the advantage of being cheaper and can be painted in the colour that

Fig 5.50 For the correct size and colour of glass eyes, see Appendix A.

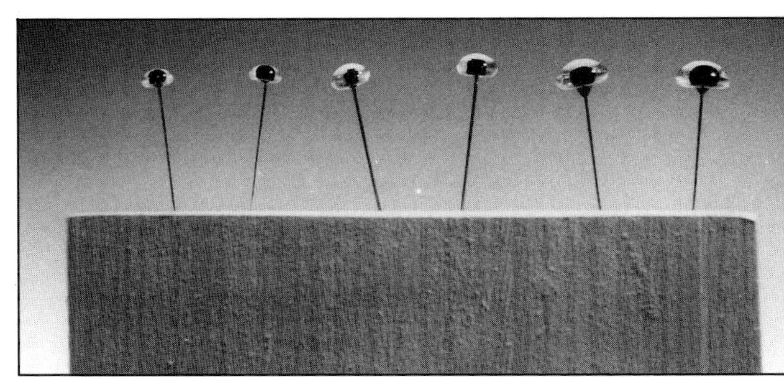

Fig 5.51 Mixing epoxy putty.

matches more closely that of the live bird. Paint is mixed to the required colour and applied to the back of the eye which is placed on a small ball of Blu-Tack or similar material to dry (see Fig 5.49).

2 The quality of glass eyes does vary, but I think it is always well worth fitting the best available. Eyes are normally sold in pairs affixed to wires, and before setting them it is advisable to cut these with wire cutters, leaving about 5/8in (15mm) of wire attached to each eye (see Fig 5.50).

3 I prefer to fix eyes in with epoxy putty. It is sold as a two-part compound as plumber's seal or modelling putty. Blend equal quantities of each part by kneading and rolling until the mixture is

Fig 5.52 Mixed, kneaded and rolled the putty is fed into the eye sockets.

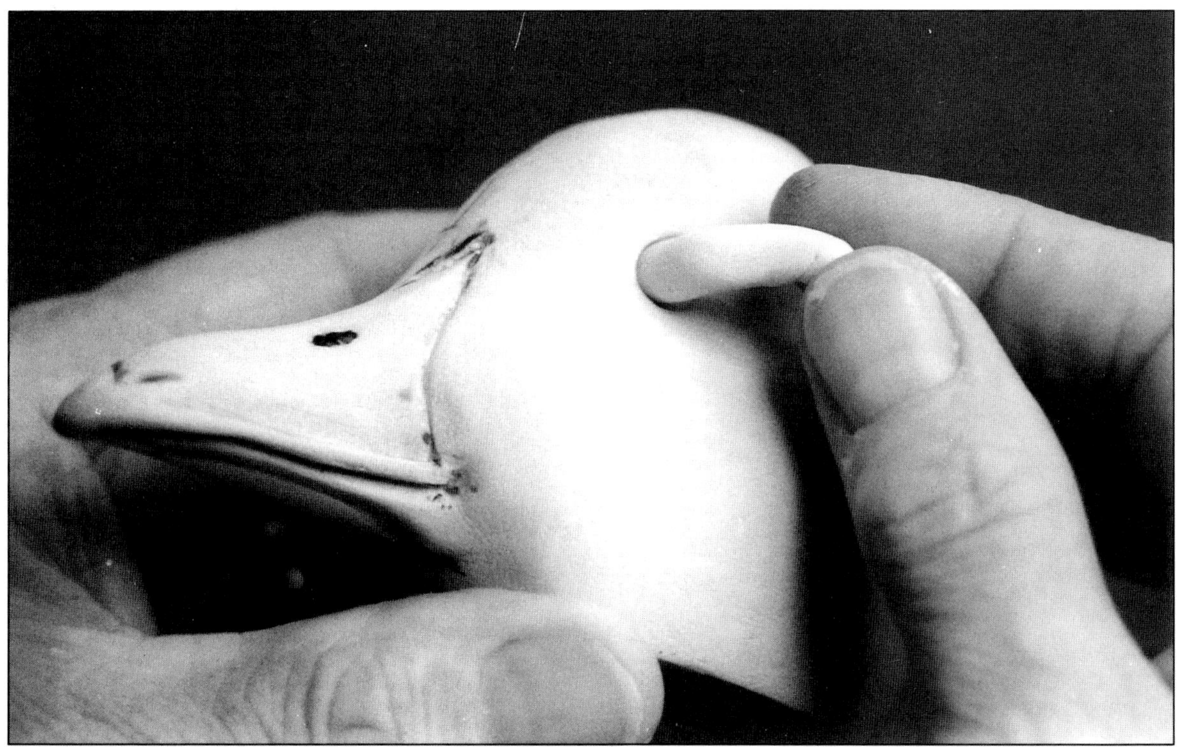

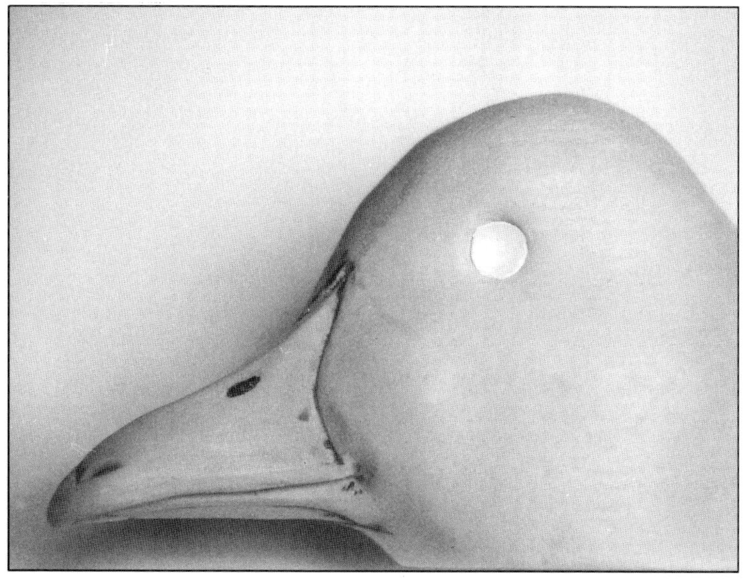

Fig 5.53 Remove surplus putty and use a round modelling tool or your finger to give a smooth concave finish.

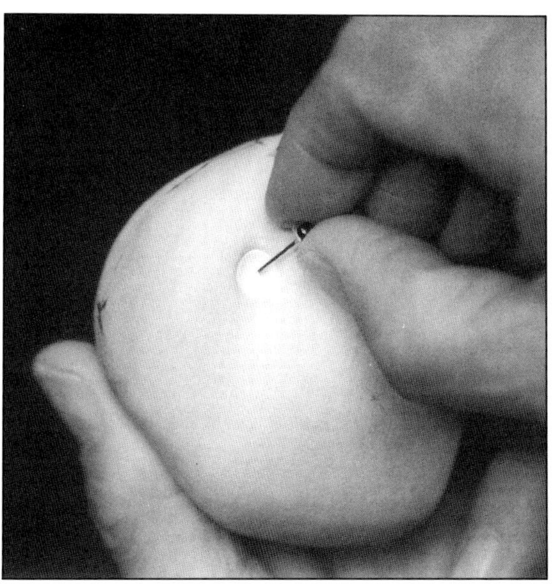

Fig 5.54 Insert the wire and press the eye firmly into place.

soft, and of an even colour throughout (see Fig 5.51).

4 Then press a small quantity into one of the eye sockets, partially filling it. Repeat the process for the other eye as it is essential to fix the final position of the eyes as a pair (see Fig 5.52).

5 With your finger, or a rounded modelling tool, press in putty to form a concave shape to receive the back of the eye (see Fig 5.53).

6 Insert the wire of the eye into the putty. Press the eye firmly into the putty until a little oozes out around the rim. Take off the surplus putty with a knife blade. Repeat the setting process immediately with the other eye, checking for alignment as you do it (see Fig 5.54).

When viewed from directly above the head it should be only just possible to see the tips of the eyes, and when viewed from the front the eyes should be level (see Fig 5.55).

Some carvers prefer to smooth or 'feather' the putty into the area around the eye with a dampened finger, but I prefer to let the putty dry thoroughly overnight, and then apply plastic wood over the putty. I then smooth this out, using a small paintbrush dipped in acetone, and this gives me a very smooth surface, on which I can cut or burn texture lines right up to the edges of the eyes.

Fig 5.55 The eyes should be level when viewed from the front.

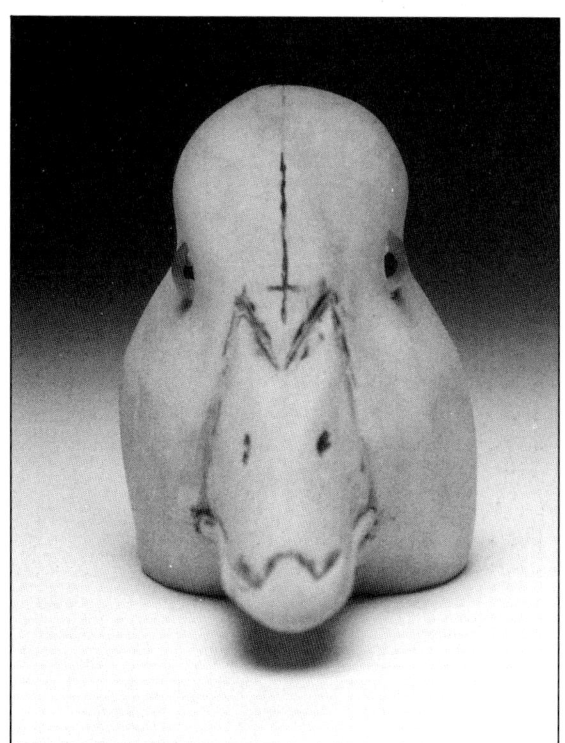

CHAPTER 6

Carving the Body

Equipment

Essential

2 pencils (HB and 2B)
Knife (fixed blade or craft)
Plastic modelling tool or knife
Paintbrush (old, size 5 or 6)

Optional

Flexible ruler
Small Surform file
Chisels, straight or skew; blade width: 1/8–1/4in (3–6mm)

Materials

2 Sanding strips; 80–120 grit and 400–600 grit; 12 x 1in (300 x 25mm)
Super epoxy glue (quick drying)
Plastic wood filler
Acetone

Useful reference material/sources

Pattern books (for details of feather groupings)
Wildlife Carver's Pattern Book. Avian Art Inc., 2388 Staunton Drive, Swartz Creek, MI 48373 USA, p. 3.
Jim Sprankle, *Waterfowl Patterns & Painting.* Greenwing Enterprises, Chester, Maryland, USA, p. 9.

Marking Out

The centre line

1 A blank for this particular carving will be symmetrical, and to help retain that symmetry, clear guide lines need to be drawn before carving is started.

At the outset, the centre line needs to be established accurately and either drawn freehand, or as I prefer to do, with a flexible ruler (see Fig 6.1). The line should be continuous around the whole body and tail.

No-go areas

2 The no-go areas, which I mark with crosses, are the high spots on the blank that, during the early stages of carving, should be avoided (see Fig 6.2). These areas correspond to the peak of the arch of the folded wings (two crosses on top of the blank) and the widest points of the duck's body, at the side pockets (one cross on each side of the blank). Later, however, when the final shape is beginning to emerge, it may be necessary to cut into, or sand down, these areas.

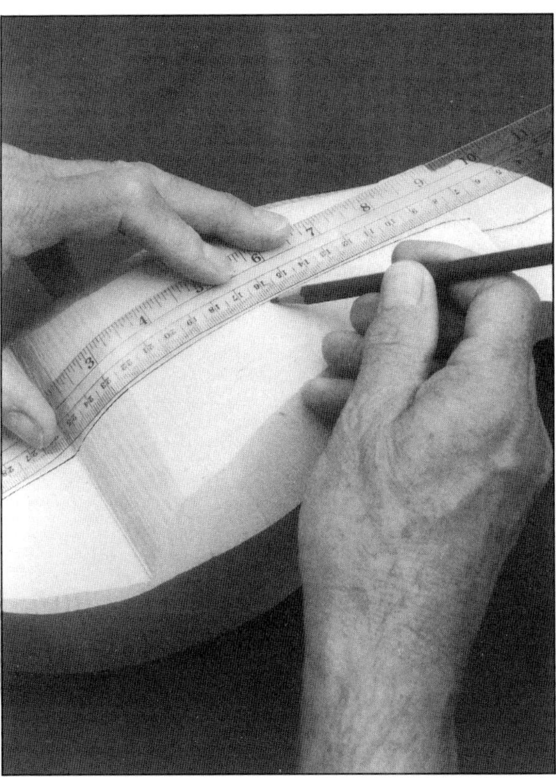

Fig 6.1 Centre line. Before starting to carve, draw in the centre line around the whole body and tail.

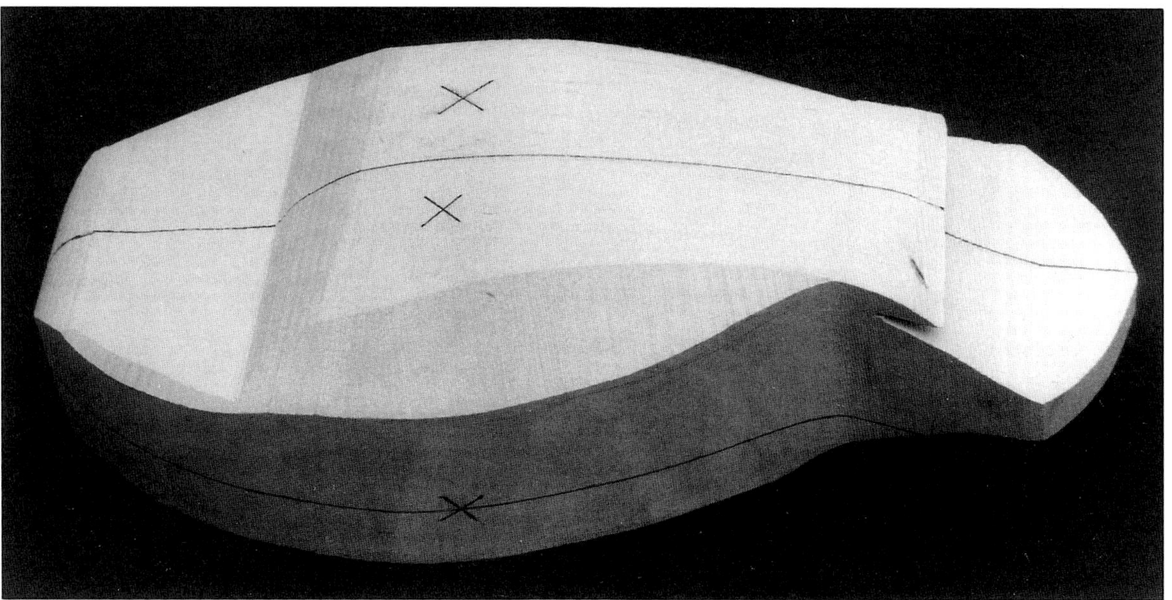

Fig 6.2 'No-go' areas. Areas marked with crosses should not be touched during early stages of carving and should be regarded as high spots.

The 'Plimsoll line'

3 One of the more elementary errors made by the novice carver is to create a straight-sided duck, sometimes dismissed in the States as a 'boxcar duck', so named for its apparent similarity to a straight-sided rail truck. To overcome this problem, I recommend drawing what I call the 'Plimsoll line' around the duck. (see Fig 6.3) The line divides the duck vertically in the proportion of approximately one third below and two thirds above the line, as measured from the water line. Viewed from either end of the duck it marks the high spot of the vertical curve of the body.

Wing areas

4 With the duck in the rest position as we are carving it, the forward part of the wings around the back and cape area form two humps. At this stage, mark these two humped areas as curves running from the centre line and continuing round the side of the body (see Fig 6.4).

Side pockets

5 The line of the wing continued to the rear of the duck and around its sides will define the side pocket areas (see Fig 6.5).

Fig 6.3 The 'Plimsoll line' drawn on the blank helps in creating the duck's curved side.

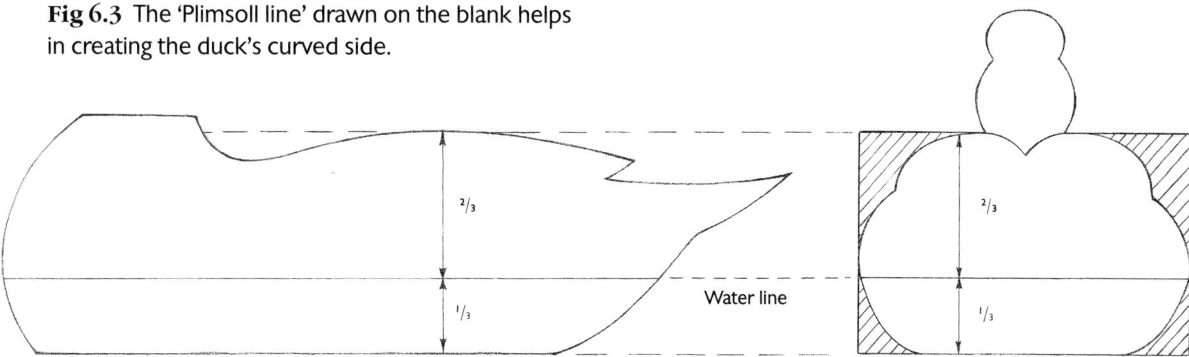

Carving the Body

1 I find in shaping the body it is better to remove all the hard edges on the blank (see Figs 6.6 and 6.7). Too much wood must not be taken off at this stage. The final required shape will not be achieved in the first series of cuts. A step-by-step approach, taking a little off at each step pays dividends.

2 Once you have removed all the hard edges you will be looking at a rounded form, and it will be much easier to assess where wood needs to be removed, and how much (see Fig 6.8).

One of the golden rules with any carving is to stop working at frequent intervals to carefully study what you have done so far. Before starting to carve again, it is a good idea to indicate on the carving where and how much wood is to be taken off at the next step.

3 When a stage in the carving has been reached approximating to the final shape, refine the shapes

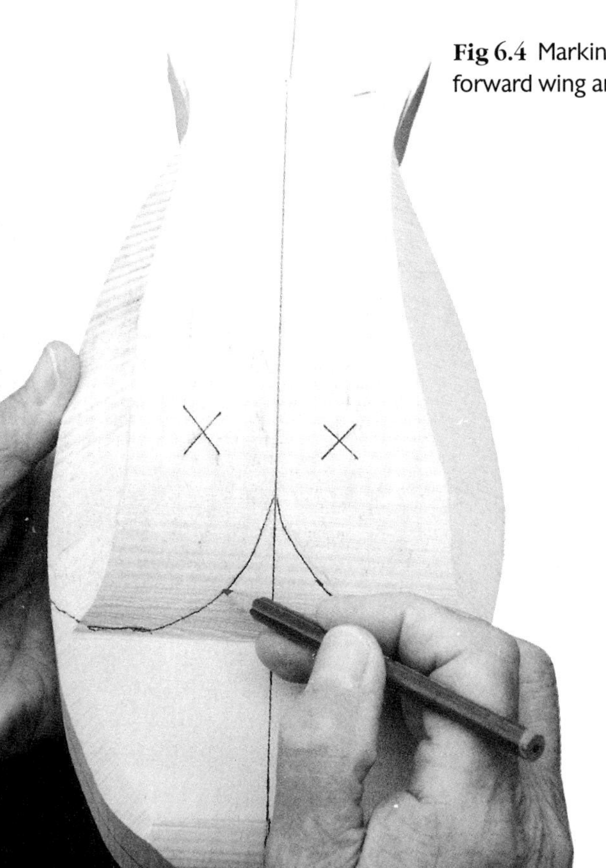

Fig 6.4 Marking the forward wing areas.

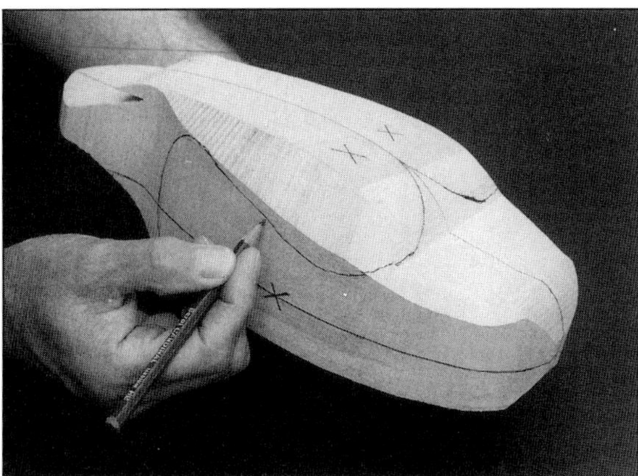

Fig 6.5 The wing area lines are extended to define the side pockets, or flanks.

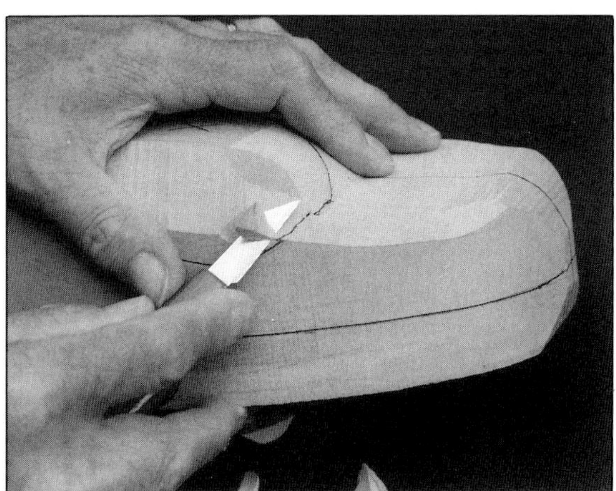

Fig 6.6 Remove all sharp edges from the blank before starting the final shaping.

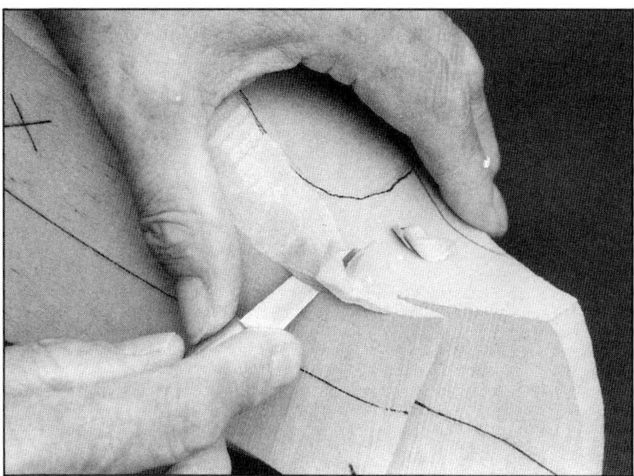

Fig 6.7 At this early stage of shaping the body, do not remove too much wood with each cut.

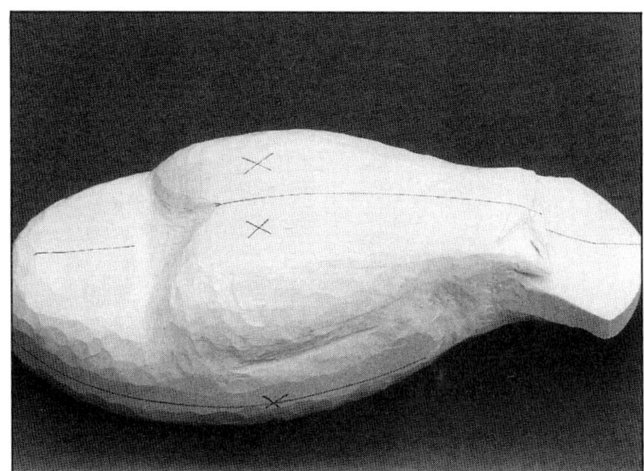

Fig 6.8 A rounded form makes it easier to assess where wood needs to be removed.

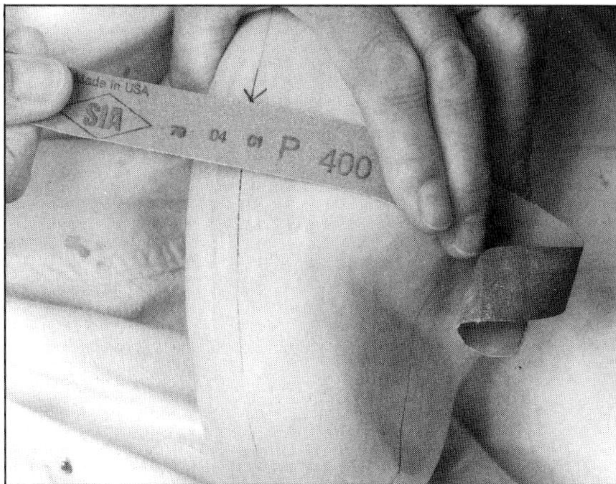

Fig 6.9 Sanding the body down using coarse, followed by fine, sanding strips.

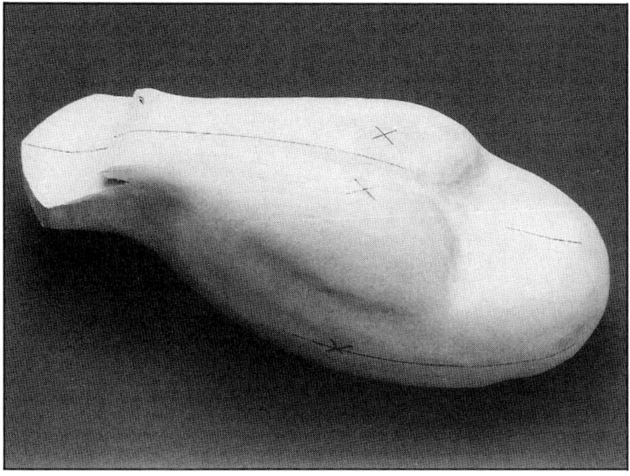

Fig 6.10 The resulting fairly smooth surface will make subsequent marking out much easier.

using a coarse sanding strip (80-120 grit) followed by a fine strip (400 grit) (see Fig 6.9).

4 You now have a reasonably smooth surface on which to mark out areas requiring further carving and to draw the feather groupings in at a later stage (see Fig 6.10).

Carving the Tail

Marking out

The tail section of the blank is always left fairly thick to allow the carver a certain flexibility in the angle or shape of the tail required in the finished carving.

Two parallel lines about 1/4in (6mm) or slightly less apart are drawn around the tail and another marking the join between the tail feathers and the upper tail coverts. These lines serve as guidelines when carving in that area. Draw shading lines (in pencil) as I have done on the edges of the wood that merge into the upper rump area (see Fig 6.11).

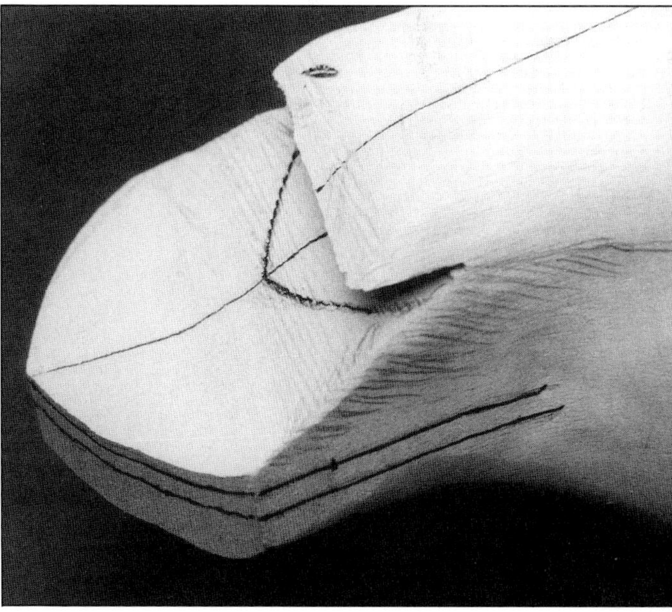

Fig 6.11 Mark out the tail thickness and the join between the upper tail coverts and the tail feathers must be marked before carving this area. Note also the shading lines.

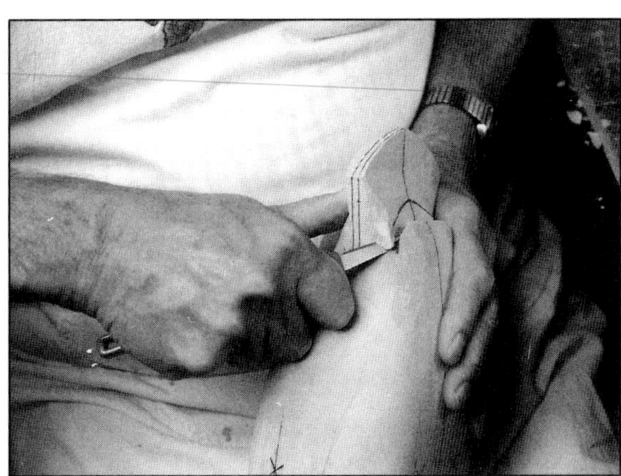

Fig 6.12 Removing the surplus wood.

Fig 6.14 Take great care when thinning the tail to prevent the wood splitting.

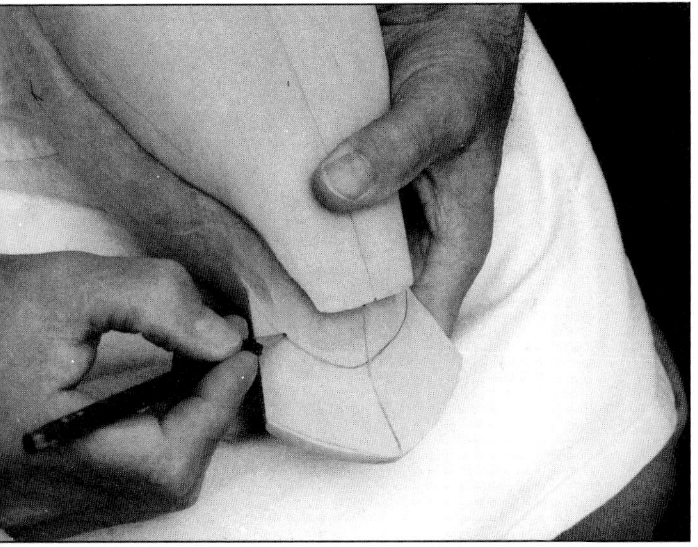

Fig 6.13 Remember to redraw guidelines which have been erased.

Carving steps

1 The surplus wood, as indicated by the shaded area in the previous photo, should be removed first. The direction of the grain in this area of the upper tail coverts makes carving it quite easy (see Fig 6.12).

2 As the carving progresses, the drawn guidelines will inevitably be erased. These should be drawn in again before carving is restarted (see Fig 6.13).

3 Reducing the thickness of the tail must be done

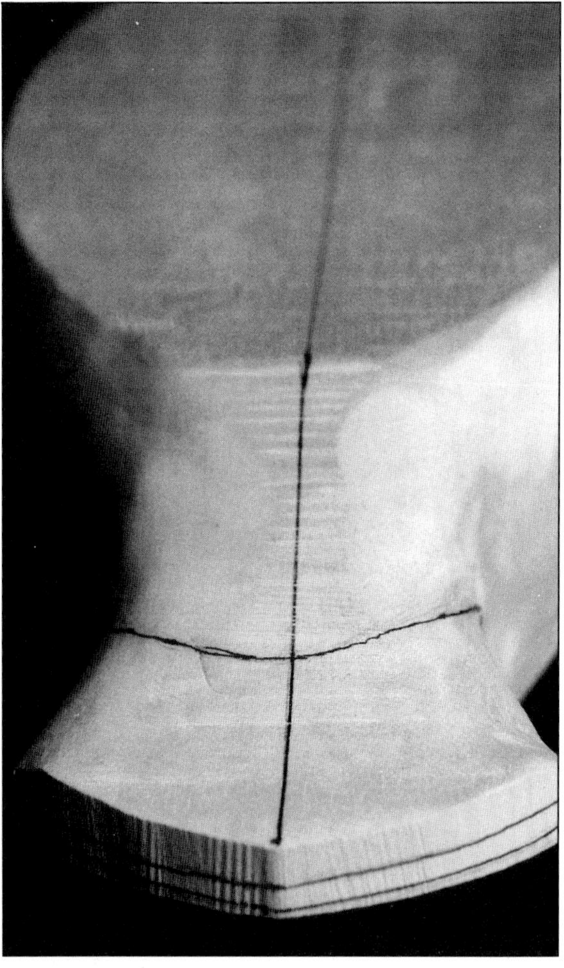

Fig 6.15 Marking out the underside of the tail to show the join between the tail feathers and the under tail coverts.

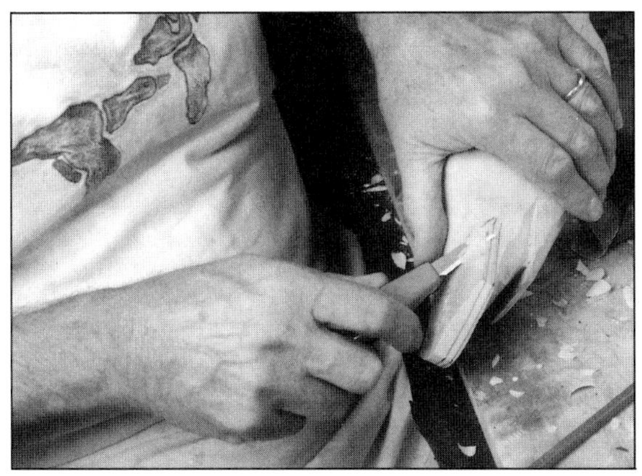

Fig 6.16 Once again take care when working on the underside of the tail to avoid splitting.
Fig 6.17 Make a vertical cut along the upper line of the side pockets and remove a sliver of wood in order to relieve the secondary feathers.

with great care, especially towards the tip where the risk of pieces splitting off must be guarded against (see Fig 6.14).

4 Mark the join between the tail feathers and the under tail coverts (see Fig 6.15).

5 Exercise the same caution as before in shaping the underside of the tail (see Fig 6.16).

Defining Secondaries and Primaries

1 In the finished carving the wings must appear to be resting over the back of the duck. To create this impression the tertial and the primary feathers of the wings must be carved in such a

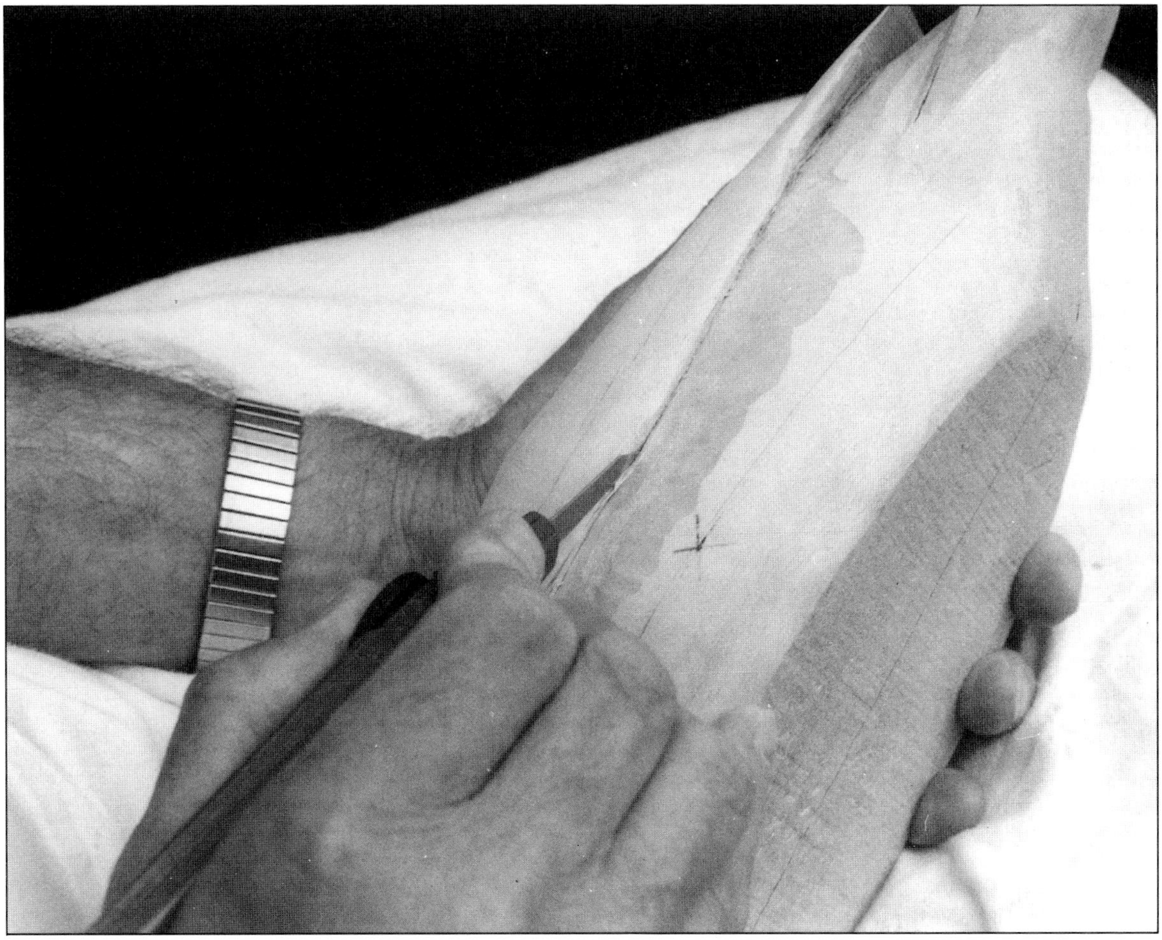

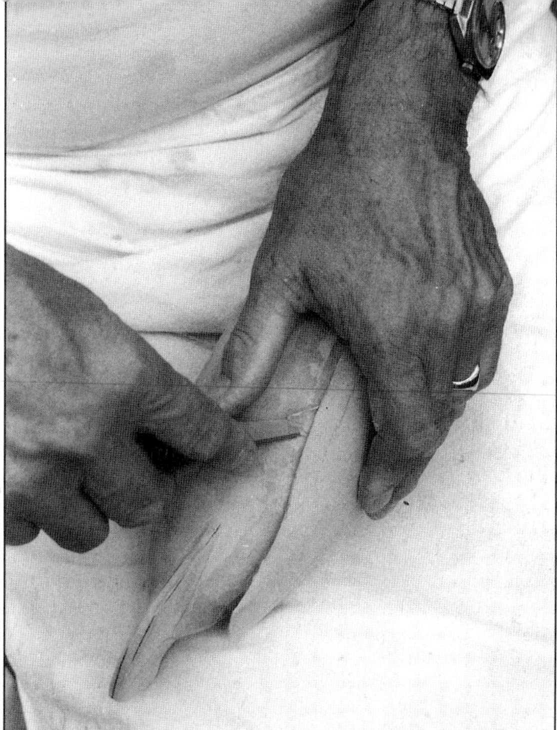

Fig 6.18 A second cut at an angle to the first throws the secondaries into relief.

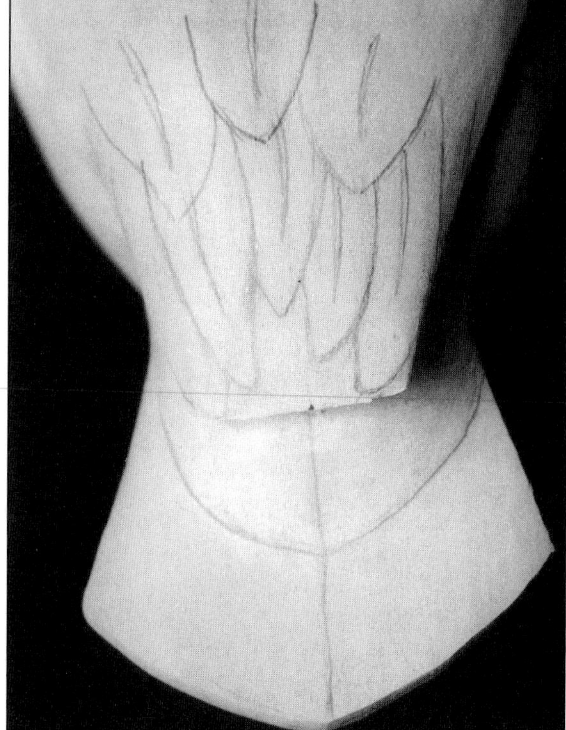

Fig 6.19 When marking the outline of the primary feathers make use of your reference sources to achieve the correct pattern.

way that they stand out from the body. To achieve this, make a cut, vertical to the surface of the wood, along the upper line that was drawn to define the side pockets (see Fig 6.17).

2 With a second cut, at an angle to the first, remove enough wood to throw the secondaries into relief (see Fig 6.18).

3 The same procedure may be used to relieve the primaries. In this case, draw in the outline of the primary feathers (see Fig 6.19).

4 Again, use the knife to undercut and define this group (see Fig 6.20).

Attaching the Head

Positioning

If the pattern for your blank has been designed with the head facing forward, the limit to which it may be angled and still retain a natural look is about 30° from the centre line. Within this limit, I suggest different positions are tried until it looks right. Then hold the head and body firmly and draw a vertical line on the head to meet another on the neck. Repeat this marking on the other side to ensure that the head is replaced in the same position when it is attached to the body (see Fig 6.21).

Fixing

To make certain that the head is firmly secured to the body, most carvers use the method outlined here. Some, however, in addition to using an adhesive, insist on fitting a dowel pin between the head and the body. Others drive a long screw up through its body and use this to tighten the head down. With this method, provided the two joined surfaces are perfectly flat, the joint between the two becomes almost indiscernible.

1 The best adhesive for attaching the head is quick drying Super epoxy glue (see Fig 6.22).

2 The compound should be applied thinly to the two surfaces being joined. Care must be taken not to spread the glue too near the edges of the joint (see Figs 6.23 and 6.24). When repositioning the head, try to avoid any glue oozing out but if it should, wipe it off immediately with a clean rag. Other wood adhesives will work just as efficiently but are less convenient to use.

3 Once the head is correctly positioned, firmly press the two surfaces together. Check frequently during the drying period that the head has not moved. If the carving is on a flat surface the risk of this happening is slight (see Fig 6.25).

Masking the joint

1 When the glue has set, cut a small V-section of

wood out from around the neck joint. This is to allow the plastic wood filler to form a wedge between the head and the neck (see Fig 6.26).

2 Using a suitable modelling tool, spread the plastic wood along the line of the joint (see Fig 6.27).

3 Using a paintbrush dipped in acetone, smooth the plastic wood out (see Fig 6.28). Acetone is available from a pharmacist or chemist. It is a highly volatile flammable liquid and should be kept in a firmly stoppered bottle away from heat or a naked flame.

As a very smooth surface is essential for texturing, it is important that the plastic wood, when dried, should present a surface as smooth as the surrounding wood. You may well have to try one or two products before finding one that meets this requirement. Plastic wood shrinks on drying, so joints and holes should be slightly overfilled to allow for this.

4 Leave the plastic wood to harden overnight to be absolutely sure it has set firmly. A 400–600 grit sanding strip will achieve a very smooth surface and the joint should be almost invisible (see Fig 6.29).

5 Some carvers recommend the use of extra fine steel wool (grade 0000) to do this, but I find that the wool leaves a fine metal dust behind that can be troublesome to remove from the surface of the wood (see Fig 6.30).

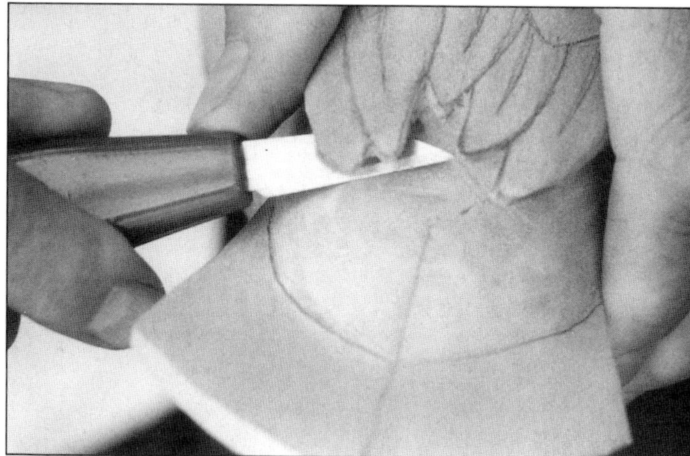

Fig 6.20 Use a knife to undercut and relieve the primary feathers.

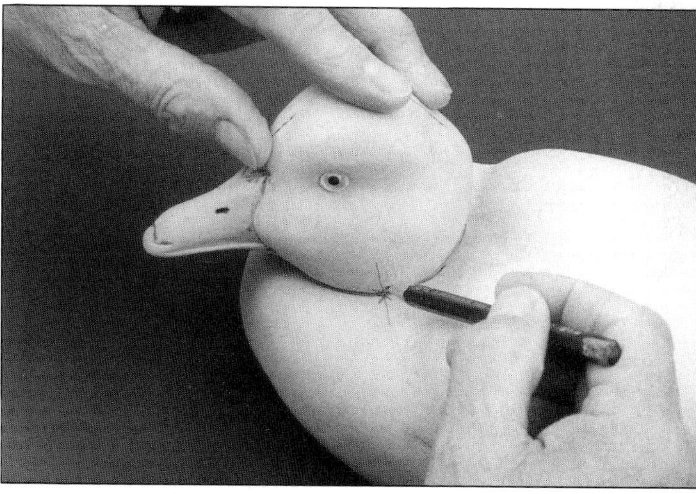

Fig 6.21 Mark the position of the head relative to the body.

Masking Defects

The latex lattice associated with jelutong, mentioned in Chapter Four can, at first sight, cause the newcomer to carving some anxiety. They appear in the most inconvenient places and seem to run right through the wood (see Fig 6.31). If the defect is longitudinal, as is the case here, cuts should be made either side of the defect, and parallel to it, to leave a V-sectioned gully. This should then be filled with plastic wood and smoothed off with a paintbrush and acetone, leaving the plastic wood slightly proud of the surrounding wood. Subsequent rubbing down with a fine sanding strip (400 or 600 grit) will ensure a completely smooth area clear of any evidence of the original defect.

However, some defects are fortunately located in wood that is subsequently removed during the carving process (see Fig 6.32). Others can be hidden quite simply by applying the techniques used to mask the head and neck joint (see 'Masking the joint').

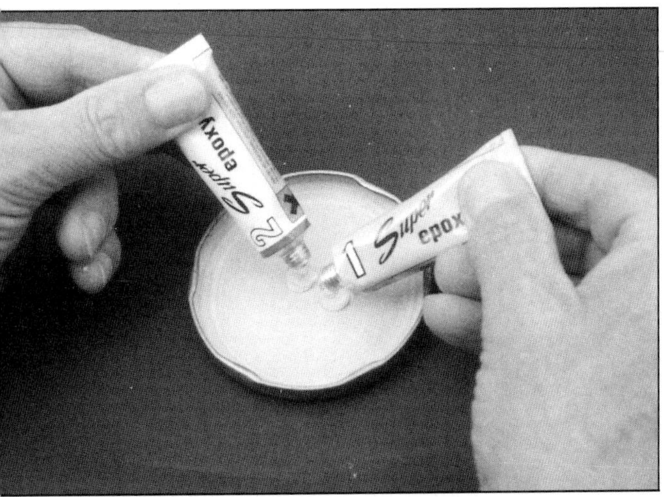

Fig 6.22 Thoroughly mix the epoxy glue.

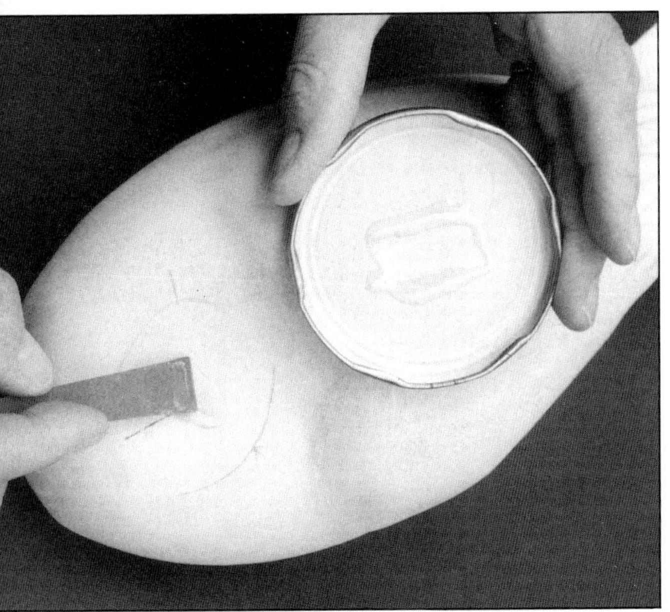

Fig 6.23 Spread the glue thinly and evenly over both surfaces.

Fig 6.24 Do not spread the glue too close to the edges.

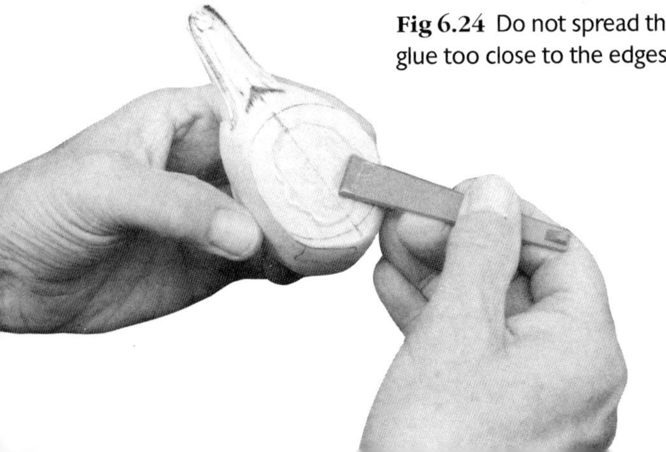

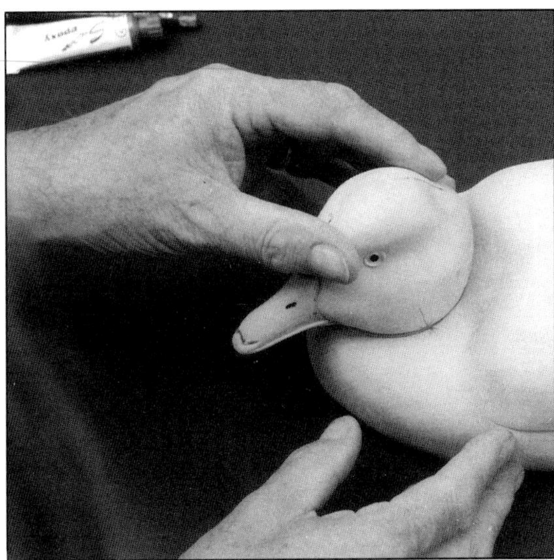

Fig 6.25 Press the two surfaces together, ensuring the head does not slide or turn as the glue dries.

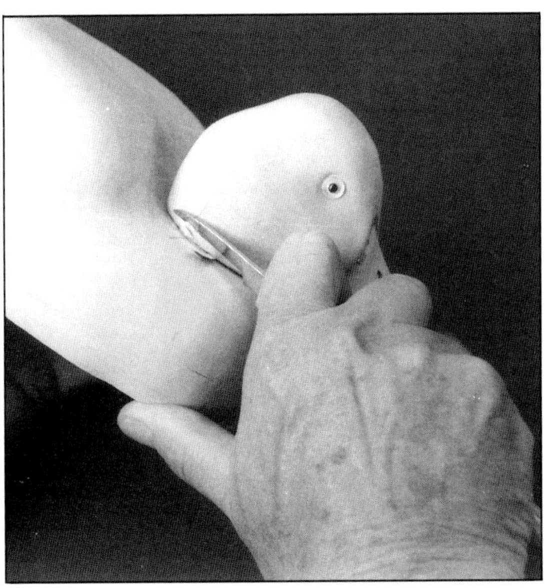

Fig 6.26 Cut a small V-section around the neck.

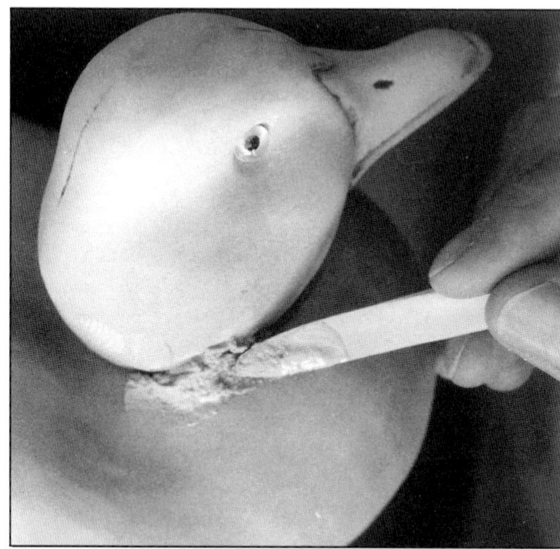

Fig 6.27 Spread plastic wood around the neck joint using a modelling tool.

Fig 6.28 Smooth out the plastic wood by brushing it with acetone.

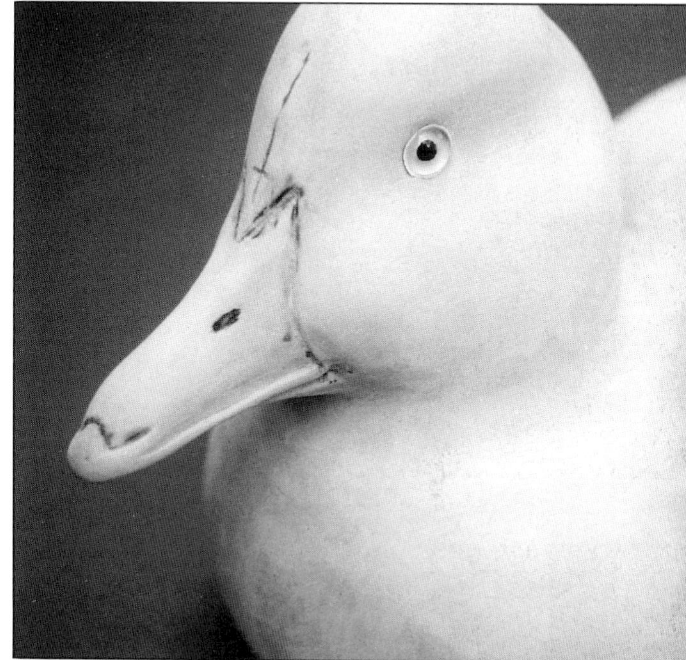

Fig 6.29 Sanding down has masked the joint and created a surface suitable for texturing.

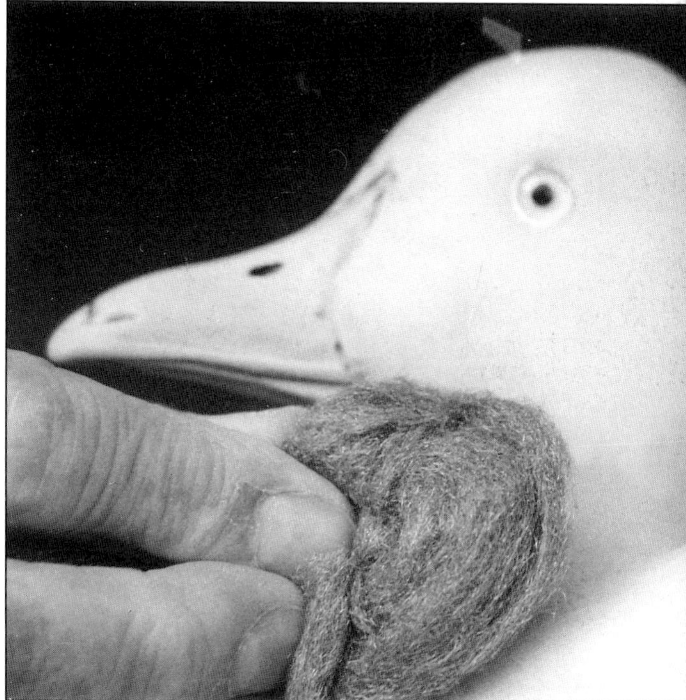

Fig 6.30 Extra fine steel wool can also be used in the smoothing process.

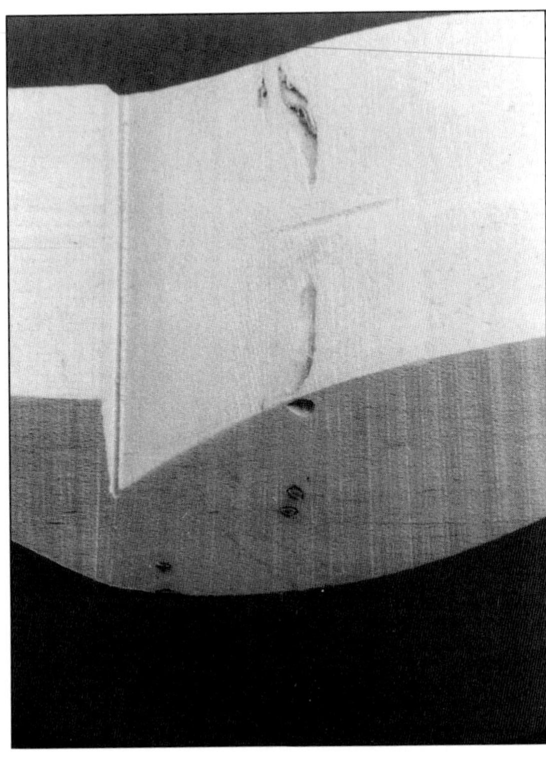

Fig 6.31 A latex lattice running through a blank can cause defects which must be concealed prior to texturing.

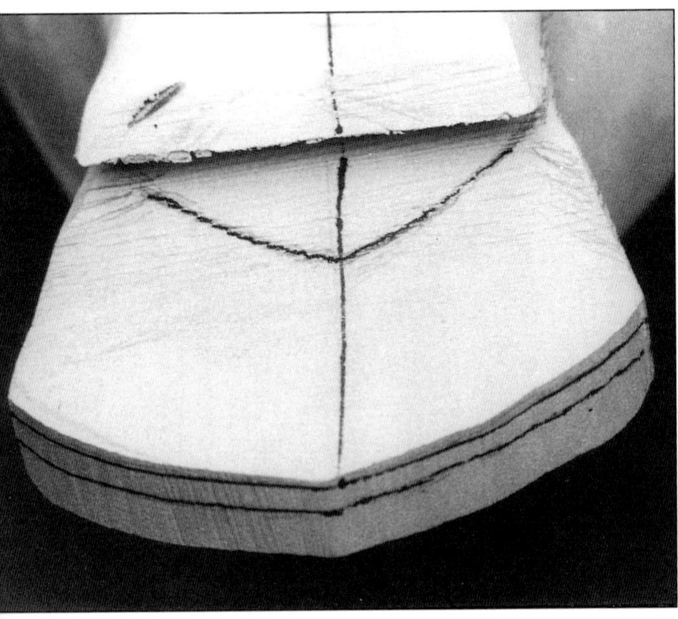

Fig 6.32 A latex cell in jelutong which will be removed as carving progresses.

Laying out the Feathers

Feather flow lines

Since a duck swims and flies, it is not surprising to find that its feathers are arranged to allow it to move through the water and the air with the maximum dynamic efficiency. Definite flow lines can be traced on the entire body and head of the duck (see Figs 6.33 and 6.34).

These should be drawn on the carving and will serve as a guide when you mark out the individual feathers. I have exaggerated the degree to which these feather flow lines need be drawn but I have done so to underline their importance (see Fig 6.35).

Subsequently, when the feather pattern is drawn on the carving, the shafts of the carved feathers must follow these flow lines.

Feather groups and patterns

In Chapter Two I wrote about the need for the carver to be aware of the characteristic feather patterns and groupings of ducks in general. When, however, a particular type is to be carved and realism is required, a close study of its feather pattern is essential.

Photographs, illustrations and patterns should be used as reference sources to ensure accuracy. In the case of the goldeneye, the drawings and photos in this chapter should be carefully followed in laying out the feather groups. The step-by-step photos in the next chapter will help you achieve the correct pattern for each type of feather.

Most ducks and birds have one or more distinguishing features. The goldeneye, for example has very distinctive scapulars, as the drawings of feather groups show (see Figs 6.36 and 6.37).

Guidelines for laying out feathers

When drawing the individual feathers on any carved bird or duck, there are guidelines which should be followed.

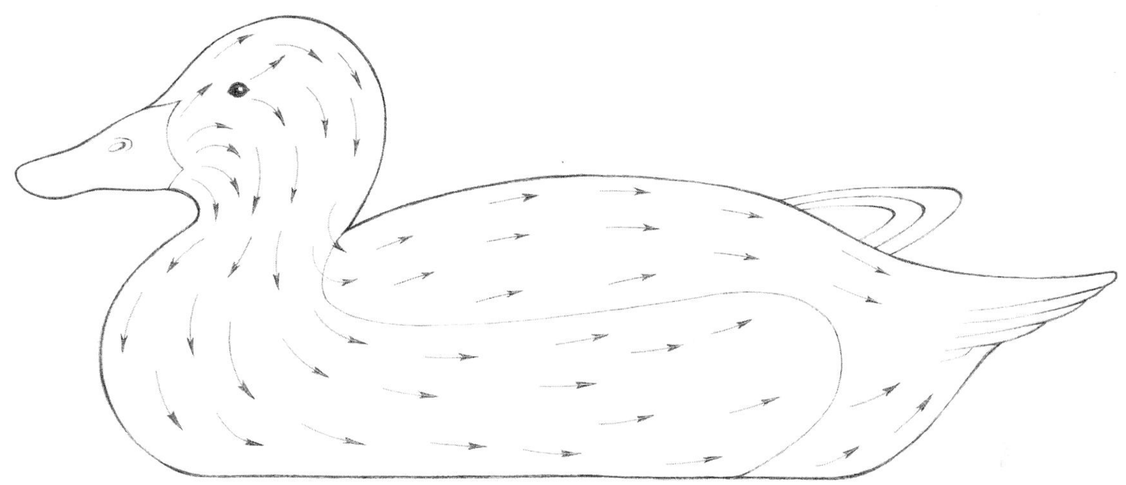

Fig 6.33 Feather flow lines.

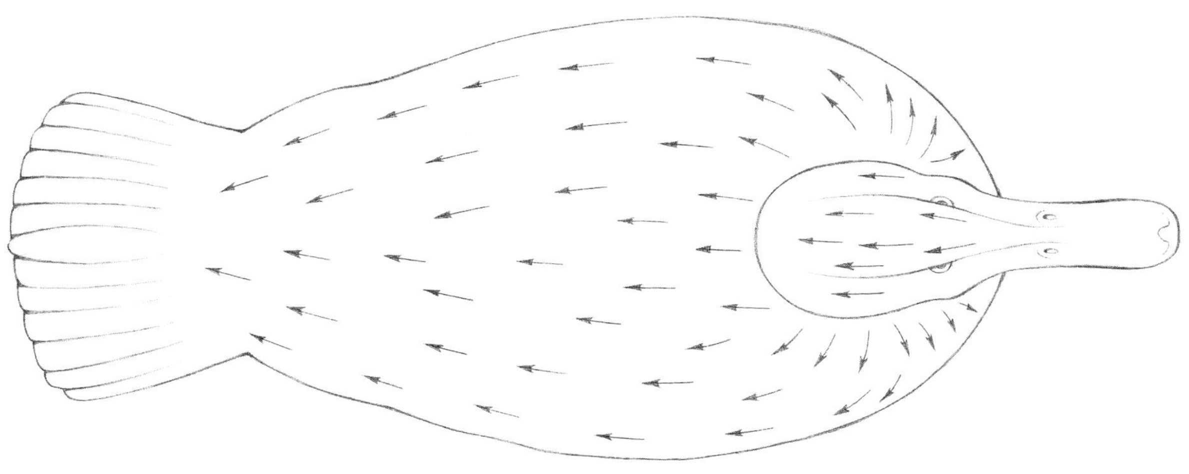

Fig 6.34 Feather flow lines.

Fig 6.35 Draw the feather flow lines on the carving as a guide.

- The feather covering of the live bird is multilayered and your carving must try to convey an impression of depth. Feathers should appear to overlay each other.
- On the live bird, feather groups, although they may have feathers of a distinctive shape or size, tend to merge into one another. They should be drawn on the carving as discrete and not too clearly defined areas.
- There is a randomness in the arrangement of any bird's feathers which is difficult to recreate on a carving. Symmetry and any tendency towards a regular pattern should be avoided.
- The body of a bird or duck is curved and therefore feathers should appear to conform to that curvature.

Steps in laying out feathers

1 It is advisable to draw the complete feather pattern of individual feathers, before embarking on any carving or texturing. From Figs 6.36 and 6.37, and from the photos that accompany this section, study the layout of specific groups of feathers, noting their relative size, shape and alignment. It is probably easier to start drawing from the head and work towards the tail, dealing with each group in turn.

2 The flow lines on the head will suffice as a guide for subsequent texturing, but these lines flow into the cape and neck area, where small rounded feathers are clearly identifiable. This type of feather also extends to the breast area (see Fig 6.39).

3 With the wings folded, the rounded feathers of the cape flow into the wing feathers. The tertials, secondaries, and primaries are much larger feathers and, when textured, have clearly pronounced quills and shafts. The goldeneye has very distinctive scapulars that make it readily identifiable (see Fig 6.40).

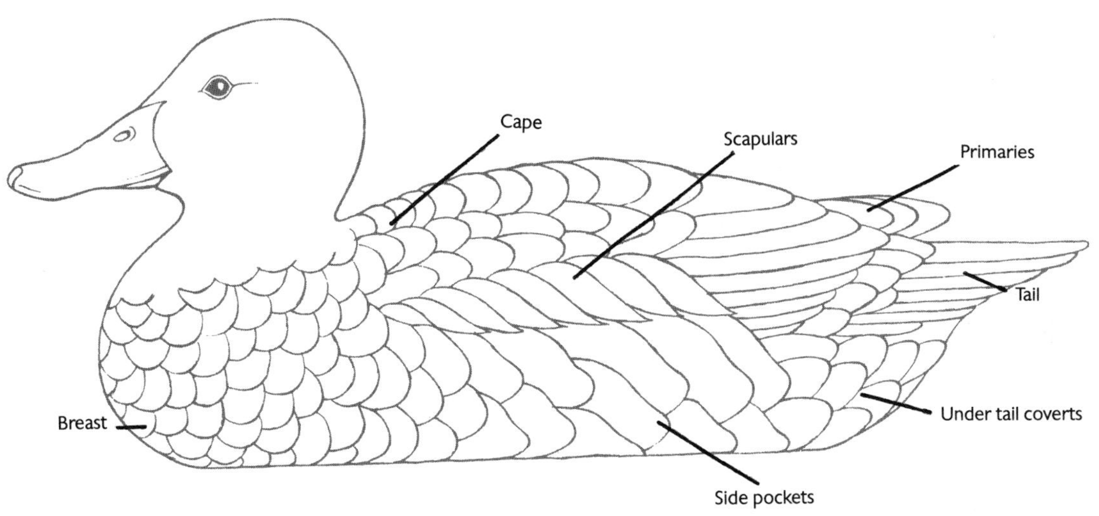

Fig 6.36 Feather groups – goldeneye.

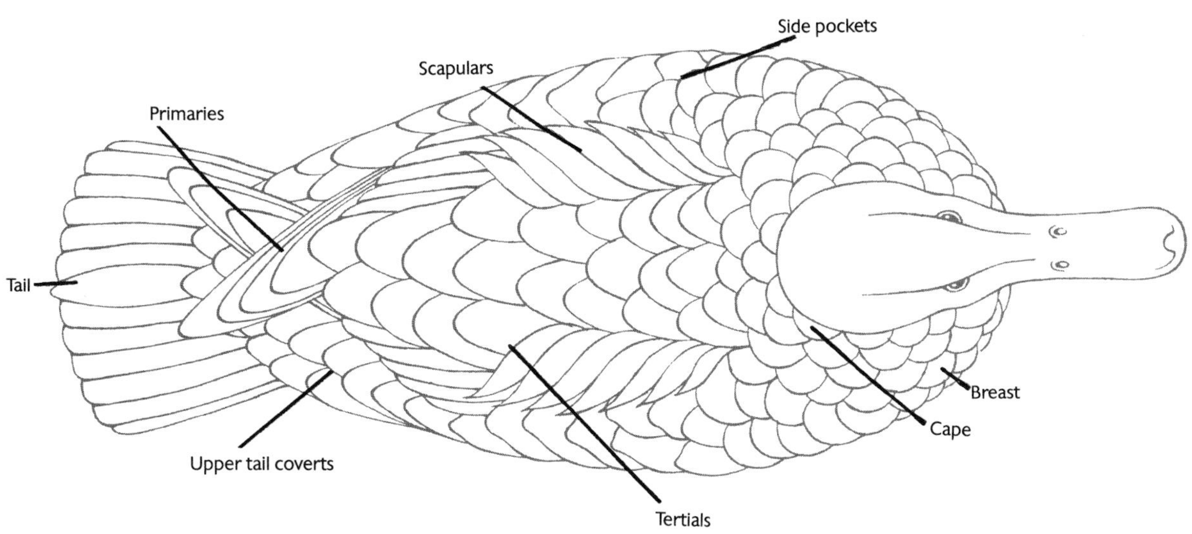

Fig 6.37 Feather groups – goldeneye.

Fig 6.38 Draw the complete feather pattern of the whole bird before further carving or texturing.

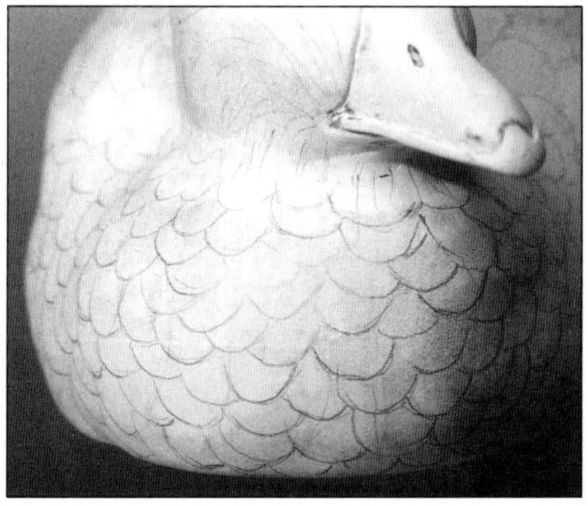

Fig 6.39 The typical rounded feathers of the neck and breast.

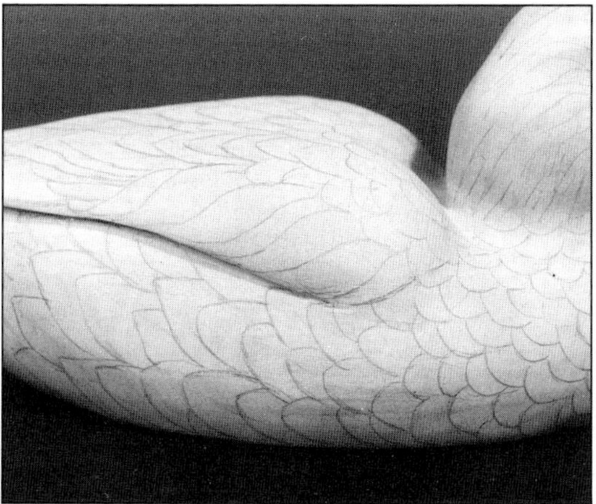

Fig 6.40 The distinctive scapular feathers of the goldeneye.

Carving the Feathers

Primaries and tertials

Most carvers prefer to carve the primaries separately and insert them later. This technique is covered in detail in volume 2 of *Wildfowl Carving*. However, some still choose to carve them from the blank, and that is the method outlined here. The primaries, having been defined and undercut (see pages 85 - 86), are now to be contoured. They have a curved profile from side to side and from front to rear. This shape is achieved by employing the technique used earlier to 'lift' the wing feathers from the body.

1 To relieve the individual feathers, run the knife vertically around the edge of each feather (see Fig 6.41). Do not cut too deeply. Then lay the knife blade almost horizontally to that cut and remove a thin slice of wood. By now you should be very familiar with this technique. With slight variations it is used throughout the whole carving process.

2 Continue to relieve the tertials and the scapulars, making the cuts less deep as you move towards the cape area (see Fig 6.42).

3 With a small loosely folded piece of sanding strip (400 grit), rub each cut along its length. This will have the effect of cleaning up the cut and rounding off the edges of the feathers (see Figs 6.43 and 6.44).

Side pockets and scapulars

1 To relieve the side pocket feathers, repeat the technique used on the primaries and tertials. The initial vertical cut should be deeper as the contours of these feathers are quite pronounced (see Fig 6.45). When the outline cuts have been made, the individual feathers should be sanded down in such a way that they appear to be curved and the sharp edges rounded off.

2 Repeat the process to relieve the scapulars (see Fig 6.46).

3 The sanding process should be continued until the surface is very smooth. The value of doing this will be fully appreciated later when texturing the surface (see Fig 6.47).

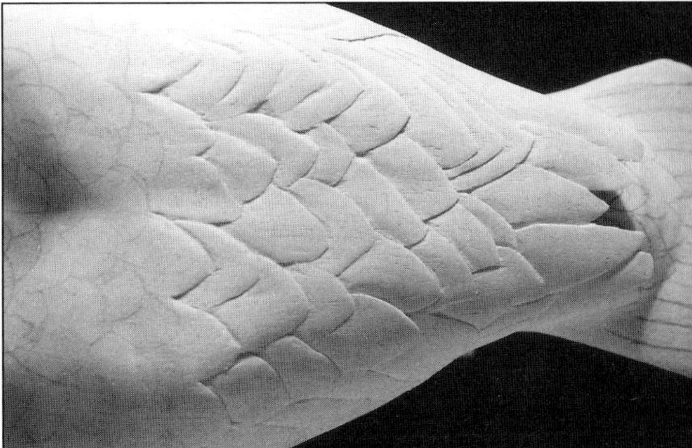

Fig 6.42 Individual feathers need not be relieved towards the cape area.

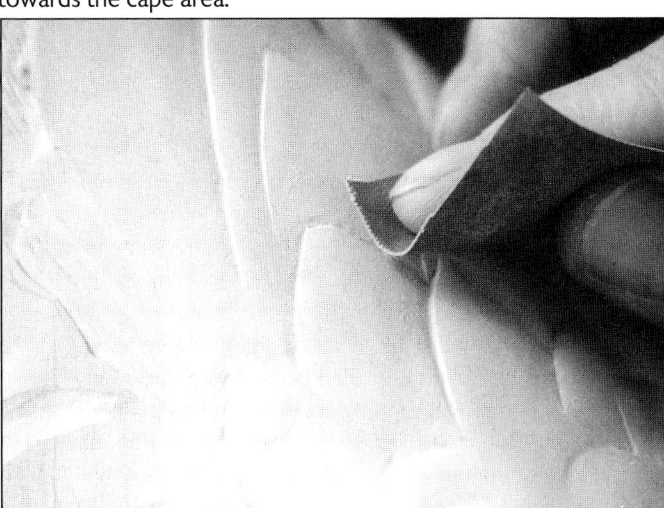

Fig 6.43 Rounding off the edges of the feathers.
Fig 6.44 The feathers after fine sanding.

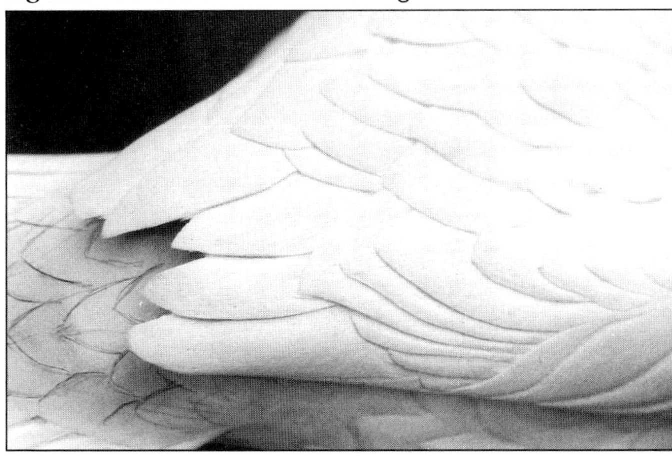

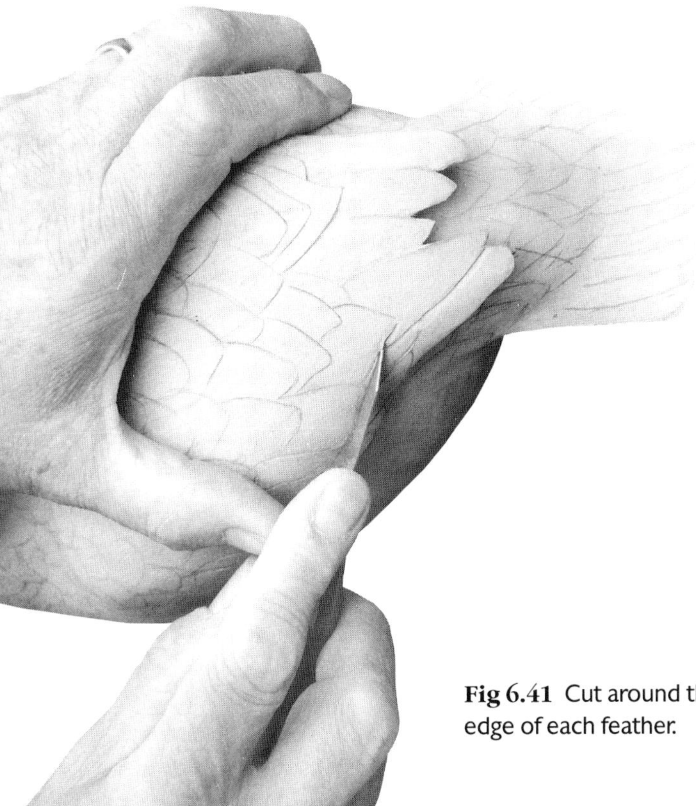

Fig 6.41 Cut around the edge of each feather.

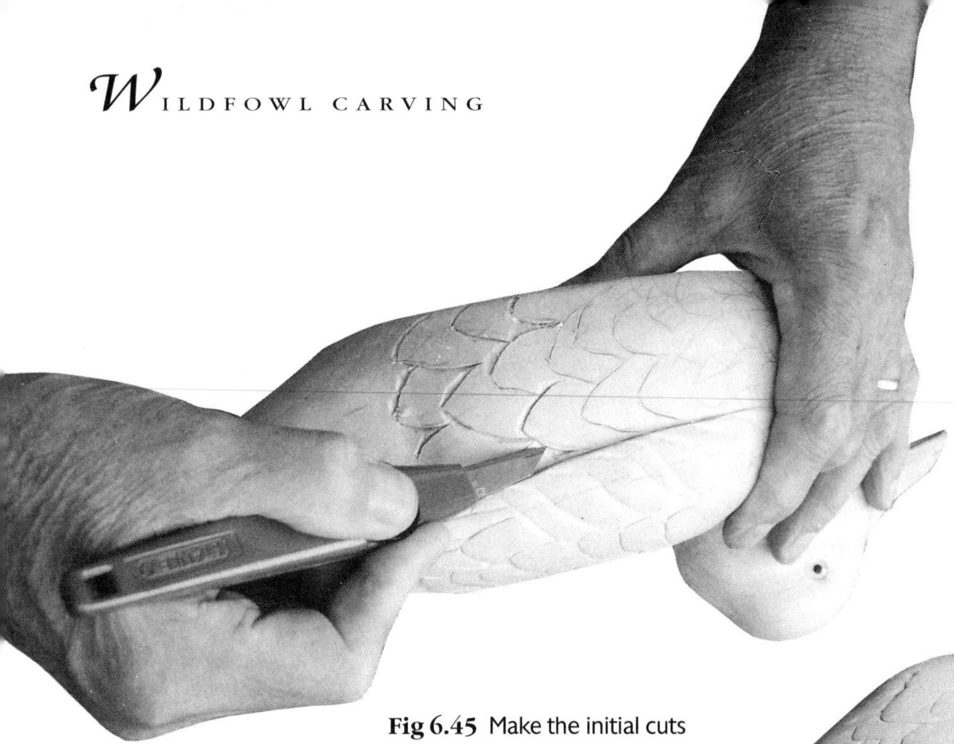

Fig 6.45 Make the initial cuts to relieve the side pocket feathers quite deep.

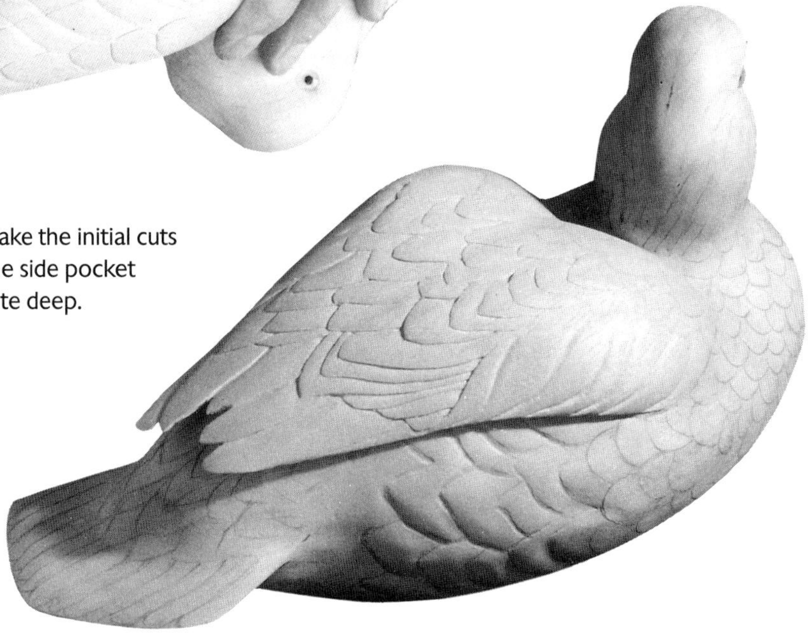

Fig 6.47 Relieved feathers should be sanded down to give a rounded effect, leaving the surface very smooth.

Fig 6.46 The scapulars and sidepocket feathers relieved.

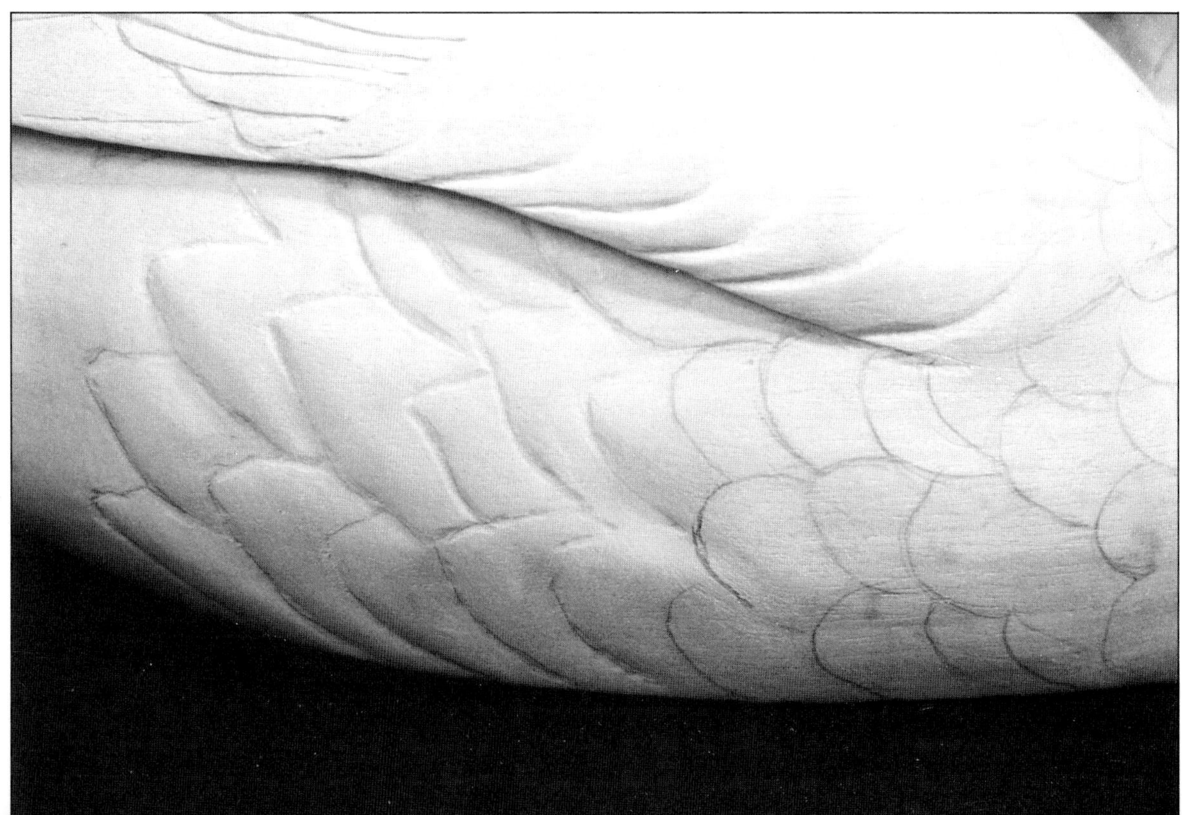

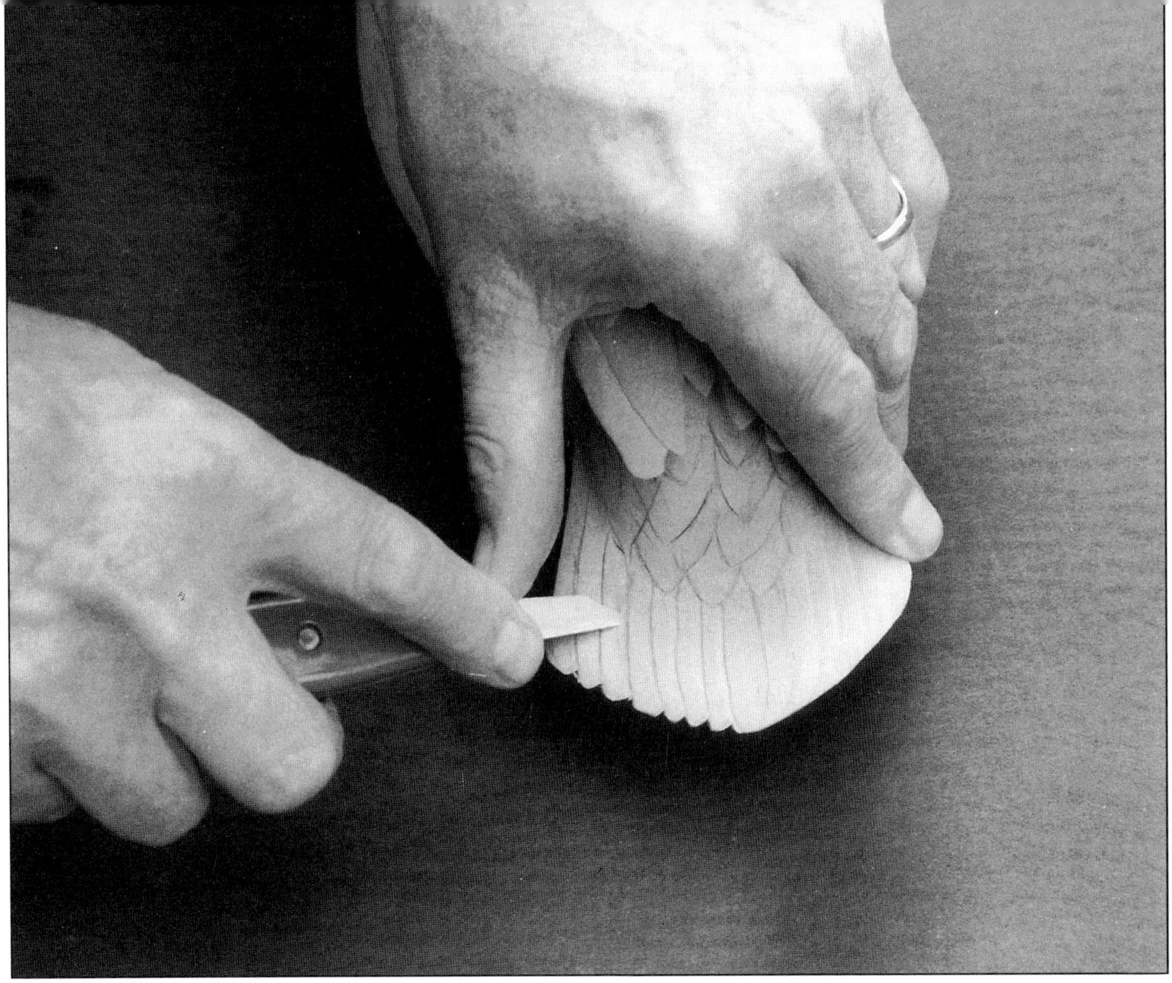

Fig 6.48 Take great care when cutting the thin wood of the tail.

The tail

1 Extreme care must be taken in relieving the individual tail feathers. The wood is very thin in this area and therefore the initial longitudinal cut along the edge of each feather must not be too deep. The second horizontal cut will remove wood easily, and the knife must be held firmly for the whole length of the cut (see Fig 6.48).

2 The tips of the tail feathers are defined with a series of V-cuts. Clean up the tips carefully using a small folded piece of fine sanding strip in the same way as before (see Fig 6.49).

Upper and lower coverts

The upper and lower coverts do not need to be relieved as they tend to merge together in a way not dissimilar to those of the head and neck.

Fig 6.49 Marking V-cuts to separate individual tail feathers.

CHAPTER 7

Basic Texturing

Equipment

Essential
Hot Tool, with standard and button tip
X-acto knife
Pencil (2B)

Optional
Heat control unit for Hot Tool
Magnifier (Opti-Visor, magnifier lamp or spectacles)

Materials
2 Sanding strips; 80–120 grit and 400-600 grit; width: 1–1 1/4in (25–30mm); length: approx 12in (300mm)
2 Pieces of well-sanded wood, approximately 4 x 4 x 3/8in (100 x 100 x 10mm)

Useful reference material/sources
Feathers (a variety of large and small feathers)

Fig 7.1 A bent rasp file being used to create texture lines after the manner of the Ward brothers.

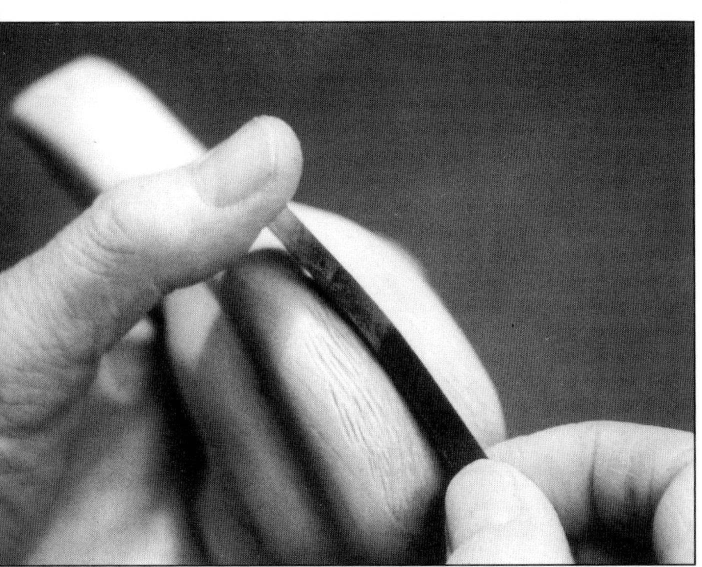

History

Texturing decoy ducks is a long established practice. Anxious that their working decoys should appear as lifelike as possible, some American and Canadian carvers of the last century used a wide variety of tools to simulate feathers.

The famous Ward brothers, who, significantly, claimed the title of 'Wildfowl Counterfeiters in Wood', working in the early years of this century, quite frequently used small triangular rasp files to add texture to their carvings. Occasionally they would heat and bend one of these files to cope with curves or tricky areas (see Fig 7.1).

Breaking up the surface of the wood not only created the illusion of feathers when viewed from above, it also had the effect of reducing the specular reflections from the painted surface of the decoys.

Chisels, gouges, knives and even axes, have all been used over the years to create some form of texturing. Even today, despite the availability of a wide range of power tool accessories designed specifically for the purpose, some carvers still use hand tools very skilfully to create feather patterns.

Prior to 1970, apart from the examples of rudimentary texturing mentioned above, most carved birds were smooth bodied. 1969-1970 saw carvers using heated tips of soldering irons and tools designed to be used in pyrography to create texture.

Unfortunately, these tools carried the heating element inside the burning tip and, therefore, the degree to which they could be sharpened to burn fine lines was severely limited.

It was in 1970 that the Reverend Jack Drake of New Mexico hit upon the idea of producing lifelike feathers by burning fine lines with the sharpened edge of an electrically heated tool.

All feather texturing is based on the principle that the soft appearance of the feathers of a live bird is brought about by the breaking up of the reflected light from the millions of fine barbs that make up the vanes of a feather. Texturing by the carver is an attempt to create a similar effect by burning or cutting closely packed fine lines into the surface of the wood.

As an indication of the accuracy and control required to duplicate in wood the primary feathers of a duck, the carver would need to be able to burn approximately 80–120 lines per inch. In practice, he or she will seldom do better than 50–60 per inch and frequently will do less. However, the limitation on the resolving power of the human eye make this density quite acceptable for most carved feathers. Even carvings with clearly visible texture lines can still be quite effective (see Fig 7.2).

Texturing: General

The aim of any texturing techniques used in carving wildfowl is to recreate the impression of delicacy and softness that characterizes the feathers of the live bird.

Heating tools

Probably the easiest and arguably the most effective, texturing is achieved by using a heating tool, with which a series of fine lines are burned into the wood.

Heating tools range from the relatively inexpensive type fitted with interchangeable tips to the far more expensive thermostatically controlled lightweight pens, to which a wide range of tips of varying shapes and sizes may be fitted.

The Hot Tool

The Hot Tool is the best known heating tool and is ideal for the beginner as it is easy to use, inexpensive, and is now available with interchangeable tips for shading and burning fine lines (see Fig 7.3).

With practice, it is possible to achieve remarkably good results with the Hot Tool, and many carvers, having used it successfully on a number of their carvings, have never felt the need to invest in a more expensive burning tool (see Fig 7.4).

A heat control unit is available as an optional extra, albeit a rather expensive one at

Fig 7.2 This merlin by Roger Jeeves shows the effectiveness of simple texturing on a well-carved bird.

almost twice the price of the tool itself. Used without it, the Hot Tool requires skill and experience to avoid excessive and uneven burning. The heat output is fairly constant, however, and if the carver takes the precaution, during pauses in texturing, to disperse the excess heat on a piece of scrap wood before applying the tool to the carving surface, the problem is solved.

The standard tip of the Hot Tool has a blunt knifelike edge which is not easy to sharpen (see Fig 7.5). As a consequence it is not possible to burn lines as thin as those obtainable with the more expensive pens.

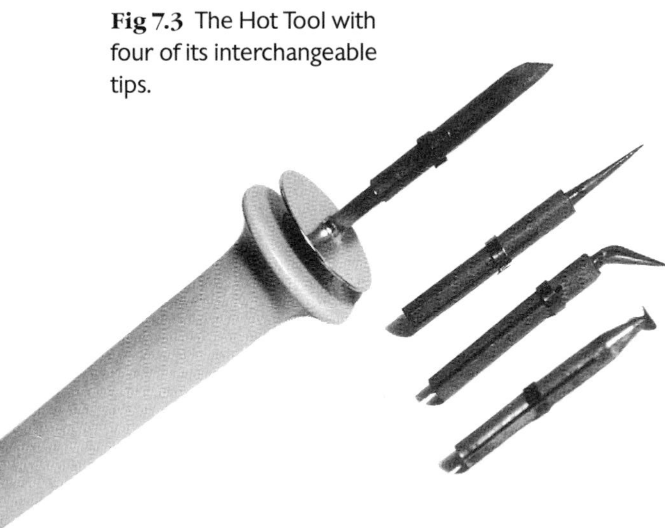

Fig 7.3 The Hot Tool with four of its interchangeable tips.

The Hot Tool is, however, very light and well balanced and is a very reliable piece of equipment.

Working Procedures

Sanding

It is absolutely essential to fine sand the surface that you intend to texture. The quality of that texturing will depend to a great extent on the degree of smoothness achieved in sanding.

A 400 grit sandpaper should be used, followed by a 600 grit to give an almost shiny finish to the wood.

Under even moderate magnification, the surface may still appear rough, and for this reason, many carvers will brush water or denatured alcohol over the wood to raise the grain and, when dried, rub the surface again with the 600 grit sandpaper.

The work area

Texturing is a time consuming technique demanding considerable patience. It requires concentration, and it is for this reason that the beginner is advised to work in sessions of no longer than one to two hours with short breaks between them. The work area should be well lit and free from any draughts, and the carver should be seated comfortably at a bench or a table.

Tips on technique

With any burning tool the heat must be allowed to create the texture. Little or no pressure should be applied when burning the wood. It is not a cutting tool. It should be held like a pen but applied almost vertically to the surface of the wood (see Fig 7.6), the tip should be used to obtain fine lines (see Fig 7.7), the edge should be used for outlining and burning in feather shafts (see Fig 7.8). Holding the pen at a shallow angle will render control over the direction of movement difficult and make the burning of fine lines impossible.

Magnifiers

Fine texturing requires good eyesight, and those of us who are not so blessed are often quite favourably surprised at the improvement in the standard of the texturing when a magnifier is used.

Magnifier lamp

A portable magnifier lamp on the bench can be extremely useful at the texturing stage, and if the lamp is fitted with an integral, colour-corrected lighting system, as the more expensive types are, it can also be very handy

Fig 7.4 The Hot Tool was used to texture this scaup.

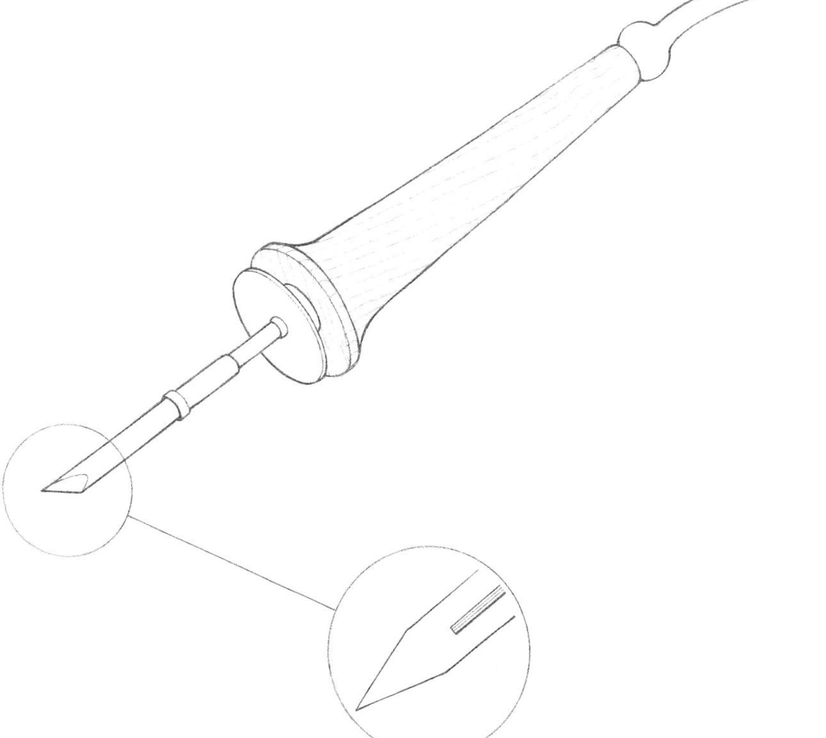

Fig 7.5 The standard tip for the Hot Tool. It's not easy to sharpen, but at its price, the Hot Tool is excellent for texturing.

when painting (see Fig 7.9). It is usually equipped with a 3-dioptre lens, giving excellent magnification at a comfortable viewing distance, and as the circular lighting is a fluorescent tube, the working area remains cool. The extension arm and the wide acceptance angle of the lens give a reasonable degree of flexibility, but the subject being worked on must remain within the rather limited field of view.

The Opti-Visor

Originally developed for the watchmaking and repairing industry, the Opti-Visor is a precision binocular headband that allows the carver to see small detail while leaving both hands free to work (see Fig 7.10). It has the advantage over the magnifier lamp of moving with the wearer's line of vision. It also offers a range of six interchangeable lenses with focal lengths from four to twenty inches, and an attachable auxiliary lens that gives additional magnification. The headband is adjustable, the lenses can be easily swung up out of the line of vision and it can be worn over spectacles.

I have used an Opti-Visor for a number of years now and found it an invaluable aid for all work involving fine detail.

Fig 7.6 The Hot Tool is held like a pen almost at right angles to the surface of the wood.

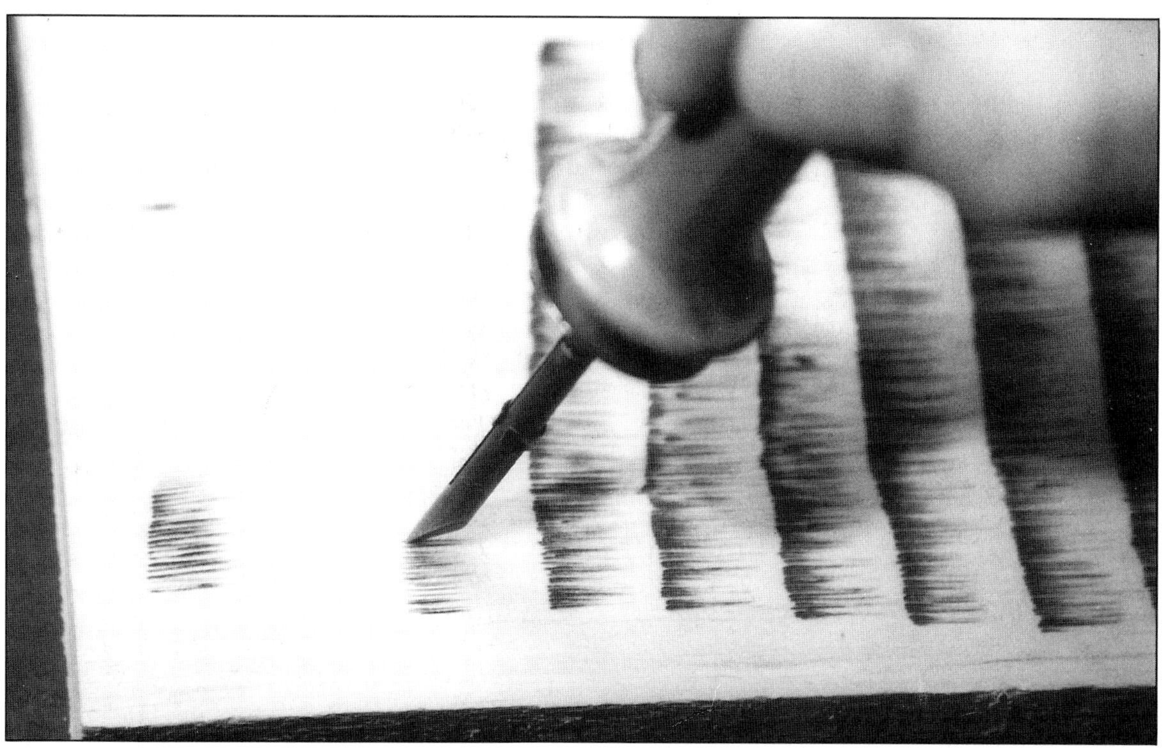

Fig 7.7 The tip of the Hot Tool used to obtain fine lines.

Fig 7.8 The tip of the Hot Tool used to burn in feather shafts.

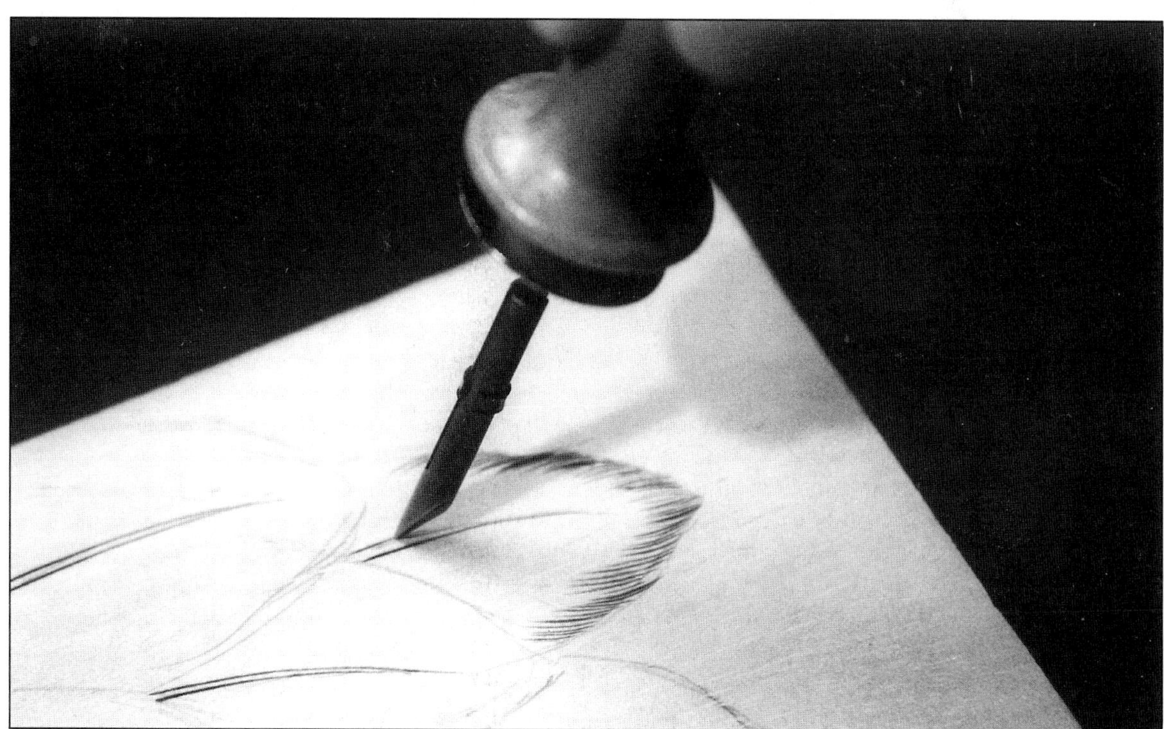

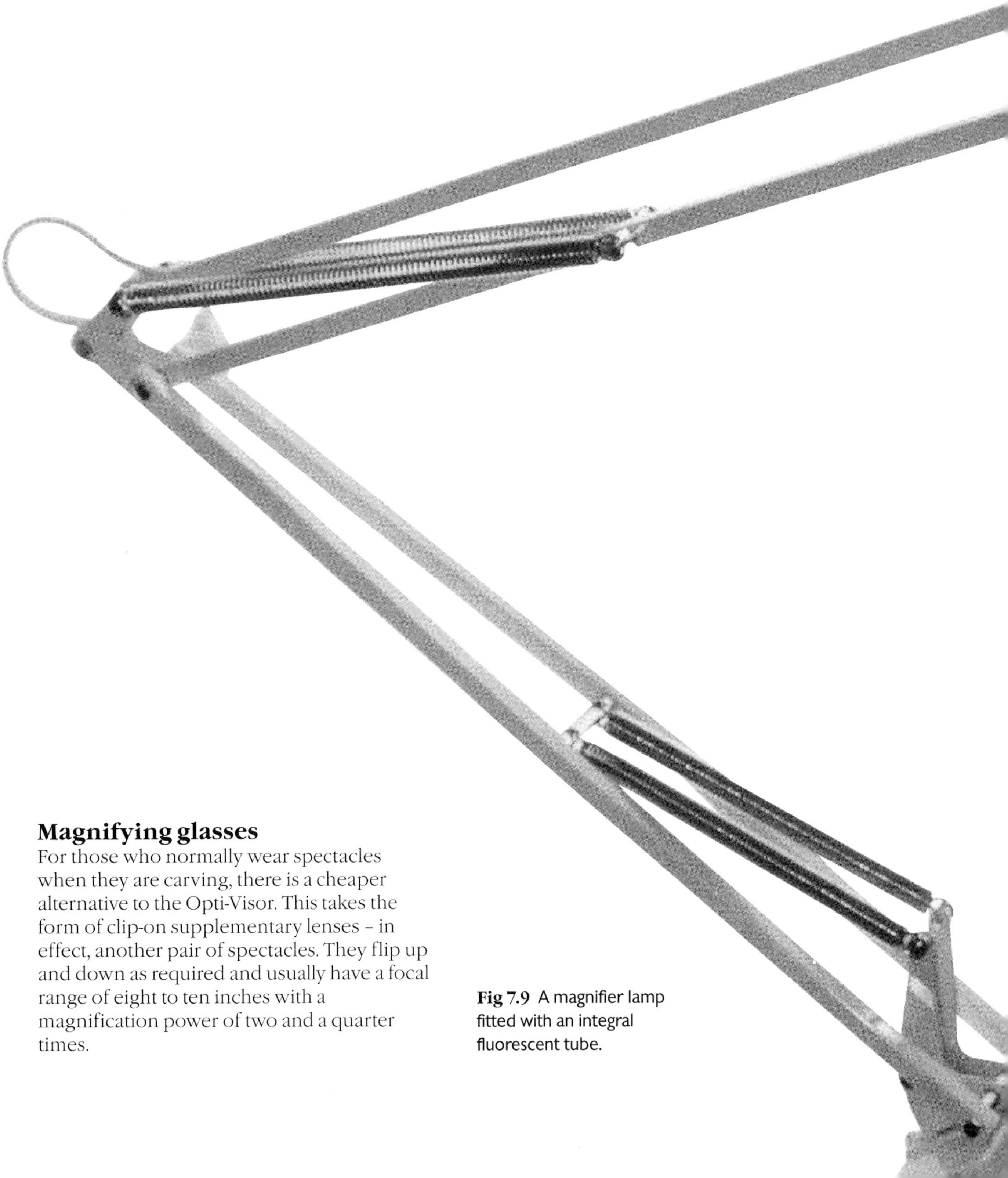

Fig 7.9 A magnifier lamp fitted with an integral fluorescent tube.

Magnifying glasses

For those who normally wear spectacles when they are carving, there is a cheaper alternative to the Opti-Visor. This takes the form of clip-on supplementary lenses – in effect, another pair of spectacles. They flip up and down as required and usually have a focal range of eight to ten inches with a magnification power of two and a quarter times.

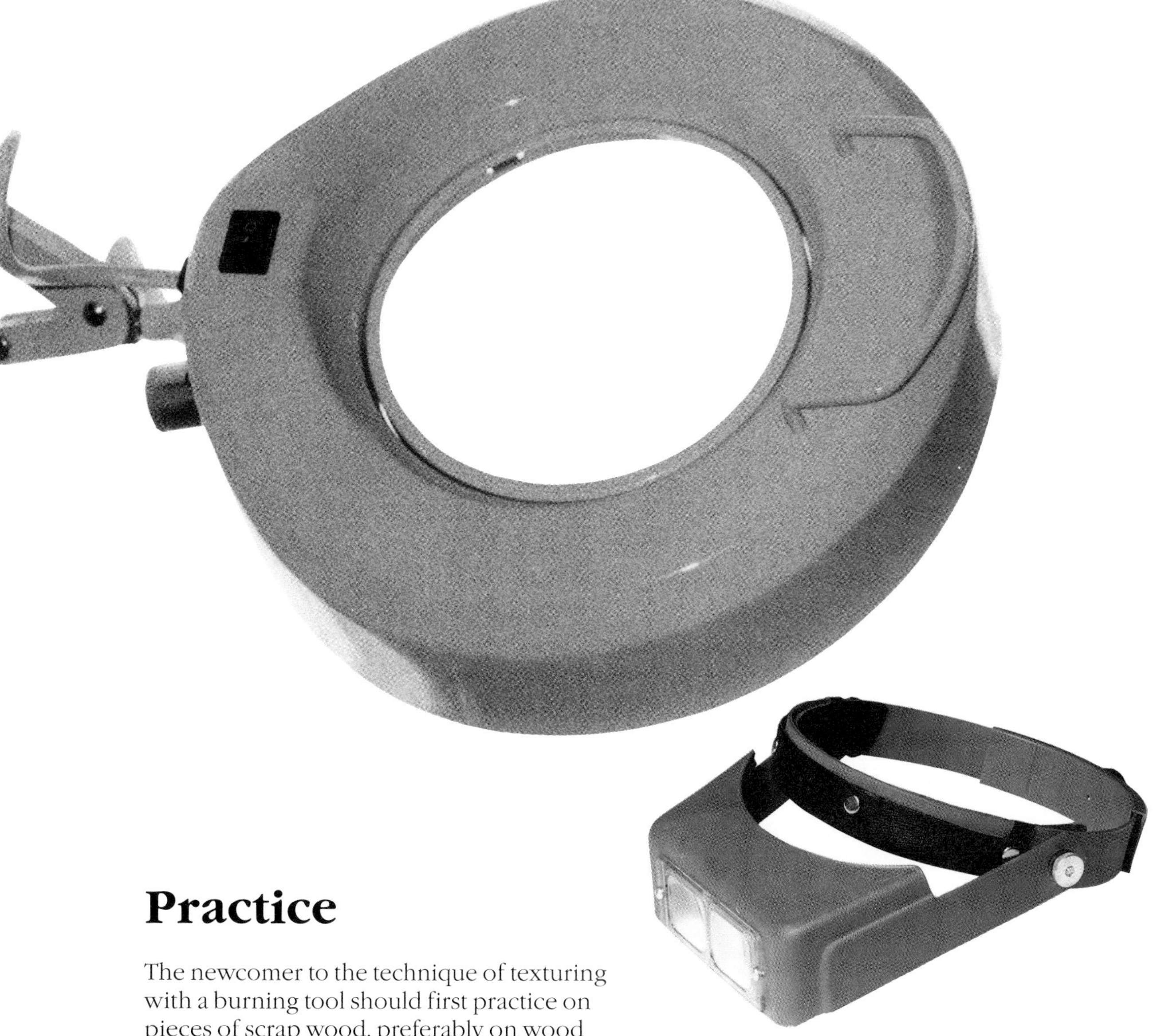

Fig 7.10 The Opti-Visor.

Practice

The newcomer to the technique of texturing with a burning tool should first practice on pieces of scrap wood, preferably on wood similar to that being used for carving. The surface of these pieces should be sanded down to provide a very smooth surface upon which to work.

Exercise 1: parallel lines

1 Having got the feel of the tool by making lines at random on the wood, an attempt should then be made to burn parallel lines using short downward strokes. This exercise should be repeated until the space between the lines is reasonably constant (see Fig 7.11).

2 Then on a separate piece of wood, an attempt should be made to burn the lines closer together (see Fig 7.12).

Exercise 2: simulating rounded feathers

1 The second exercise I recommend to the novice is burning lines to simulate the small rounded feathers of the breast and neck. When this is done well, the individual feathers will appear to be contoured, as they are on the live bird (see Fig 7.13).

2 Since all the surfaces of a carved duck or bird are curved, these exercises should be repeated on scraps of wood having curved surfaces (see Fig 7.14).

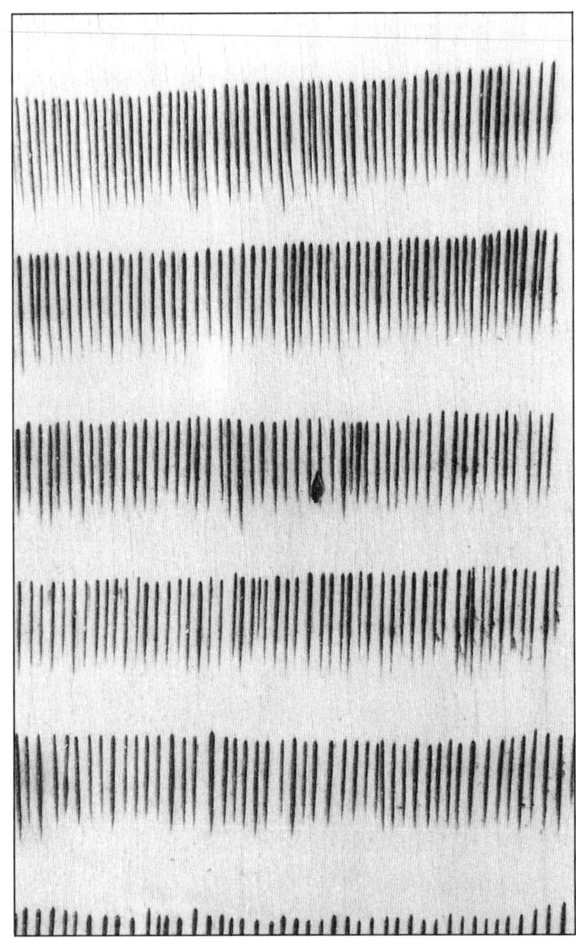

Fig 7.11 Practice using the Hot Tool, beginning with a series of parallel lines.

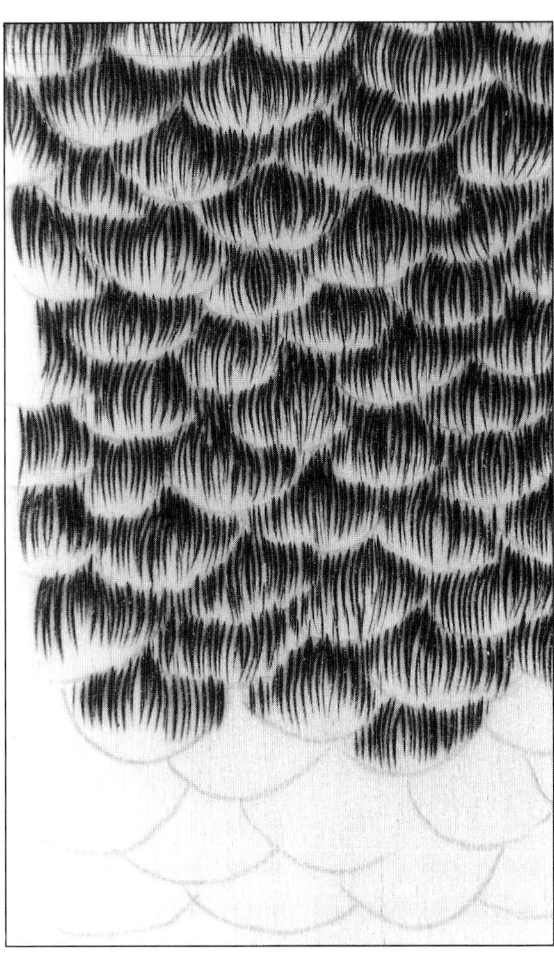

Fig 7.13 Practice texturing small rounded feathers to produce a contoured effect.

Fig 7.12 Then try burning the lines closer together.

Fig 7.14 Repeat the exercises on curved surfaces.

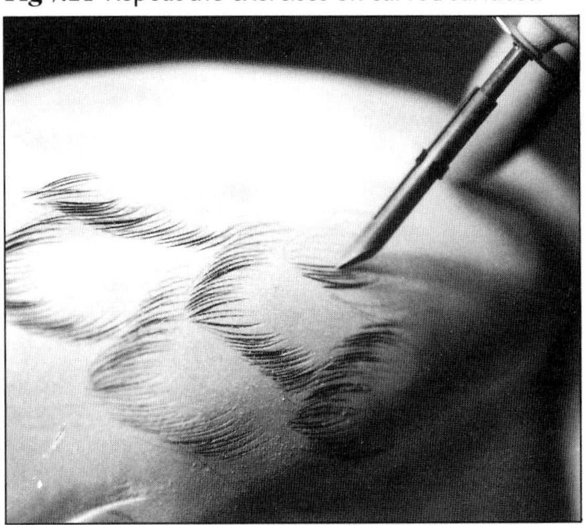

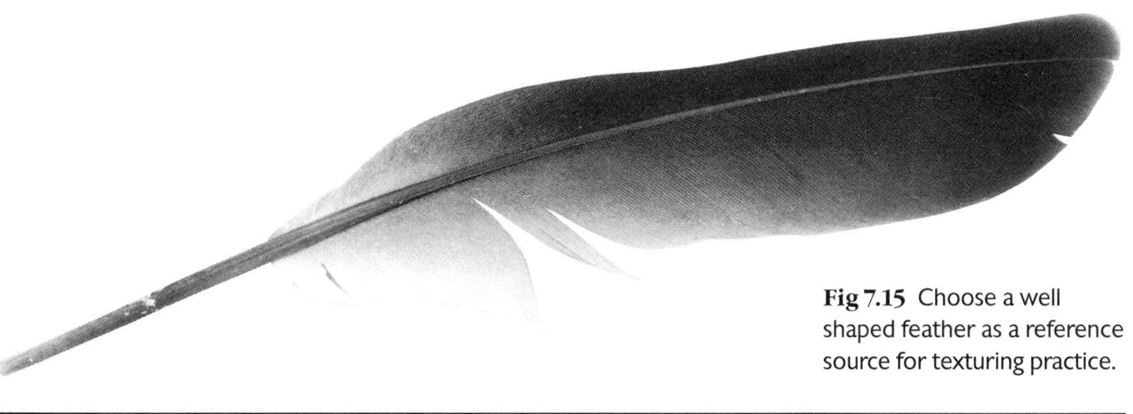

Fig 7.15 Choose a well shaped feather as a reference source for texturing practice.

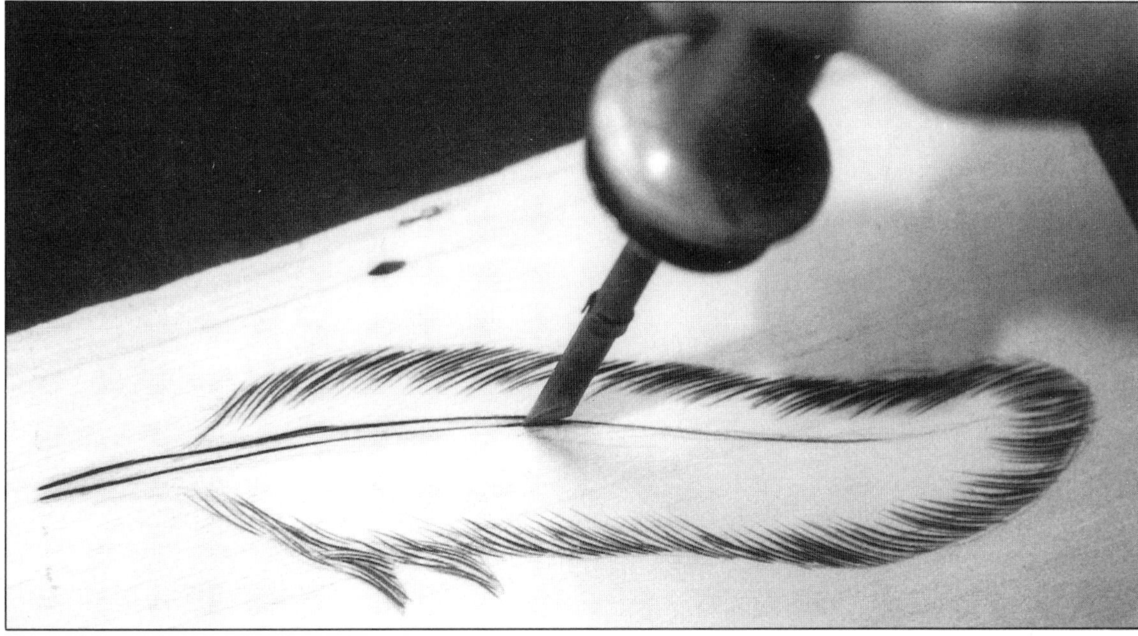

Fig 7.16 Defining the shaft with the tip of the Hot Tool.

Fig 7.17 Burning the lines from the shaft and the edge separately.

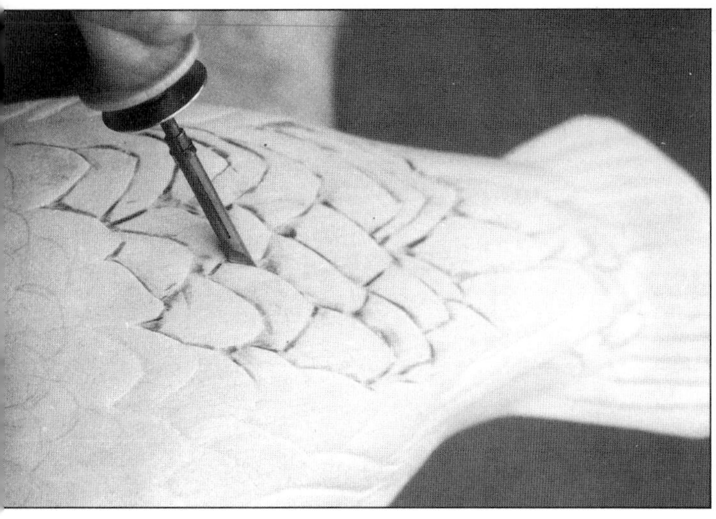

Fig 7.18 Outline the larger feathers using the Hot Tool.

Exercise 3: an individual feather

1 Most wildfowl carvers have a collection of feathers which they can use as a reference source. The novice should start collecting and identifying a wide range of feathers. From this collection, select feathers with a distinctive shape (see Fig 7.15). Trace the outline on a previously sanded piece of wood and draw in the shaft and some of the barbs including any splits.

2 Use the Hot Tool to define the shaft, starting at the quill end of the feather and drawing the edge of the tool towards the tip in one movement. Repeat this, trying to keep the sides of the quill parallel and the lines of the shaft convergent towards the tip (see Fig 7.16).

Fig 7.19 Splits can alter the shape of feathers.

3 If the vanes of the feather are too wide to burn in one stroke, start burning in each barb at the quill and lift off the tool towards the centre of the vane. Turn the piece of wood through 180° and burn in the same barbs, starting this time at the edge of the feather and drawing the tool towards the centre of the vane (see Fig 7.17).

Precautions

Choice of wood

Texturing wood with pronounced grain, such as pine or cedar is not recommended. The burning tip has a tendency to dig into the softer areas of wood between the grain lines, resulting in a marked unevenness in the textured surface.

Plastic wood

Similarly, plastic wood will burn more easily than solid wood and, therefore, when texturing, the tool should be moved over the surface more quickly and, if possible, more lightly. Invariably there will be a noticeable change in the colour of the texturing in this area, but this will be masked during the painting.

Texturing the Goldeneye

Outlining feathers

Before texturing it may be necessary to redraw those feathers that have been erased. It will also help with the subsequent texturing if the larger feathers, the tertials, secondaries, primaries and those on the flanks of the duck are outlined using the Hot Tool (see Fig 7.18).

Splits

1 The barbs of any feather are hooked together and held by the interlocking action of the barbules and barbicels (see page 17). When these separate, as they tend to do towards the tip of the feather, and even more so nearer the water line, splits are created. The continuity of the barbs is broken and in some cases even the shape of the feather is altered (see Fig 7.19).

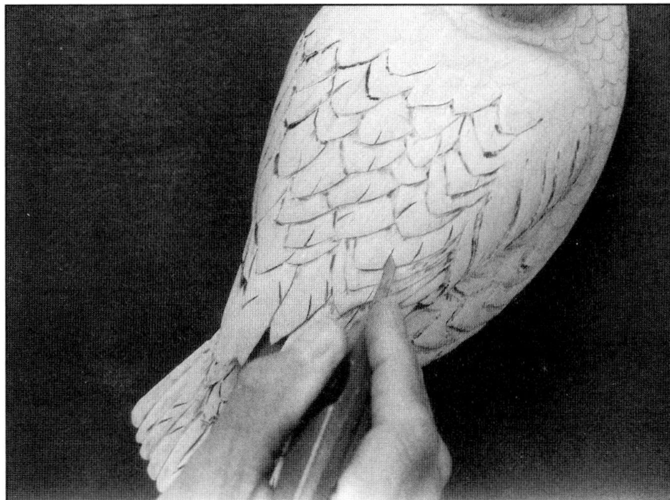

Fig 7.20 Cutting out feather splits with a sharp knife.

2 Splits invariably start near the shaft of a feather and follow the curve of the barbs, widening out towards its edge. The simplest way to create splits in a carved feather, having first marked them out with a pencil, is to remove a very fine wedge-shaped piece of wood, cutting the sides of the wedge at an angle to the surface of the wood with a sharp-bladed knife (see Fig 7.20).

3 An X-acto knife, fitted with a new blade, is recommended where splits are to be created in some of the smaller feathers and on other feathers where the curve of the barb is quite pronounced (see Fig 7.21). Splits should not be cut too deeply, and it is preferable to err on the side of having too few than too many.

The Hot Tool may also be used to burn in splits, but care must be taken to retain the characteristic wedge shape of the split and to follow the curve of the barbs.

Marking out

Before starting to texture, those feather shafts that are clearly visible should be drawn in with a pencil. In doing so, it must be remembered that they are rarely straight and should all follow the flow lines that were established when marking out the feathers in Chapter Six. Gentle curves in the shafts will go a long way to enhance the illusion of softness of the feathers.

It is also advisable at this stage, to draw in a sample selection of barbs in each group of feathers to serve as a guide. Not only will the pencil marks help to indicate the curved lines the barbs should take, but also the angle at which they should lie relative to the shaft. With more complicated feather patterns this is not always obvious.

Tail feathers

1 With the tail feathers in the closed position, it is only the centre feather that will be seen as a complete feather (see Fig 7.22). The remainder overlap one another, and in consequence the shafts are seldom visible. Occasionally, for instance during preening, the tail feathers may be fanned out, and then almost all the shafts are seen (see Fig 7.23).

2 Since the shafts and barbs have already been drawn in (see above 'marking out'), texturing the tail feathers is not a difficult task. The shaft of the centre feather should be defined using the technique illustrated in 'Exercise 3: an individual feather', page 108 (see Fig 7.24).

After outlining the shaft, some carvers, in order to make it more pronounced, recommend laying the tip of the burning tool on its side and running it along the shaft, or alternatively, moving it in a wiping motion towards the edge of the vane.

3 When burning in the barbs, start each stroke as close to the shaft lines as possible. With the remaining feathers, start each burn where the adjacent feather overlaps, and draw the tip towards the edge of the feather. The tail feathers, being very thin, are vulnerable and the tips can easily be broken. When working on any other

Fig 7.21 Using an X-acto knife to cut a split.

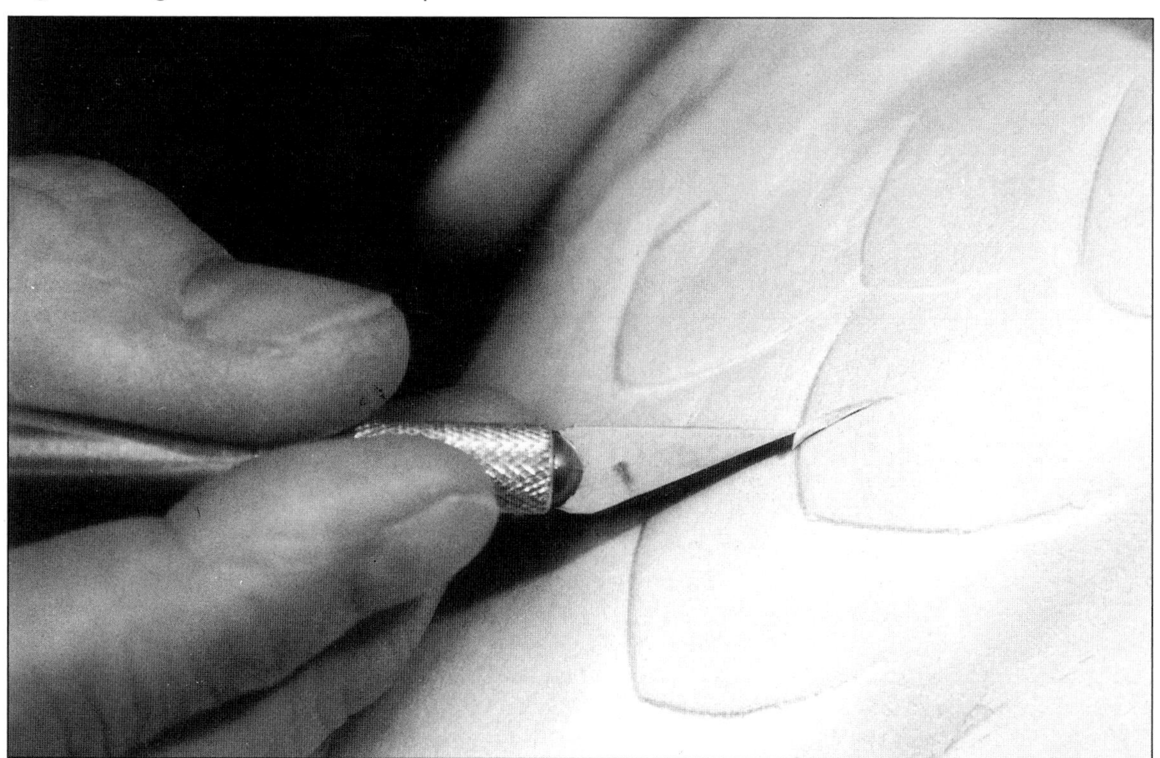

Fig 7.22 When the tail is in the closed position only the centre feathers are completely visible.

Fig 7.23 Almost all the shafts become visible when the tail feathers are fanned out.

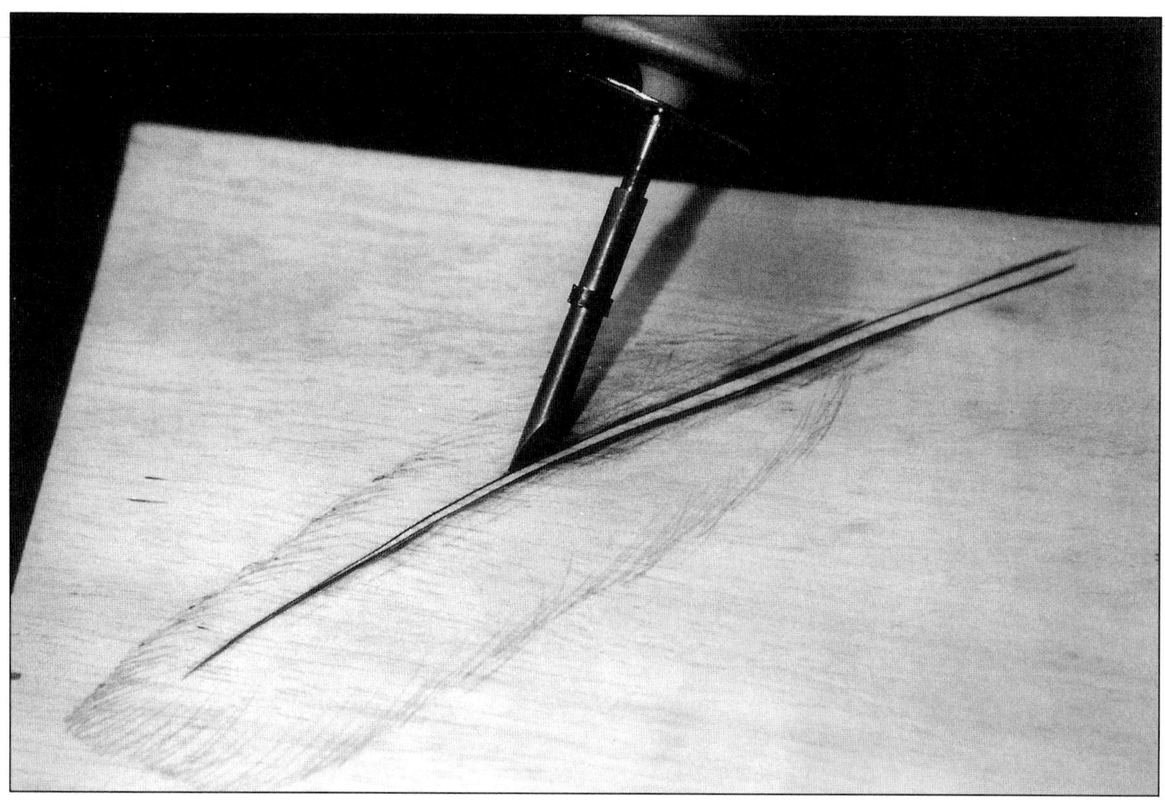

Fig 7.24 Using the Hot Tool at an angle to throw the shaft into relief.

Fig 7.25 When working on other areas of the carving, protect the tips of the tail feathers.

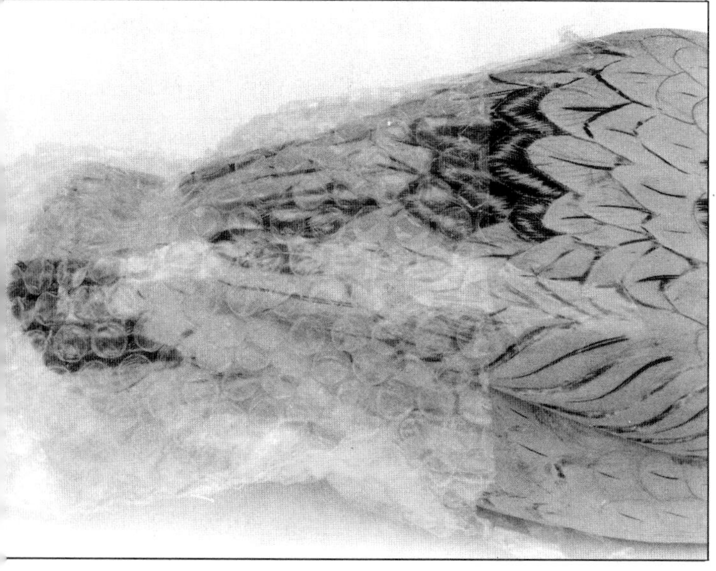

Fig 7.26 Primaries are the longest of the feather groups.

Fig 7.27 Damage to the primary feathers of a blackbird.

area of the carving, it is advisable to protect them with a soft cloth or bubble plastic sheeting taped to the body (see Fig 7.25).

Primaries

1 In the attitude in which the goldeneye has been carved in this book, the primaries extend from under the tertials and secondaries and have been carved *in situ*. They are not inserts. Primaries are flight feathers and are the longest of all the feather groups (see Fig 7.26). In older birds the tips of the these feathers are quite often damaged and badly split, as are the primaries from a wing of an old blackbird shown in Fig 7.27.

2 The shafts of the primaries are quite long and each side must be burnt in one continuous stroke. A good tip, therefore, is to just catch your breath before you touch down with the burning tip then hold it for the length of the stroke.

For the barbs, work from the shaft towards the edge of the feather. If the vane is too wide to accomplish this in one stroke, lift the tip off towards the centre of the vane and repeat the process starting at the edge of the feather.

Tertials and secondaries

On the larger of these feathers, where the shafts are clearly visible, the same technique used to burn in the shafts of the primaries and the tail feathers should be applied (see Fig 7.28). Towards the cape area, however, where the feathers become smaller and the shafts less obvious, one stroke of the burning pen will usually be all that is required to define them. In the cape area itself and around the neck, the shafts of the smaller rounded feathers are barely discernible, and therefore there is no need to burn them in at all.

Fig 7.28 Define the shafts of the larger tertial and secondary feathers with the Hot Tool.

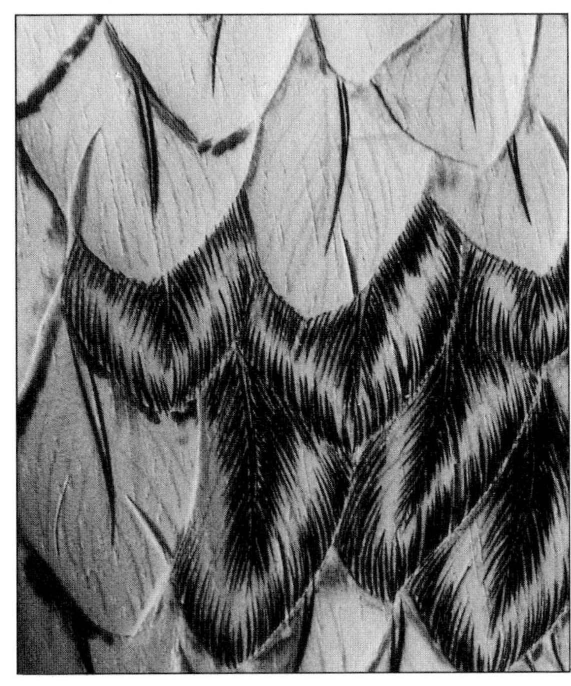

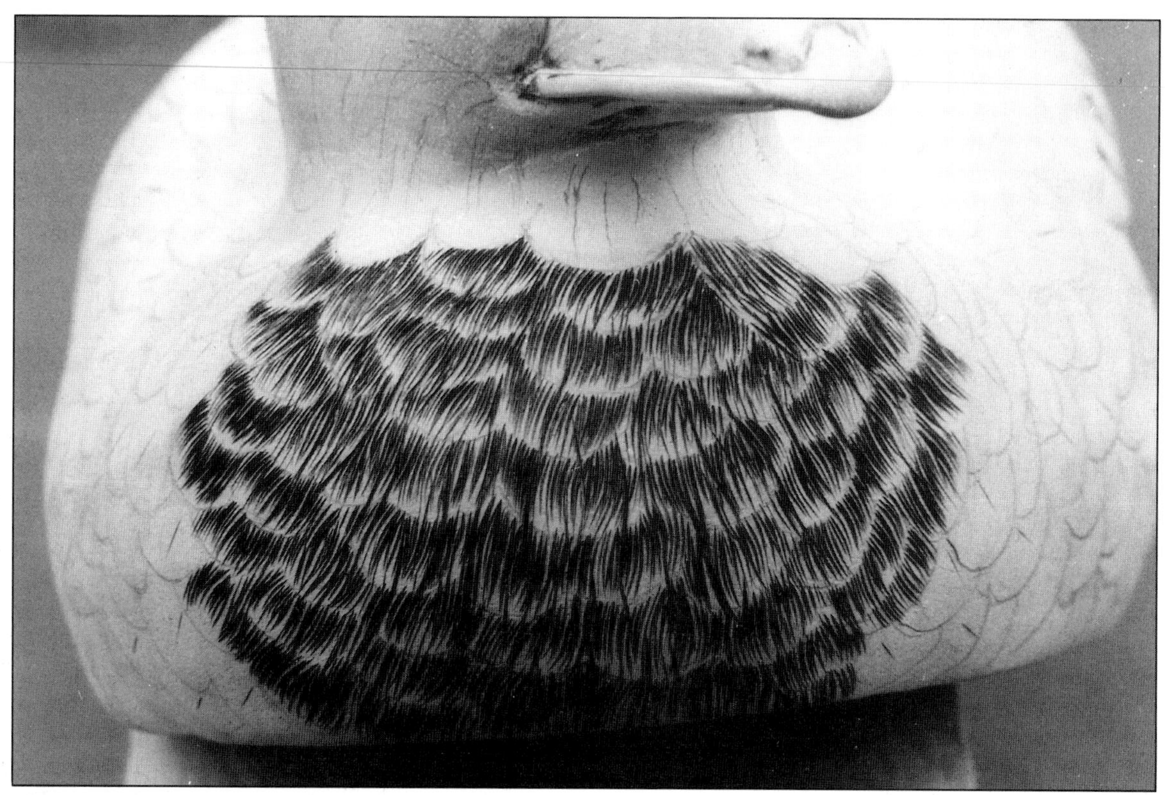

Fig 7.29 Start burning in the breast feathers at the neckline and progress downwards in short strokes.

Fig 7.30 Burn in the feathers on the head and neck with short strokes, following the flow lines.

Fig 7.31 The flank feathers have prominent shafts and sweep up towards the tail.

Fig 7.32 The goldeneye's scapulars make it readily recognizable.

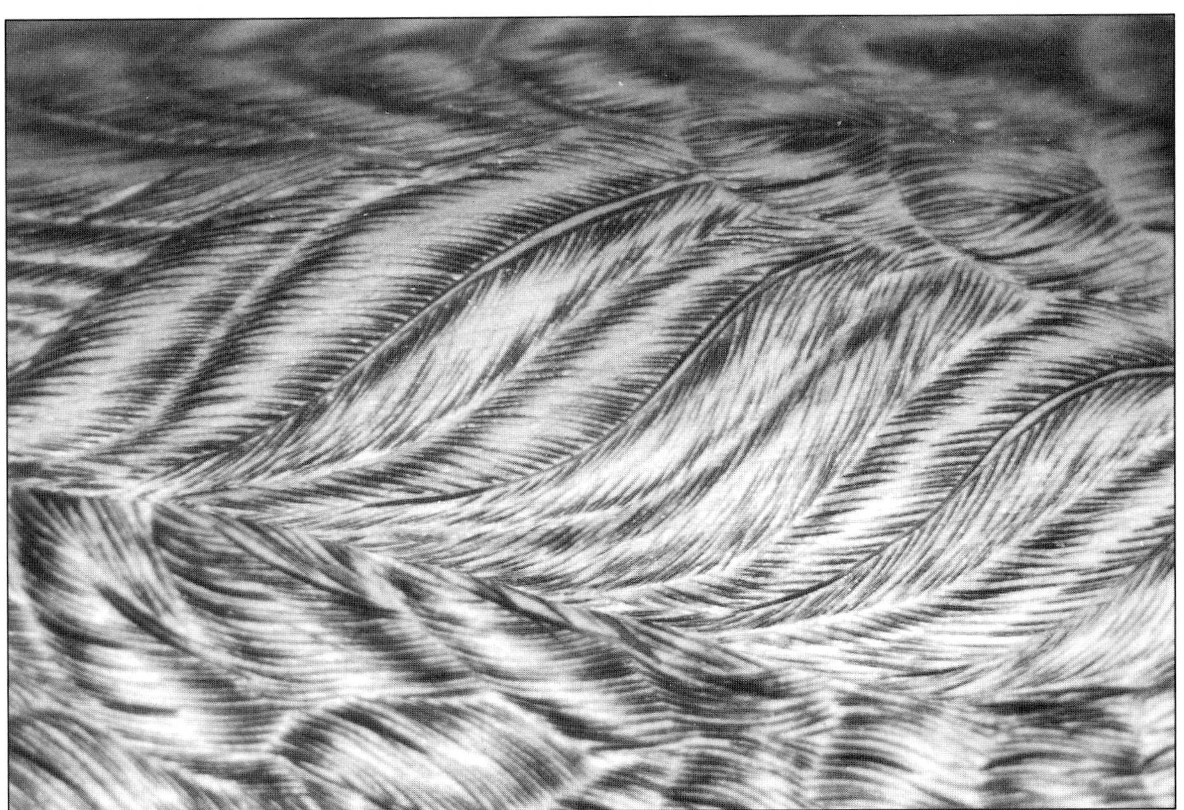

Breast feathers

The small rounded breast feathers emerge from the even smaller and more compact feathers around the neckline and extend into the larger feathers on the flanks. If the pencilled outlines of the feathers have been erased, they should be redrawn, and I have found it very helpful to reinforce the flow lines with a light touch of the burning tool. Burning should start at the neckline using short downward strokes of the burning tool, creating an overall fanlike pattern (see Fig 7.29).

Head and neck

The feathers on the neck and head are so small and dense that they appear more like hair than feathers, and can be simulated by a series of short strokes of the burning tool. These strokes should follow the general direction of the flow lines and be at varying angles to them (see Fig 7.30).

Flank feathers

The feathers on the flanks extend from the breast to the side pockets, where they are much larger

and have pronounced shafts (see Fig 7.31). The latter should be 'raised' by applying the same technique as that used on the primary feathers, taking care to ensure that they are gently curved and that they follow the feather flow lines along the side of the body to the rump area.

Scapulars

The scapulars on the goldeneye are quite distinctive, both in colour and in shape (see Fig 7.32). With the wings closed, they appear white with fine black lines running through them at an angle to the body. The individual feathers form S-shaped curves, and, where visible, the shafts should be burnt in to follow those curves.

The rump

The rump feathers present few texturing problems, except where they extend under the primary feathers. The button tip, available as an optional extra with the Hot Tool, should be used to texture the area (see Fig 7.33).

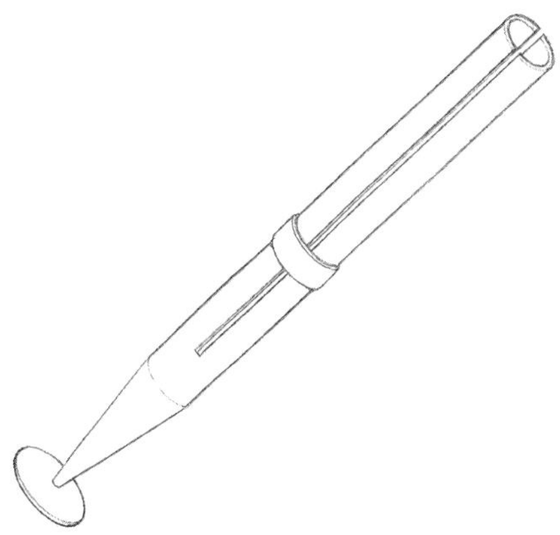

Fig 7.33 The button tip for the Hot Tool, ideal for texturing in awkward corners.

Cleaning

Creating texture by burning, however carefully it is done, always leaves behind fine carbon particles. When the burning is complete, a semi-stiff brush should be used to clean out the texture lines, lightly brushing in the direction of the lines. An old soft toothbrush is ideal for this. The carving is now ready to be prepared for painting (see Fig 7.34).

Fig 7.34 The fully textured carving is now ready to paint.

CHAPTER 8

Introduction to Painting

Painting aims to match the colours on the carving with those of the live bird. To represent those colours is not easy, since what appears to be a monochromatic group of feathers, e.g., black or white, on closer inspection is revealed as having subtle shades of different colours in them.

Painting should not be regarded as a separate stage, but as a continuation of the carving and texturing stages, and as complementary to them. Painting should enhance the contours and texture lines previously created and enhance the highlights and shadows that add to the impression of depth and softness.

Paints

The carver's choice is normally between oils or acrylic paints, and the novice is recommended to choose acrylics, as in my experience they are more versatile, dry more quickly and are more convenient to use than oils.

The paint is an acrylic polymer emulsion: solid particles of resin suspended in water droplets. On evaporation the solid particles are deposited on the surface of the wood, forming a transparent film that is both porous and flexible.

Available in tube or jar, acrylics are of a soft, creamy consistency that is easily diluted with water. When wet, the paint can be cleaned up with water, but when dry, it becomes water insoluble and the dried, hard surface can then be overpainted.

Other reasons for choosing acrylics are:

- They are non-toxic, odourless and non-non-flammable.
- They dry quickly.
- They are translucent and give a high degree of brilliance, depth and lightness.
- They can recreate the subtleties of the many shades and nuances of colour found in the plumage of birds.
- They have a consistency of colour, and the colours can be mixed together without any adverse chemical or colour reaction.

Acrylic paints for artists were introduced in America in the fifties and are now available in a wide range of colours. Winsor & Newton, in their current catalogue, offer some 75 different colours, and Jo Sonja lists a choice of over 65. The beginner, however, is advised to buy, at first, only those colours needed for the immediate project on which he is intending to work. For example, to paint the goldeneye, only the colours listed at the beginning of the next chapter are required (see page 124).

In time, with the completion of more projects and the acquisition of more colours, the carver will find that the colours occurring most frequently are: burnt umber, burnt sienna, raw sienna, yellow ochre (or oxide), ultramarine blue, brilliant green, cadmium and Indian red, and of course, titanium white and Mars black.

Colour theory

A little knowledge and understanding of basic colour theory will always be of help to the wildfowl carver, particularly when it comes to mixing and matching colours.

Explanations of colour theories can, however, be very confusing, since the scientist and the artist differ at the outset over basics. To the colour photographer and scientist, the primary colours are red, green and blue. A mixture of red and green light projected onto a white screen will produce orange. Red and blue light will produce magenta, and blue and green light will produce cyan.

The painter, however, regards red, yellow

Right: Ruddy turnstone by Derek Richards.

Mallard with young by Philip Nelson.

Tufted blue by Roger Jeeves.

Right: Mallard in flight by Judith Nicoll.

Pintail Decoy by Bob Leatherby.

Kingfishers by David Patrick – Brown.

Little Owl by Jane Brewer.

Left: Great Northern Diver by Jim Pearce.

Mallards for the Queen by Jim Pearce.

Dotterel by M. Wood.

Left: Wood duck by David Shelton.

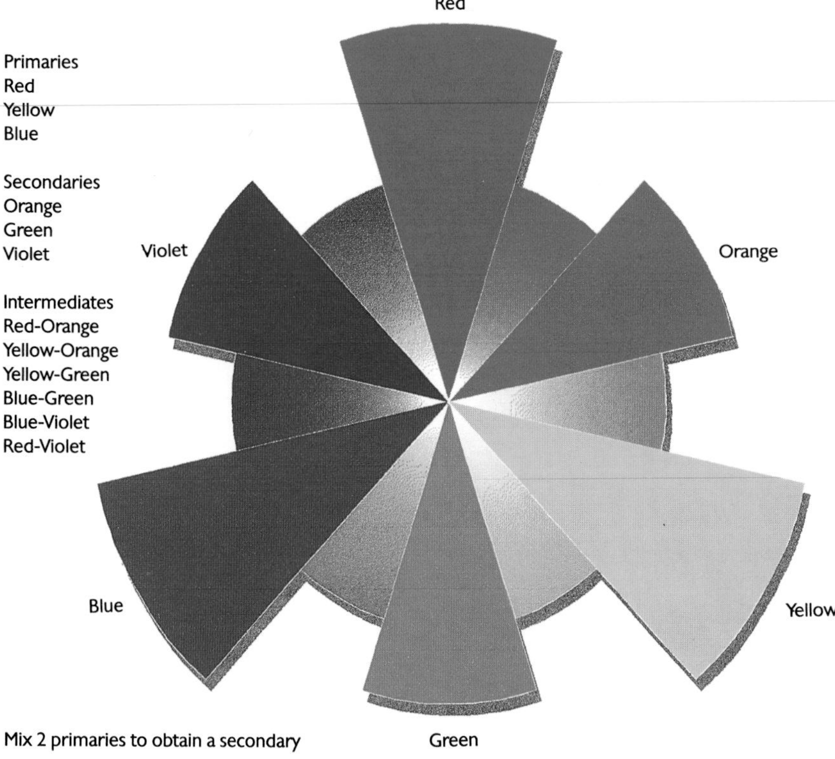

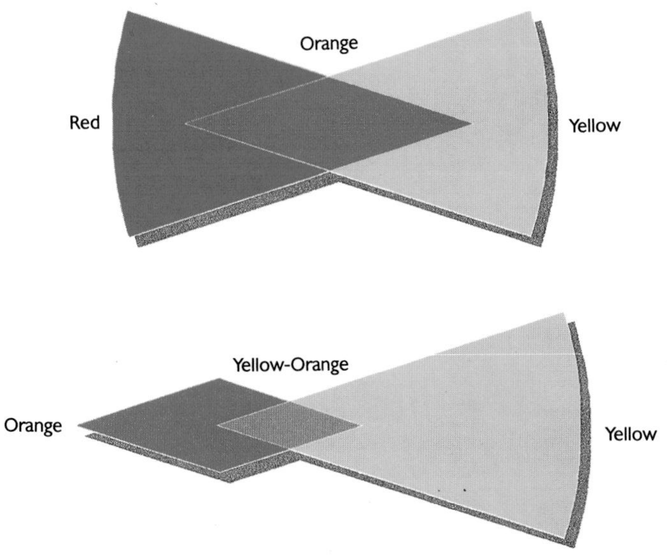

Fig 8.1 Colour wheel, showing how primary colours are mixed, in varying proportions, to achieve secondary and intermediate colours.

Fig 8.2 Samples of various pigments on gessoed jelutong. One row shows the colour straight from the tube, the other row shows diluted washes.

and blue as the primary colours. It is with the mixing of these so called 'pure' colours, that the wildfowl carver is concerned.

Red + Yellow	=	Orange
Yellow + Blue	=	Green
Blue + Red	=	Violet (Magenta)

The paint pigments approximating to these primaries are cadmium red, cadmium yellow and ultramarine blue. Figure 8.1, the colour wheel, (shown in the colour section opposite) illustrates the mixing together of the primaries (red, yellow and blue) in equal proportions to create the secondaries (orange, green and violet) and, by varying the proportions in a mixture of those secondaries, the intermediaries.

Only experimentation will demonstrate the range and nature of the colours it is possible to achieve. Carvers may wish to devise their own colour wheels or refer to colour charts and wheels published by paint manufacturers.

The beginner will have difficulty in predicting exactly how a particular colour straight from the tube or jar will appear when it dries. Even colours having the same name but coming from different makers may well exhibit subtle variations in hue.

For this reason, when I first started carving, I painted a series of colour patches on pieces of jelutong that had been previously sanded down and primed with gesso (see Fig 8.2). One row of patches represents a range of saturated colours straight from the tubes. The other row, next to the first, represents diluted washes of the same colours.

Since the surface of the wood had been sanded and primed, the patches have not only served as a colour guide, they have also given me some idea of the finish to be expected when the paint is dry.

Equipment and materials

For the beginner, choosing the right equipment and materials needed to master the basic technique of painting, from amongst the enormous range of products available, can be both frustrating and potentially expensive.

Brushes

With brushes for instance, the beginner is faced with a bewildering range from which to choose. There are at least 14 generally accepted shapes for brush heads alone, each one available in a variety of fibres.

Although for many years brushes were only available in natural materials, e.g., sable, squirrel, ox, hog etc., more recently synthetic fibres have been introduced, which many carvers actually prefer to use with the fast-drying acrylics.

Sizes

The size of a brush is indicated on the handle, but unfortunately these sizes are not standardized across the ranges made by different manufacturers. Nevertheless, they do serve as a reasonable guide: the lower the number, the finer the brush. For anything other than the more specialized tasks, brushes between sizes 0–12 will be found to serve the needs of the wildfowl carver.

Shapes

The shape and length of the bristles dictates the use to which the brush is best suited. Rounds and filberts are the most commonly used brushes and are particularly effective on the relatively larger areas of colours. Flats, having flattened, squared or angled heads are particularly suitable for defining areas or sharp edges. Very fine brushes are used where very small areas or fine lines are to be painted.

Quality

It is generally accepted that the very best quality brushes have Kolinsky sable hair bristles, but this quality is reflected in the high prices that these brushes command. The improvements made in the quality of synthetic fibre brushes have narrowed the gap between them and those made with natural hair.

The soundest advice for beginners choosing brushes is to buy the best they can afford; buying cheap brushes is false economy. At the outset a small range of brushes will be required. I recommend the following starter kit of brushes.

Starter kit (brushes)

Shown in Fig 8.3.

A sealant brush

If a sealant is to be applied, a large, cheap brush should be used. It should be kept

Fig 8.3 A suggested starter kit of brushes for: *(a)* sealants, *(b)* large washes, *(c)* general purpose, *(d)* and *(e)* small areas and fine lines.

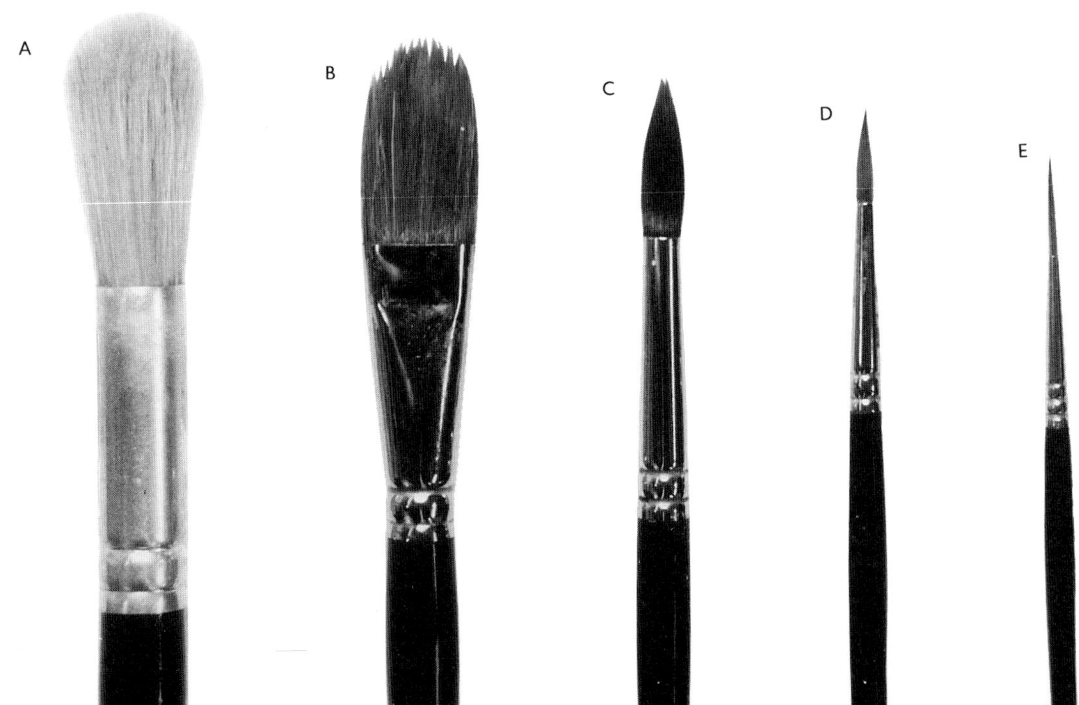

exclusively for this purpose and cleaned immediately after use in white spirit or turpentine.

It is very difficult to clean brushes used to apply sealant, and all too frequently they have to be thrown away, hence the seemingly contradictory advice to both take special care of it and to buy a cheap brush for this purpose.

B Large wash-brush
A broad size 10–12 is ideal for applying an undercoat (gesso) or laying down large areas of paint. Its relatively stiff bristles ensure that when brushed in the direction of the textured lines, no excess paint will remain to clog up the grooves.

C General purpose brush
For the beginner, the majority of painting may be done satisfactorily using one or two round or filbert brushes, sizes 7–9. The most expensive, top quality brushes will probably have sable bristles, but good quality brushes made of synthetic fibres either used alone or in combination with natural hair, are also available and will serve the painter well.

D & E Fine brushes
For the finest detail work a size 1 or 2 sable brush is recommended. With any brush, the colour holding capacity is important. A short flat brush head will hold considerably less paint than a larger round-headed brush. Generally, cheaper, poorer quality brushes also tend to hold less paint.

Caring for brushes
Top quality brushes are expensive, and therefore taking care of them is important. By following these simple guidelines, brushes will keep in good condition.

- Always wash brushes immediately after use. Remove any paint from the fibres, the ferrule and the handle. Use only cool water, as hot water may cause the paint to coagulate. Shape up the brushes after cleaning (see Fig 8.4).

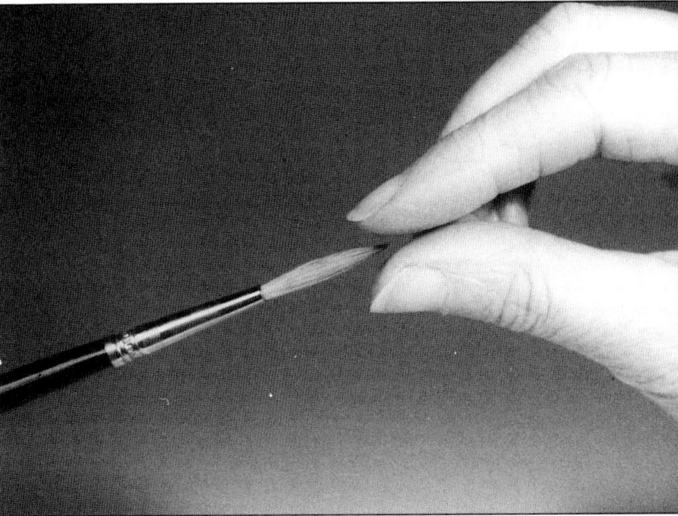

Fig 8.4 Reshape brushes after cleaning.

- Never leave a brush loaded with paint for any length of time. If you are called away, leave the brush in water and dry it out immediately on returning.
- Never leave brushes resting on their bristles. Stand them head uppermost in a pot or jar.
- In use, the brush should be stroked across the surface and not scrubbed.
- If for any reason paint does dry into the bristles it can be removed by dissolving the paint in methylated spirits and washing gently in warm soapy water.
- Never mix paint with a brush, always use a palette knife.
- Never leave brushes submerged or soaking in water for a long time, as moisture can enter the handle and crack the wood.

Miscellaneous equipment and materials

Palette
Any white palette or even a white saucer will serve as a perfectly adequate receptacle in which to mix paint. For the method of mixing I advocate in this book, a sheet of glass

approximately 2ft x 18in (60cm x 45cm) and 1/4in (6mm) thick makes a very good surface on which to work and is an excellent palette upon which to mix paints.

Palette knife

A good quality stainless steel palette knife is a sound investment. Cheap metal knives tend to rust and contaminate mixed paint with fine particles of that rust, while plastic palette knives are far less effective in use than stainless steel ones.

Paper towelling and clean rags

A roll of paper towelling and one or two small pieces of clean rag should be kept handy for drying brushes and mopping up spilt paint.

Water

A plentiful supply of clean water must be readily available when using acrylic paints. A large container (a bucket, preferably) for washing off brushes and a jar or pot of clean water for thinning down paint is the minimum requirement.

A Raphael water container, with its twin compartments for water and grooves on which to rest brushes is a very convenient, but not essential piece of equipment for the beginner (see Fig 8.5).

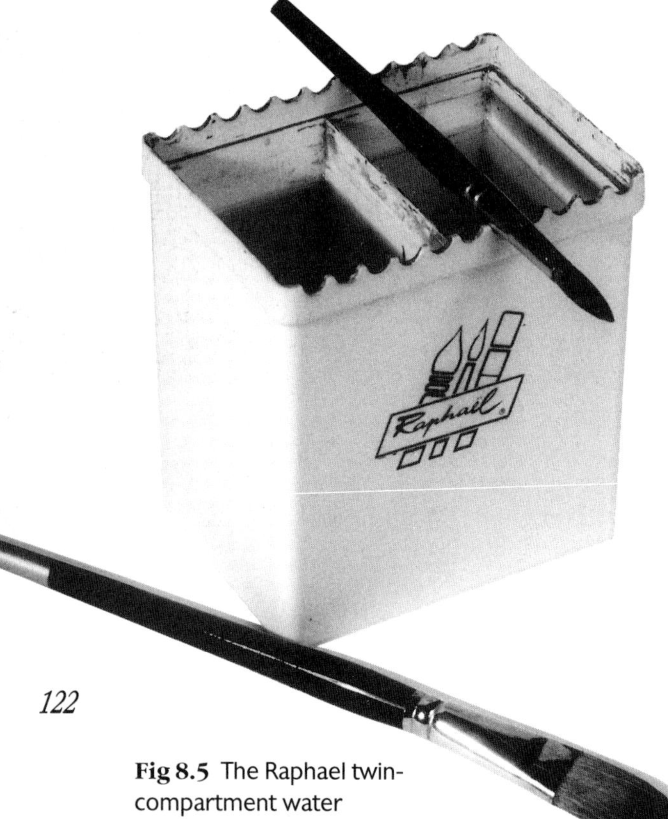

Fig 8.5 The Raphael twin-compartment water container.

Support for carving

When painting, the carving should be handled as little as possible. Apart from the obvious risk of spots of paint being accidentally transferred from the fingers to the surface, perspiration and grease can be left behind - even with clean hands - to affect the surface adversely.

Any turntable device, provided it has a stable base and revolves freely, will suffice as a support for the carved bird while it is being painted. A potters' wheel, suitably adapted, can be used, and on a number of occasions I have found a simple and inexpensive cake-icing stand extremely effective.

However, for the majority of painting jobs, a simple wooden 'keel' made from scrap wood affixed to the base of the carving with two small dabs of epoxy glue will provide a convenient handle. A piece of wood, 1 x 1 x 4in (25 x 25 x 100mm) not only serves as a handle, but also allows the painter to rest the carving on the bench without it touching the work surface. The keel is easily knocked off when the painting is completed (see Fig 8.6).

The work area

Lighting

The workbench must be well and evenly illuminated. The preference must be for natural light, although not direct sunlight, but where this is not possible, or where the light level is low, artificial light should be even and 'shadowless'.

The colour quality of the light could also be important when painting. Colour-corrected lighting (daylight tubes) fluorescent or a blue tungsten daylight lamp ensure consistent lighting and make good substitutes for natural daylight.

Cleanliness

Even the smallest particle of dried acrylic paint may spoil any surface that may have taken a great deal of time and trouble to paint.

Palettes and brushes must be thoroughly cleaned, and water changed frequently. If the glass palette method is used, any dried paint must be scraped off and the glass wiped clean after each stage in the painting. Before the painting process is begun, a proprietary brand of window cleaning fluid sprayed on the glass will make cleaning that much easier.

Application

Good painting will improve good carving, but it will not redeem bad carving. Conversely, bad painting can ruin an otherwise well-carved bird.

Details added during the carving process can be enhanced by the careful use of paint. Darker shades of paint used in recesses and splits will accentuate them and greatly add to the impression of depth and softness.

Reference sources for colour

Accuracy is paramount in this type of woodcarving, and, as with the carving stages, reference sources are invaluable. Good quality colour photographs and illustrations should be collected and filed along with any other information about the bird or duck being carved.

Videos of wildfowl are readily available and are another good reference source, but by far the best source is a study skin. This is simply a partially stuffed and preserved skin of a dead bird, and since the brightness in the colours of plumage is retained, it can be used for ensuring accuracy when painting the carving. Study skins are available on loan from the Wildfowl and Wetlands Trust, Slimbridge, Gloucestershire., England.

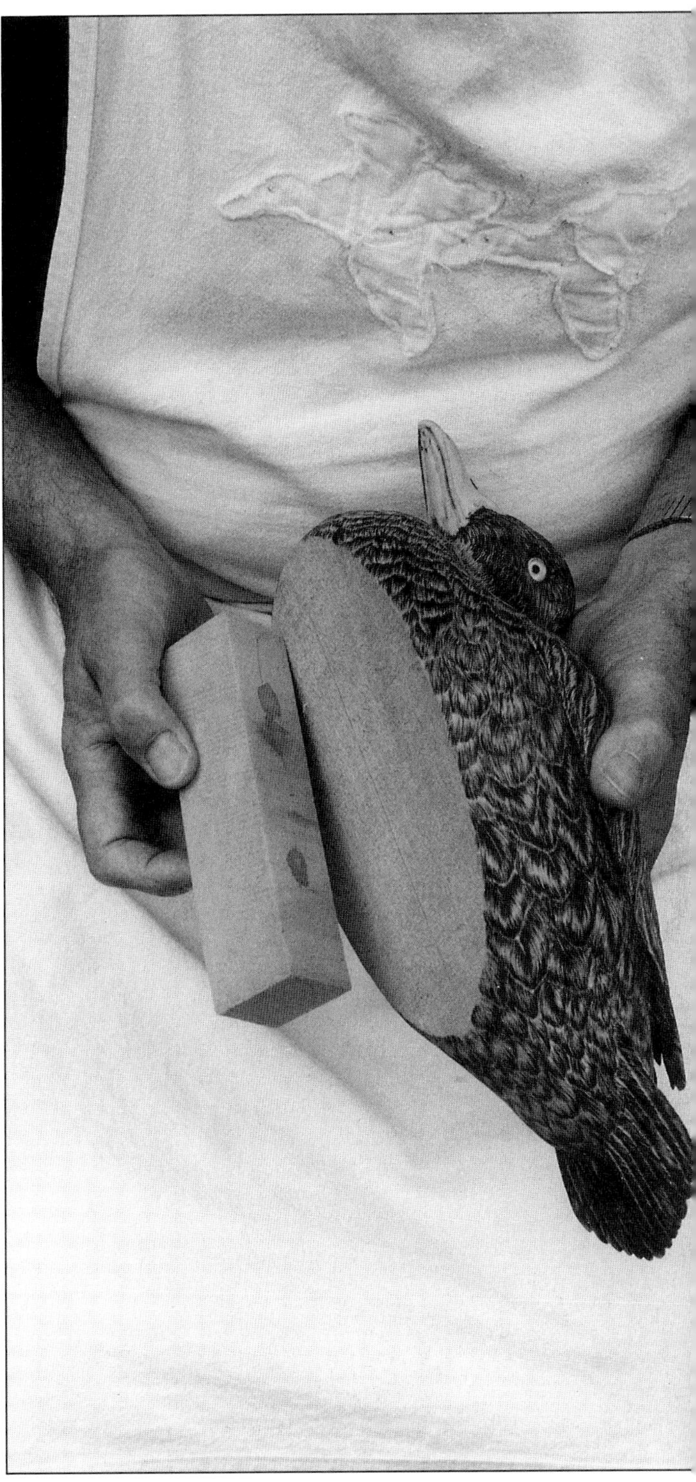

Fig 8.6 A wooden 'keel' affixed to the base of the carving serves as a convenient handle.

CHAPTER 9

Painting the Goldeneye

Equipment

Essential

2 Water containers
Paintbrushes: 1 Artists' hog filbert, size 10–12
1 Round watercolour brush, size 7–9
1 Round watercolour brush, size 1–2
1 (cheap) 1/4in (6mm) brush (for sealant)
1 Toothbrush (old)
Palette knife

Optional

Dual water container
Sheet of thick (32 gauge) glass, approximately 22 x 18in (550 x 450mm)
Daylight bulb
Stay-Wet palette or 35mm film containers (4 or 5)
Hair dryer

Materials

Acrylic Paints: gesso
titanium white
ultramarine blue
burnt sienna
raw umber
burnt umber
pearlescent green
glazing medium (to replicate the sheen on the duck's bill)
Sealant or shellac
Clean rags
Window cleaning fluid (for glass sheet)
Roll of paper towels
Piece of wood for 'keel', approximately 4 x 1in (100 x 25mm)

Useful reference materials/sources

Study skin (goldeneye drake)
Photographs and/or illustrations

Colours for the goldeneye

The following colour mixtures are recommended for the goldeneye:

Base coat	Gesso, raw umber (a trace)
Head: white patch	Titanium white with a trace of ultramarine
Back: rump, tail	Ultramarine blue, burnt sienna (1:1)
Head	Ultramarine blue, burnt sienna (3:2) Pearlescent green
Bill	Ultramarine blue, Burnt sienna (2:3) Glazing medium
Eyes	Cadmium yellow
Tonal wash	Burnt umber (very diluted)

Preparation

However carefully the texturing has been carried out, there will always remain a few particles of wood and/or carbon left behind. If you have not already done so (see 'Cleaning', page 117), clean the surface of the carving with a semi-stiff brush to remove this charred residue and any specks of dust. Be careful not to damage any of the fine detail. An old toothbrush will do this job very effectively.

Sealing

Before painting the wood, it is advisable to treat it with some form of sealant. However, because gesso itself acts as a primer and a sealant, some carvers prefer not to do so. Unless a sealant is used, there is always a risk that water-based paint will cause the grain to fuzz up and ruin an otherwise smooth surface. The sealant reduces the rate at which the wood loses or absorbs moisture, and it helps to fill in the open grain of the wood. I normally use a shellac sealer, which I dilute 50:50 with thinners for the first and second coats. It is a sticky, white, cloudy solution that must be stirred well before use. It can be used liberally on an untextured carving, giving the surface an attractive sheen. For textured surfaces it should be used sparingly – three coats is normally sufficient – as the thickness of the total paint layers must be kept to a minimum. For this reason an aerosol spray such as Krylon 1301 or 1302, which give a very fine clear coating, may be preferred (see Fig 9.1).

Applying the sealant

Use a large brush to stroke the sealant on in the direction of the barbs and the feather flow lines.

Fig 9.1 Apply a sealant, brushing in the direction of the feather flow lines.

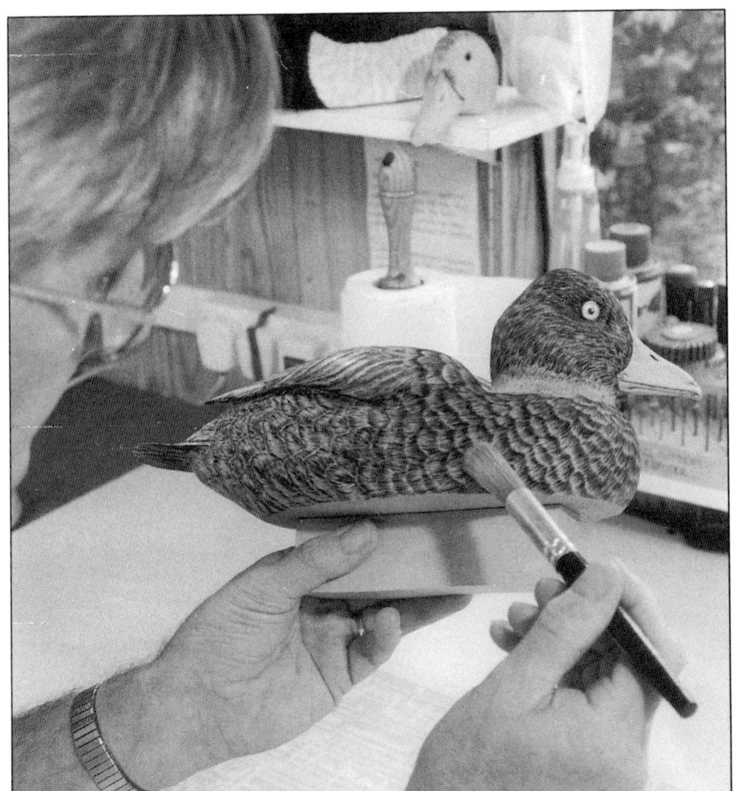

Fig 9.2 Apply thinned gesso primer in a series of washes.

Priming

Gesso is an acrylic primer that dries quickly, leaving a pure white, matte surface that very effectively bonds with the subsequent applications of acrylic colours. Its chalky base absorbs some of the sheen from the acrylic finish, giving the surface a flatter finish.

If too little gesso is used the subsequent sheen will become obtrusive, giving the feathers an unnatural glossy appearance. If too much is used the textured surface will become clogged.

1 Dilute the gesso with water to the consistency of milk and apply with a soft bristled brush, taking care to avoid a build up in the textured lines.Use an artist's hog filibert or similar brush (size 10–12). Many carvers will add a trace of another colour to the gesso to assist in the subsequent colouration of the plumage. In the case of the goldeneye, I add the merest trace of raw umber (see Fig 9.2).

2 Allow each coat to dry out thoroughly before applying the next. The carving may need as many as four or five coats of gesso, but judgement of

Fig 9.3 Make sure the feather texture is still clearly visible after the final coat of gesso.

just how many only comes with experience (see Fig 9.3).

Marking out colour areas

The areas of different colours on the plumage of the goldeneye are clearly delineated and not difficult to mark out.

With a soft pencil, the neckline should be very lightly drawn in, together with that defining the area of the cape and the scapulars. The limit of the large, white feathers of the side pockets was set at the carving stage and therefore presents no problem and need not be pencilled in.

White patches – head

The distinctive white patches on the head do need to be marked in carefully. They should be checked for size, shape and symmetry before painting begins (see Fig 9.4).

Mixing and matching paint

The mixing of paints to match the colours of a bird's plumage is very imprecise and is very much a question of trial and error. Where a mixture of two or more colours has been indicated in this book, I have adopted the convention of stating the proportion of the colours to each other. Thus, ultramarine blue and burnt sienna (3:2) represents a mixture of three parts ultramarine blue to two parts burnt sienna. These ratios should only be used as a guide. The final decision must rest with the painter and should be based on a trial of that final mix on a piece of scrap wood, sanded and gessoed to replicate the surface of the carving.

To ensure that the paint is thoroughly mixed, a palette knife must be used (see Fig 9.5).

Fig 9.4 Use a soft pencil to mark in the distinctive white patches on the head of the goldeneye.

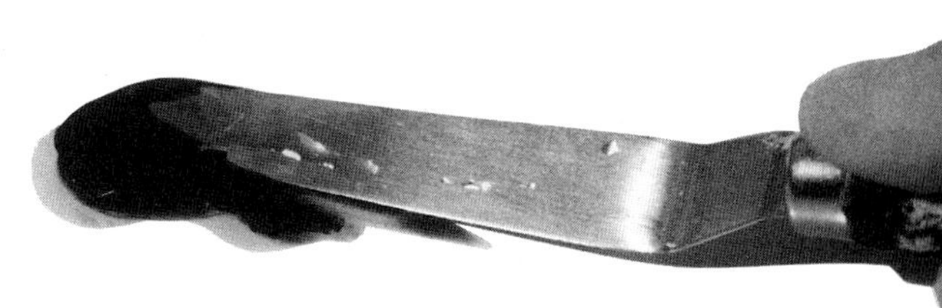

Fig 9.5 Mix colours thoroughly with a palette knife.

Storing mixed acrylic paint

Like the manufacturers of mustard who admit that the major part of their profits come from the mustard left on the plate, the paint firms make a large proportion of their money from 'incorrect' colour mixes that individuals, like me, reluctantly wash down the drain.

It is therefore all the more frustrating to find that, having at last achieved the right colour, the paint has dried out before the painting is finished. I have found that a Rowney's Stay-Wet palette with its plastic dish and semipermeable membrane, works well (see Fig 9.6). Replacing the lid after use will ensure paint remains moist for a reasonable length of time.

However, I prefer to use my own solution to this problem. Put the mixed paint, ready for use and before dilution, into a 35mm film container, taking the precaution to label it clearly. Information on the label should include the type of bird, the part of the carving for which the paint has been mixed and the details of the mix. For example: male mallard, bill, undercoat, gesso, yellow oxide (4:1).

With the lid tightly in place, the paint will remain in a perfectly usable state for many weeks or even months, and the paint can be used as often as you wish over that period. The containers are readily available, as they are normally thrown away (see Fig 9.7).

Fig 9.6 It is possible to keep acrylic paints wet for days or even weeks with the Stay-Wet palette.

Fig 9.7 Acrylic paint stored in 35mm film containers will remain usable for several months.

Another suitable airtight container, fulfilling the same purpose as the plastic film container for storage of mixed paint, is the baby food jar. They are somewhat larger, however, and consequently a larger air space is left above the surface of the paint.

Even cling film stretched over the top of the palette on which the paint has been mixed will help keep it moist overnight.

Applying the Paint

The breast, flanks and head patches

The paint, thinned to the consistency of skimmed milk on the glass palette, is applied with the appropriate brush. In the case of the goldeneye, these white areas should be tackled first using a size 7–9 round bristle brush.

The paint must always be applied in the direction of the flow lines and along the length of the feather barbs to avoid obscuring the texture, and in a series of thin washes which are absorbed into the textured surface, giving it a characteristic translucent quality.

Painting is time consuming and requires the same degree of patience as that

Fig 9.8 The effect of painting a textured surface using single and multicoat techniques.

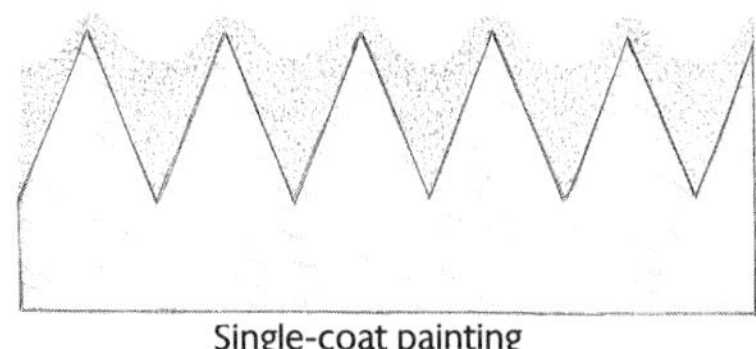

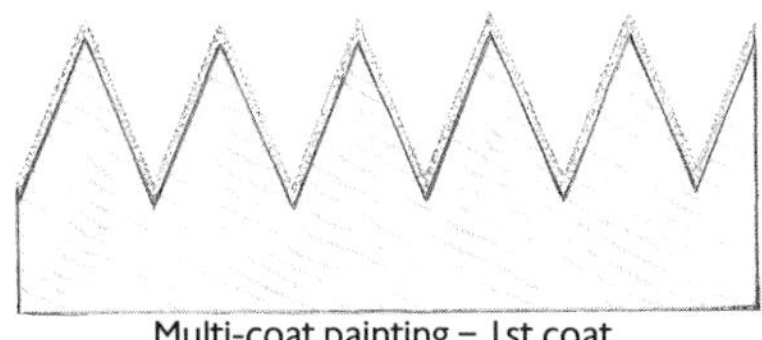

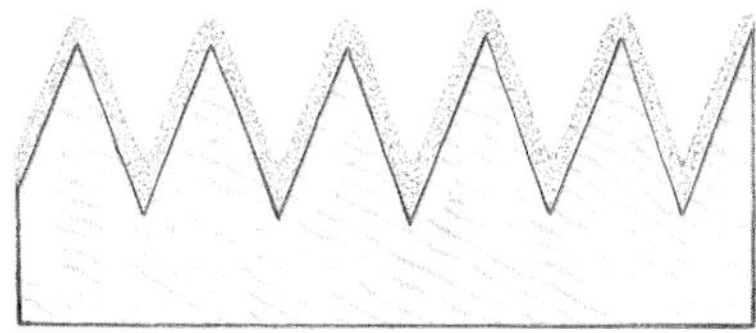

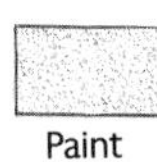

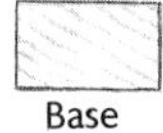

Fig 9.9 Painting the rump.

demanded of the carver when texturing.

I am often asked by students 'why is it necessary to apply many coats of thinned paint instead of using a single thick coat?' The softness in appearance of natural feathers is largely due to the breaking up of the reflected light from the barbs of those feathers. Having created a textured surface to simulate that effect, nothing should be done that would mask it.

One single coat of thick paint to achieve the required colour would considerably reduce the reflective surface area of the carved feathers. Thick paint tends to fill in the burned grooves, and although the colour may be correct, the texture will have been impaired and the softness of the feathers lost.

If, on the other hand, a thin wash is applied and allowed to dry, a small amount of the solid pigment is evenly laid down over the

Fig 9.10 'Pulling' colours – white to black . . .

whole exposed surface. The required colour is achieved by a succession of these applications of thin washes (see Fig 9.8).

Back, rump, tail and head

Using this multicoat technique, painting the larger areas of the goldeneye is fairly straightforward. Having painted the white areas (breast, flanks and the white head patches), the back, rump and tail can now be tackled.

Using a similar-sized brush as that used on the breast and flanks, apply the black paint (ultramarine and burnt sienna 1:1) in thin washes. The appearance of these areas after the first two coats is a very disappointing 'dirty brown' colour and there may be a temptation to apply a thicker mix of paint. Patience, however, will be rewarded, as there is always a marked change in the appearance of the paint after the third, fourth or fifth coat. The final richness of colour is achieved without any loss in translucency or texture (see Fig 9.9).

'Pulling' colours

Where adjacent colours come into contact, the feathers tend to overlap in places and create a broken line between them.

To recreate this effect, a very thin brush (size 1 – 2) is used to alternately 'pull' one colour into the other along the length of this line. An irregular pattern must be created and it will invariably be necessary to repeat the process more than once to simulate a natural overlap of feather barbs.

I On the goldeneye, the 'pulling' colours technique is used where the feathers of the sidepockets meet the rump feathers, the edge of the scapulars and around the neck and shoulders. Note that white paint is pulled into black and

Fig 9.11 . . . and black to white.

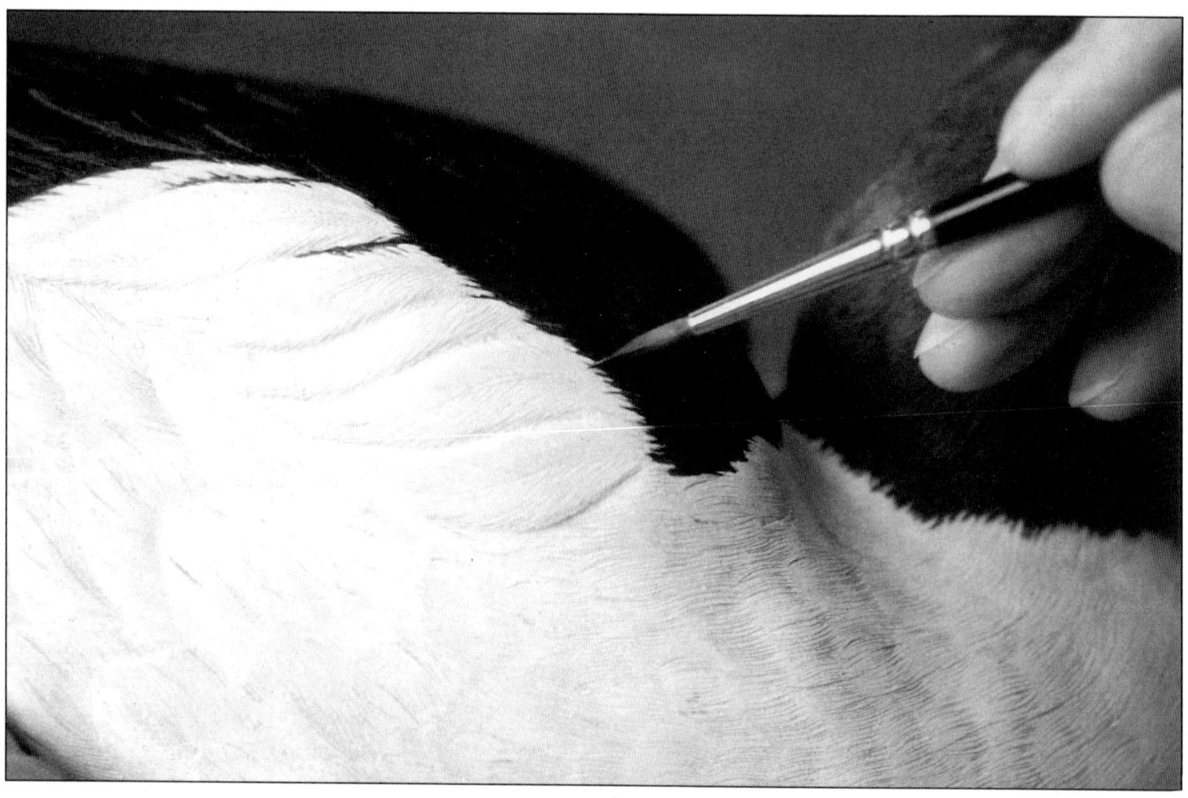

black paint into white! (see Figs 9.10 and 9.11).

2 The edges of the white head patches are treated in exactly the same way (see Fig 9.12).

Painting and glazing the bill

The bill is first painted with a mixture of ultramarine blue and burnt sienna (2:3) to give a brown-black hue. Then when the required colour in achieved and dry, the glazing medium is applied.

Glazing is a technique applied to produce a semi or high gloss to the dried surface of the paint, and is used to replicate the sheen on the duck's bill. Acrylics will normally dry with a matte finish, and to achieve a semigloss appearance a glazing medium in dilute form is applied to the painted surface when it is dry.

Glazing medium is a viscous liquid that is,

Fig 9.13 Take care not to overglaze the bill.

Fig 9.12 Head patches – 'pulling' black paint into the adjacent area of white.

Fig 9.14 Iridescence – making perlescent paint with the original head paint.

invariably, a milky white colour. It must be diluted and applied using the same multicoat technique that is used with the acrylic colours. The dried coating is transparent.

Care must be taken not to overglaze the bill, otherwise it will have a very high, unnatural looking gloss (see Fig 9.13).

Iridescence

A number of ducks have patches of bright, rainbow-coloured feathers, which appear to change colour as the bird moves or are viewed from different angles. The goldeneye for example, has a distinctive green iridescent plumage on the head.

1 For the beginner, to recreate these interference patterns of colour applying pearlescent paint from a tube, suitably diluted, is recommended as being the easiest method and one producing very good results.

For the iridescent effect on the goldeneye's head, the diluted mixture should be added to the paint previously used on the head (ultramarine blue and burnt sienna (1:1)) (see Fig 9.14).

2 Apply the mixture in the same way as the acrylic colours, that is, build up the desired degree of iridescence with successive coats. The pearlescent paint must be used sparingly to avoid the final result looking garishly bright (see Fig 9.15).

Drying

To reduce the drying times between applications of paint a small hand-held hair dryer is extremely useful.

The warm air will accelerate the drying process but the hair dryer must not be held too close to the painted surface, otherwise there is a risk of the paint drying unevenly or even blistering (see Fig 9.16).

Toning washes

When painting is completed and dried, a neutral colour toning wash should be applied liberally over the white areas. This will have the effect of throwing the textured surface into greater relief by accentuating the recesses at the feather splits. A very, very weak solution of burnt umber, diluted to look like dirty water, is used, and great care taken to ensure an even distribution over the whole surface.

When the toning wash has dried the keel should be gently knocked off, and the goldeneye carving will be completely finished (see Fig 9.17).

Fig 9.15 Iridescence – applying pearlescent paint.

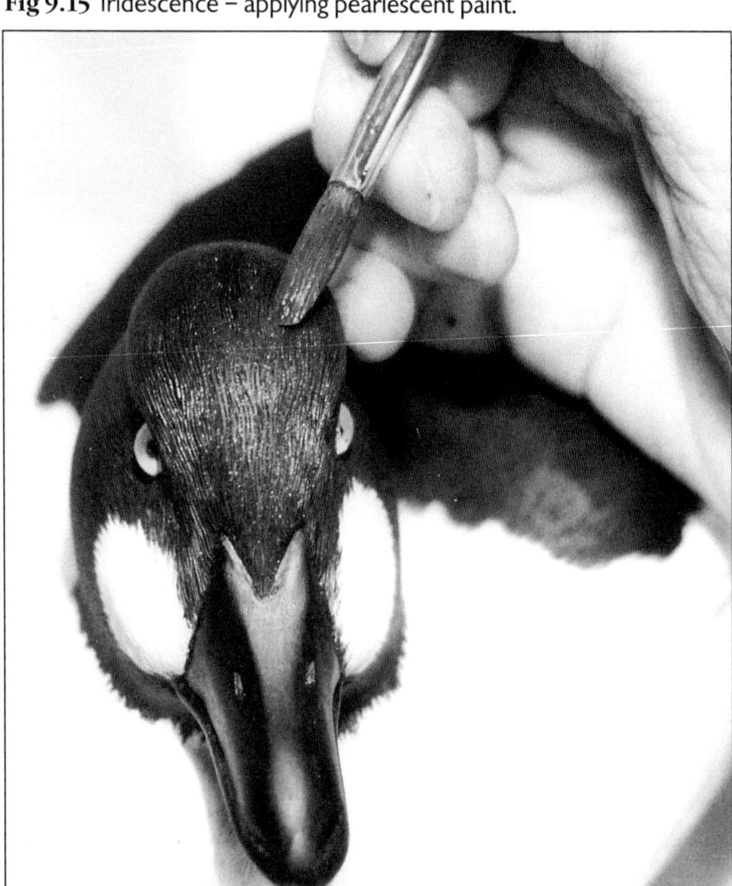

Fig 9.16 A small hand-held hair dryer will accelerate the drying process.

Fig 9.17 Once the keel has been removed the goldeneye is completed!

APPENDIX *A*

Body sizes, eye colours and eye sizes

The following table lists the body sizes, eye colours and sizes of a selection of the better known birds of Europe and the United States of America. The names are arranged in five main categories, conforming to those generally accepted for most carving competitions.

The information in this table was culled from several authoritative texts, which are listed in the bibliography for those wishing to do further research.

NOTE: In the planning and early stages of any carving, establishing the scale and the correct proportions is very difficult. It is for this reason that the body size figures have been included.

WATERFOWL SPECIES	SIZE (CM)	EYE COLOUR	EYE SIZE (MM)
DUCKS			
Black, American	55–60	Dark brown	9
Bufflehead	32–39	Medium brown	8
Canvasback (M)	50–58	Deep red	10
Canvasback (F)	50–58	Medium brown	10
Eider, Common (M)	50–70	Dark brown	10
Eider, King	48–64	Dark brown	9
Eider, Spectacled	50–58	Dark brown	10
Eider, Steller's	44–48	Dark brown	8
Ferruginous or White-Eyed Pochard (M)	36–42	Whitish grey	8
Ferruginous or White-Eyed Pochard (F)	38–42	Dark brown	8
Gadwall	45–55	Dark brown	9
Garganey	38–42	Medium brown	7
Goldeneye, Common (M)	42–50	Lemon yellow	9
Goldeneye, Common (F)	42–50	Pale yellow	9
Goldeneye, Barrows (M)	42–50	Light yellow	9
Goldeneye, Barrows (F)	42–50	Greenish yellow	9
Goosander or Common Merganser (M)	55–65	Reddish brown	10
Goosander or Common Merganser (F)	55–65	Medium brown	10
Harlequin	35–45	Dark brown	8
Long-Tailed or Old Squaw (M)	38–48	Brown	8
Long-Tailed or Old Squaw (F)	38–48	Yellowish brown	8
Mallard (M)	50–65	Dark brown	9
Mallard (F)	50–65	Light brown	9
Mandarin	40–50	Reddish brown	8
Masked	32–38	Dark brown	7
Merganser, Chinese	42–50	Whitish grey	8
Merganser, Hooded (M)	42–50	Light yellow	8
Merganser, Hooded (F)	42–50	Light brown	8
Merganser Red-Breasted	52–58	Reddish brown	9
Pochard (M)	42–48	Reddish orange	8
Pochard (F)	42–48	Light brown	8
Pochard, Baers (M)	42–46	Greyish white	8
Pochard, Baers (F)	42–46	Dark brown	8
Pochard, Red-Crested (M)	53–57	Red	9
Pochard, Red-Crested (F)	53–57	Dark brown	9

Pintail, Northern	51-66	Dark brown	9
Redhead (M)	50-52	Yellow-orange	9
Redhead (F)	50-52	Light brown	9
Ring, Necked	35-45	Yellow-orange	8
Ruddy	35-43	Dark brown	8
Scaup Lesser	42-46	Yellow	8
Scaup Greater	42-52	Yellow	9
Scoter, Common or Black	44-54	Dark brown	8
Scoter, Surf (M)	45-55	Greyish white	9
Scoter, Surf (F)	45-55	Dark brown	9
Scoter, Velvet or White-Winged (M)	50-58	Greyish white	9
Scoter, Velvet or White-Winged (F)	50-58	Dark brown	9
Shelduck (M)	58-67	Dark reddish brown	9
Shelduck (F)	58-67	Brown	9
Shelduck, Ruddy	60-68	Dark brown	9
Shoveler, Northern (M)	44-52	Yellow	9
Shoveler, Northern (F)	44-52	Light brown	9
Smew	38-44	Brown	7
Spotbill	58-62	Brown	9
Teal, Baikal	34-38	Dark brown	7
Teal, Blue-Winged	37-41	Medium brown	7
Teal, Cinnamon (M)	38-43	Reddish brown	7
Teal, Cinnamon (F)	38-43	Dark brown	7
Teal, Falcated	48-55	Medium brown	8
Teal, Greenwinged	34-38	Medium brown	7
Teal, Marbled	38-42	Medium brown	7
Tufted (M)	40-45	Lemon yellow	8
Tufted (F)	40-45	Pale yellow	8
Wigeon, American	45-56	Medium brown	8
Wigeon, European	45-56	Medium brown	8
Wood (M)	43-51	Deep red	9
Wood (F)	43-51	Medium brown	9
Whistling, Black-Bellied	51-56	Medium brown	9
Whistling, Fulvous	51-56	Medium brown	9
Whiteheaded	44-48	Medium brown	8
GEESE			
Barnacle	58-70	Dark brown	10
Bean	72-90	Dark brown	11
Brent	56-60	Dark brown	9
Canada	90-110	Greyish brown	12
Egyptian	62-72	Light brown	9
Greylag	75-90	Medium brown	12
Lesser Whitefronted	66-80	Dark brown	10
Pink-Footed	60-75	Medium brown	10
Red-Breasted	52-55	Dark brown	9
Snow	65-84	Dark brown	11
SWANS			
Bewick	115-130	Medium brown	10
Mute (M)	140-160	Dark brown	12
Mute (F)	140-160	Dark brown	11

Whooper (M)	140–160	Dark brown	12
Whooper (F)	140–160	Dark brown	11
BUZZARDS			
Eurasian	50–56	Dark brown	12
Long-Legged	52–65	Dark brown	12
Rough-Legged	50–61	Dark brown	13
EAGLES			
Bald	82–100	Straw yellow	16
Black and White Hawk	52–62	Medium brown	13
Booted	45–52	Medium brown	12
Golden	75–95	Yellowish brown	16
Ornate Hawk	60–65	Medium brown	14
Short-Toed	63–68	Dark yellow	14
White-Tailed Sea	70–90	Medium brown	14
FALCONS AND KESTRELS			
American Kestrel	24–30	Dark brown	8
Common Kestrel	32–35	Dark brown	8
Gyr Falcon	51–59	Dark brown	14
Merlin	28–32	Dark brown	10
Northern Hobby	32–36	Dark brown	9
Peregrine	38–49	Dark brown	11
HARRIERS			
Hen	45–52	Dark yellow	9
Marsh (M)	46–56	Dark yellow	10
Marsh (F)	46–56	Light yellow	11
Montagu's (M)	40–45	Bright yellow	9
Montagu's (F)	40–45	Light yellow	10
HAWKS			
Common Black	45–60	Brown	12
Cooper's	38–51	Red	10
Grey	35–42	Medium brown	9
Harris'	46–59	Medium brown	12
Northern Goshawk	50–65	Yellowish brown	13
Northern Sparrowhawk	28–38	Orange-yellow	9
Red-Tailed	51–62	Light brown	13
Red-Shouldered	40-52	Dark brown	12
Sharp-Shinned	26–32	Reddish brown	9
KITES			
American Swallow-Tailed	58–62	Dark brown	12
Black	55–60	Light brown	12
Red	58–65	Reddish brown	12
Western Honey Buzzard	52–59	Yellow	12
Osprey	52–60	Yellow	14
OWLS			
Barn	33–36	Very dark brown	11

Burrowing	18–26	Light yellow	9
Eagle, Eurasian	50–72	Orange-yellow	16
Eastern Screech	18–24	Light yellow	9
Elf	13–15	Light yellow	9
Great Grey	63–66	Light yellow	14
Great Horned	45–55	Light yellow	12
Hawk	35–40	Light yellow	12
Little	21–23	Light yellow	10
Long-Eared	34–37	Orange-yellow	11
Pygmy	15–18	Very Light yellow	6
Saw Whet	17–19	Orange-yellow	9
Scops, Eurasian	18–20	Pale yellow	9
Short-Eared	35–40	Light yellow	11
Snowy	55–65	Light yellow	19
Tawny, Eurasian	36–40	Very dark brown	16
Tengmalm's	19–23	Light yellow	9
Ural	52–58	Very dark brown	12
GAME BIRDS			
Capercaillie (M)	84–90	Reddish brown	12
Capercaillie (F)	60–65	Reddish brown	10
Doves, Collared	28–32	Dark red	6
Doves, Mourning	28–30	Medium brown	6
Doves, Rock	32–36	Orange	8
Doves, Stock	30–35	Dark brown	8
Doves, Turtle	26–30	Yellow	6
Grouse Black (M)	50–55	Dark brown	10
Grouse Black (F)	40–45	Dark brown	9
Grouse Red	33–40	Dark brown	9
Grouse Ruffed	38–44	Dark brown	9
Grouse Willow	36–42	Dark brown	9
Partridge, Grey	30–33	Reddish brown	7
Partridge, Red-Legged	33–36	Reddish brown	7
Partridge, Rock	33–38	Reddish brown	7
Pheasant (M)	76–90	Greyish white	9
Pheasant (F)	52–65	Medium brown	8
Pheasant Golden (M)	90–110	Greyish white	10
Pheasant Golden (F)	60–70	Medium brown	8
Pheasant, Lady Amtherst's (M)	115–150	Greyish white	10
Pheasant, Lady Amtherst's (F)	60–70	Medium brown	8
Pigeon, Wood	40–42	Light yellow	9
Ptarmigan	32–36	Dark brown	8
Quail	16–18	Reddish brown	5
SONGBIRDS			
Blackbird	24–26	Dark brown	6
Blackbird, Red-Winged	18–19	Dark brown	5
Bluebird, Eastern	14–19	Dark brown	6
Blackcap	13–16	Dark brown	4
Bobolink	16–18	Medium brown	5
Brambling	14–15	Very dark brown	4
Bullfinch	14–15	Dark brown	4

Bunting Cirl	15–16	Medium brown	4
Bunting Corn	17–18	Dark brown	5
Bunting Lapland	14–16	Dark brown	4
Bunting Reed	14–16	Dark brown	4
Bunting Snow	16–17	Dark brown	4
Cardinal, Red-Crested	18–20	Dark brown	5
Cardinal, Northern	20–23	Dark brown	5
Catbird, Grey	19–21	Dark brown	5
Chaffinch	14–16	Medium brown	4
Chickadee, Black-Capped	12–14	Dark brown	4
Chough, Red-Billed	35–40	Dark brown	7
Cuckoo, Eurasian	32–35	Yellow	7
Dipper	17–18	Light brown	5
Dunnock	14–15	Light brown	4
Fieldfare	24–26	Dark brown	6
Firecrest	8–9	Dark brown	3
Flycatcher, Pied	12–13	Dark brown	4
Flycatcher, Spotted	13–14	Dark brown	4
Goldcrest	8–9	Dark brown	3
Goldfinch	11–13	Dark brown	4
Grackle, Common	28–33	Whitish yellow	6
Greenfinch	14–15	Dark brown	4
Hawfinch (M)	16–17	Whitish red	5
Hawfinch (F)	16–17	Light brown	5
Hoopoe	27–29	Medium brown	5
Jackdaw, Western	32–34	Whitish grey	7
Jay	33–36	Whitish blue	8
Kingfisher	15–16	Dark brown	6
Kingfisher, Belted	28–30	Medium brown	8
Lark, Crested	18–20	Dark brown	4
Lark Sky	17–19	Dark brown	4
Linnet	13–14	Dark brown	3
Magpie, Black-Billed	42–48	Dark brown	8
Martin, House	12–13	Dark brown	4
Martin, Sand	12–14	Dark brown	3
Mockingbird	23–28	Light yellow	6
Nightingale	15–17	Medium brown	5
Nuthatch	13–14	Medium brown	4
Oriole, Golden	24–26	Reddish brown	6
Pipit, Meadow	14–15	Dark brown	4
Pipit, Rock	14–16	Dark brown	4
Pipit. Tree	14–16	Dark brown	4
Raven, Common	60–65	Very dark brown	12
Redstart, Black	14–15	Dark brown	4
Redstart	13–14	Dark brown	4
Redwing	20–22	Dark brown	6
Robin, European	13–15	Very dark brown	4
Robin, American	23–28	Very dark brown	6
Roller, European	30–32	Greyish brown	8
Rook	44–46	Very dark brown	9
Serin	11–12	Dark brown	3
Siskin	11–12	Dark brown	3

Sparrow, House	14–15	Dark brown	4
Sparrow, Tree	13–14	Medium brown	3
Starling	20–22	Medium brown	6
Stonechat	12–13	Medium brown	4
Swallow	16–22	Dark brown	4
Swift	16–17	Very dark brown	6
Tanager, Scarlet	15–17	Dark brown	5
Thrasher, Brown	24–26	Orange brown	5
Thrush, Missel	26–28	Dark brown	7
Thrush, Song	22–24	Dark brown	6
Tit, Bearded (M)	16–17	Bright yellow	4
Tit, Bearded (F)	16–17	Orange yellow	4
Tit, Blue	11–12	Very dark brown	3
Tit, Coal	10–11	Dark brown	3
Tit, Crested	11–12	Reddish brown	3
Tit, Great	13–14	Very dark brown	4
Tit, Long-Tailed	13–14	Dark brown	3
Tit, Marsh	11–12	Dark brown	3
Tit, Willow	11–12	Dark brown	3
Treecreeper	12–13	Dark brown	3
Wagtail, Grey	18–20	Very dark brown	4
Wagtail, Pied	17–18	Very dark brown	4
Wagtail, Yellow	16–17	Very dark brown	4
Warbler, Cetti's	13–14	Medium brown	4
Warbler, Dartford	12–13	Orange red	4
Warbler, Garden	13–15	Dark brown	5
Warbler, Grasshopper	12–13	Light brown	4
Warbler, Icterine	13–14	Dark brown	4
Warbler, Marsh	12–13	Greyish brown	4
Warbler, Reed	12–13	Medium brown	4
Warbler, Savi's	13–14	Light brown	4
Warbler, Sedge	12–13	Light brown	4
Warbler, Willow	10–12	Dark brown	3
Warbler, Wood	12–13	Dark brown	4
Waxwing	17–18	Reddish brown	6
Wheatear	14–15	Dark brown	4
Whinchat	12–13	Reddish brown	4
Whitethroat	13–15	Orange-brown	4
Whitethroat, Lesser	13–14	Light brown	4
Woodlark	14–16	Light brown	4
Woodpecker Acorn	19–21	Whitish grey	5
Woodpecker, Great Spotted	20–24	Reddish brown	6
Woodpecker, Green	30–32	Whitish grey	8
Woodpecker, Lesser Spotted	14–15	Reddish brown	4
Woodpecker, Northern Wryneck	16–17	Light brown	5
Woodpecker, Pileated	38–48	Light yellow	7
Woodpecker, Red-Cockaded	17–19	Reddish brown	5
Woodpecker, Red-Headed	18–20	Reddish brown	5
Woodpecker, Three-Toed	20–23	Reddish brown	6
Wren	9–10	Dark brown	3
Yellowhammer	16–17	Dark brown	4

SHOREBIRDS			
Avocet, Pied	42-46	Reddish brown	8
Coot, Black	42-44	Red	7
Crake, American Black	16-18	Medium brown	4
Crake, Corn	26-28	Light yellow	6
Crake, Spotted	22-24	Medium brown	5
Crane, Common (M)	110-120	Bright red	14
Crane, Common (F)	110-120	Orange red	14
Crane Demoiselle	90-100	Bright red	12
Crane Whooping	120-130	Light yellow	16
Curlew (M)	50-62	Dark brown	9
Curlew (F)	50-60	Dark brown	10
Curlew, Stone	40-42	Orange yellow	9
Dotterel	20-22	Dark brown	8
Dunlin	16-19	Dark brown	5
Egret, Cattle	48-52	Medium brown	8
Egret, Great	85-100	Yellow	9
Egret, Little	56-64	Yellow	8
Flamingo, Greater	125-145	Yellow	9
Godwit, Bar-Tailed	35-40	Dark brown	6
Godwit, Black-Tailed	38-44	Dark brown	7
Heron, Great Blue	100-125	Yellow	13
Heron, Grey	90-102	Yellow	12
Heron, Purple	75-90	Orange yellow	12
Heron, Squacco	45-50	Yellow	7
Moorhen	30-35	Red	6
Oystercatcher	40-45	Red	9
Phalarope, Grey	19-22	Dark brown	5
Phalarope, Red-Necked	17-19	Darl brown	4
Plover, Golden	25-30	Dark brown	8
Plover, Grey	28-30	Dark brown	8
Plover, Kentish	16-18	Dark brown	6
Plover, Little Ringed	14-16	Dark brown	5
Plover, Ringed	18-20	Dark brown	6
Rail Clapper	32-46	Reddish brown	8
Rail Water	27-29	Reddish brown	6
Ruff (M)	26-30	Dark brown	7
Ruff (F)	22-26	Dark brown	6
Sanderling	18-22	Dark brown	5
Sandpiper, Common	18-22	Dark brown	5
Sandpiper, Green	22-24	Dark brown	5
Sandpiper, Purple	20-22	Dark brown	5
Sandpiper, Wood	18-22	Dark brown	5
Snipe, Common	24-28	Dark brown	6
Snipe, Jack	18-20	Dark brown	5
Spoonbill, White	76-80	Red	10
Spoonbill, Roseate	80-82	Red	10
Stork, White	100-115	Dark brown	12
Whimbrell	40-43	Dark brown	8
Woodcock	32-36	Dark brown	9
SEABIRDS			
Albatross	84-90	Dark red	12

Little Auk	20–24	Very dark brown	6
Cormorant, Double-Crested	75–90	Dark green	10
Cormorant, Great	80–100	Dark green	11
Cormorant, Pygmy	46–56	Dark brown	7
Diver, Black-Throated	56–72	Red	12
Diver, Great Northern	70–80	Red	14
Diver, Red-Throated	52–65	Red	11
Fulmar, Northern	45–50	Dark brown	11
Gannet, Northern	88–92	Light yellow	12
Grebe, Black-Necked	26–34	Red	7
Grebe, Great Crested	46–52	Red	8
Grebe, Little	25–30	Reddish brown	5
Grebe, Pied-Billed	30–38	Brown	6
Grebe, Red-Necked	40–45	Reddish brown	8
Grebe, Slavonian	30–35	Red	6
Guillemot, Common	40–45	Brown	10
Guillemot, Black	30–35	Brown	7
Gull, Black-Headed	36–40	Reddish brown	8
Gull, Common	40–45	Dark brown	10
Gull, Franklin	32–38	Dark brown	9
Gull, Glaucous	60–70	Light yellow	12
Gull, Great Black-Backed	64–70	Light yellow	12
Gull, Herring	54–60	Yellowish-light grey	11
Gull, Iceland	50–57	Yellow	11
Gull, Lesser Black-Backed	52–56	Yellowish-light grey	11
Gull, Little	26–30	Dark brown	6
Gull, Mediterranean	35–40	Dark brown	9
Kittiwake	39–42	Dark brown	8
Pelican, American White	128–180	Whitish yellow	14
Pelican, Brown	110–135	Whitish yellow	12
Pelican, Great White	145–175	Reddish brown	14
Petrel, Leach's	19–22	Dark brown	5
Petrel, Storm	14–16	Dark brown	4
Petrel, Wilson	16–20	Dark brown	5
Puffin, Atlantic	28–31	Greyish white	7
Shearwater, Cory's	42–48	Dark brown	9
Shearwater, Great	42–50	Dark brown	9
Shearwater, Little	25–30	Dark brown	8
Shearwater, Manx	30–38	Dark brown	8
Shearwater, Sooty	40–45	Dark brown	9
Skua, Arctic	38–45	Dark brown	8
Skua, Great	52–65	Dark brown	10
Skua, Long-Tailed	48–58	Dark brown	8
Skua, Pomarine	48–53	Dark brown	9
Tern, Arctic	30–39	Dark brown	7
Tern, Black	22–25	Dark brown	5
Tern, Common	24–36	Dark brown	7
Tern, Caspian	48–60	Dark brown	10
Tern, Little	22–26	Very dark brown	5
Tern, Roseate	30–38	Dark brown	6
Tern, Sandwich	42–46	Reddish brown	8

APPENDIX *B*

CHARACTERISTICS OF A SELECTION OF CARVING WOODS

NOTE: 'Fine' refers to texture and 'straight' to grain

Wood	Main source	Colour	Texture	Grain	Carving characteristics	Rating
Alder (H)	Europe - grey alder - black alder, W America - red alder	Pale to bright Orange	Fine	Fairly straight (no distinct 'figure')	Saws easily, works well with sharp tools gives a good finish.	*
Apple (H)	Europe, W Asia, Americas	Pale pink	Very fine	Irregular, spiral, often twisted	Heavy and hard, takes fine detail, stains and polishes well, splits easily, attractive natural colour.	**
Ash (H)	Europe, Japan, N America	White - pale pink	Medium	Straight but can be wavy	Strong, saws well, gives a good finish, can be steam bent, better where detail is not required, available in large sizes.	**
Balsa (H)	S America	Whittish pink	Fine	Straight	Very light, low strength, bends easily, works well with very sharp tools, excellent for model making.	**
Basswood (H)	See under lime					***
Beech (H)	Europe, Japan, N America W Indies	White to pale brown	Fine and even	Straight	Strong, works well, subject to fungal growth during drying to produce attractive black, gold and red streaks. Referred to in the trade as 'spalting' and is in fact the first stage in rotting. Can be seen in a number of hardwoods.	*
Birch (H)	Europe, Canada	Yellow - light brown	Fine	Straight	Heavy and hard. Similar to oak. Not ideal for detailed carving. Polishes well.	*
Boxwood (H)	Europe, Asia, S Africa	Pale yellow	Very fine and even	Straight but sometimes twisted	Takes very fine detail, high density and hardness enhances its value to the carver.	**
Cedar (S)	Middle East - Lebanon, India - Deodor, N Africa - Atlas	Pale brown	Coarse	Well defined growth rings	Inclined to be brittle and to check and crack, requires very sharp tools, gives good finish but not suitable for texturing, very strong.	*
Cedar (S) (Atlantic white)	USA	Creamy white	Medium	Straight	Easy to work, ideal for hunting decoys, polishes well, not readily available.	**

CHARACTERISTICS OF A SELECTION OF CARVING WOODS

NOTE: 'Fine' refers to texture and 'straight' to grain

Wood	Main source	Colour	Texture	Grain	Carving characteristics	Rating
Cherry (H)	Europe, America (Black cherry)	Pale pinkish brown	Fine	Straight	Prone to gumstreaks, carves well but not easily, good finish, not available in large sizes.	**
Chestnut (H) (sweet)	Europe, America, Mediterranean, Japan	Pale brown	Medium	Straight but often spiralled	Easier to work than oak, has tendency to split, carves well, takes a good polish.	*
Cypress (S)	Europe, America, SE Africa, Australia New Zealand	Brownish red	Fine	Straight	Light, very knotty, goes lovely honey gold colour on exposure to air, works easily.	*
Dogwood (H) (Cornel)	USA and some European countries	Creamy white – soft pink	Fine to medium	Straight	Strong, can be worked to feather thinness, bends easily, sands well, popular with US carvers.	**
Elm (H)	America – rock and white, Europe – wych; Japan – nire	Pale brown	Medium to coarse	Irregular, well defined growth rings	Can be carved but better for non-detailed work, can be steamed and bends easily. Polishes well.	*
Fir (S) (Douglas and Scots)	N America, S and C Europe, C and E Asia	Creamy white – pale brown	Medium	Straight	Needs very sharp tools, not strong, brittle but reasonably easy to work.	*
Holly (H)	Most temperate and tropical zones	Greyish-white but variable	Very fine	Straight but irregular	Very heavy, hard wood that will take fine detail, can be stained to resemble ebony.	**
Jelutong (H)	SE Asia (Malaysia), Indonesia	Whitish-yellow	Very fine	Straight, wood marred by latex trace cavities	Soft and weak wood but excellent for carving, takes very fine detail. Accepts paint well.	***
Laburnum (H)	C and S Europe	Light to dark brown	Fine	Straight	Very hard, works well, can have 'oyster shell' pattern, when cut across end of grain, very heavy but carves well, available in large pieces.Polishes well.	**
Larch (S)	N America N Asia	Light brown	Medium	Straight	Very knotty and resin can cause problems.	*

CHARACTERISTICS OF A SELECTION OF CARVING WOODS

NOTE: 'Fine' refers to texture and 'straight' to grain

Wood	Main source	Colour	Texture	Grain	Carving characteristics	Rating
Lime (H)	Europe, Canada, Asia, America - basswood	Almost white	Fine and uniform	Straight	Not strong but is one of the easiest woods for carving, takes very fine detail. Basswood tends towards 'wooliness' when using burrs. Lime and basswood accept paint well.	***
Mahogany (H)	Africa	Pale reddish-brown	Medium	Intertwined giving very distinctive character	Can be used for carving, polishes well. Beware the African brown woods sometimes sold as mahogany. They have an interlocked grain and can be very difficult to carve.	*
Mahogany (H)	American	Deep reddish brown	Medium	Normally straight but can be irregular	Heavy, gives excellent finish and fine detail, polishes well.	**
Oak (H) white	Japan, USA, Europe	Pale yellow brown	coarse	Straight	Dense and hard to work if quick grown, lighter and easier to work if slow grown.	*
Oak (H) red	N America, Iran, Europe	Pinkish	Coarse	Straight	Dense and difficult to carve.	*
Pear (H)	Europe, Asia, America	Pale pinkish brown	Very fine	Straight	Strong, difficult to work, very sharp tools required, good finish, takes fine detail, arguably best English carving wood.	**
Pine (S) (pitch pine)	Southern USA, Carribean	Light brown, reddish brown	Fine and even	Straight	Sap tends to leach out, texturing difficult as heat draws out resin, grain width gives uneven texturing, suitable for unpainted carvings, polishes to high lustre.	**
Pine (S) yellow or white	USA - Western white and sugar, Siberia - yelow pine	Straw coloured	Fine and even	Straight	Works easily, not strong, popular carving wood, ideal for 'slicks', has large knots, unsuitable for texturing.	**
Poplar (H) (aspen)	Temperate zones, N America - cotton wood	White	Fine and even	Straight	Will carve with very sharp tools, not strong, splits easily.	*

CHARACTERISTICS OF A SELECTION OF CARVING WOODS

NOTE: 'Fine' refers to texture and 'straight' to grain

Wood	Main source	Colour	Texture	Grain	Carving characteristics	Rating
Spruce (S)	USA, Europe	Creamy white	Fine	Straight	Few knots, suitable for slicks, polishes well, subject to resin leaching, can be very hard and dense, mellows in colour to a golden hue.	**
Sycamore (H)	Europe, America	Pale yellowish brown	Fine	Straight	Hard, takes fine detail, good carving wood.	**
Tupelo (H)	E and S America	Yellow to pale brown	Fine and even	Irregular and often intertwined	Not very strong. Light and soft. Excellent for wildfowl carving. Inconsistencies in density. Available in large pieces.	***
Walnut (H)	Europe N, C and S America	Greyish brown with grey black	Medium Medium	Straight but often wavy	Carves well. Gives excellent finish.	**
Yew (S)	Europe, Asia, N Africa	Reddish brown	Very fine and even	Irregular and twisted	Strong. Quite hard. Heavy can be carved and takes fine detail. Very pretty wood. Polishes well.	**

NOTE: (S) Softwood
(H) Hardwood

Carving Rating ***Excellent
**Very good
*Satisfactory/good

The carving ratings apply more particularly to wildfowl carving where knives and power tools tend to be used more often than chisels and gouges.

BIBLIOGRAPHY

Berkey, Velma, Barry and Richard, *Pioneer Decoy Carvers.* Tidewater Publishers, Cambridge, MD, 1977.

Burk, Bruce, *Game Bird Carving.* Winchester Press, Clinton, NJ, 1988.

Burnie, David, *Bird -Eyewitness Guide.* Dorling Kindersley in Association with the Natural History Museum, London, 1988.

Burton, Robert, *Bird Flight.* Facts on File Ltd, Oxford, 1990.

Chapell, Carl and Sullivan, Clark, *Wildlife Woodcarvers.* Stackpole Books, Harrisburg, PA, 1986.

Fisher, James (ed.) and Parsley, John, *Thorburn's Birds.* Peerage Books, London, 1985.

Freethy, Ron, *Secrets of Bird Life.* Blandford Press, London, 1990.

Gooders, John and Boyer, Trevor, *Ducks of Britain and the Northern Hemisphere.* Dragon's World, London, 1989.

Gould, John. *Birds of Great Britain.* Bloomsbury Books, London, 1986.

Hume, Rob and Boyer, Trevor, *Owls of the World.* Dragon's World, London, 1991.

Kingshott, Jim, *Sharpening, The Complete Guide.* Guild of Master Craftsman Publications, Lewes, 1994.

Lambert, Terence, *Birds of Shore and Estuary.* Collins, London, 1979.

LeMaster, Richard, *The Great Gallery of Ducks.* Contemporary Books, Chicago, 1985.

Newton, Dr Ian and Olsen, Penny (eds), *Birds of Prey.* Merehurst Press, London, 1990.

Perrins, Dr Christopher and Middleton, Dr Alex, *Encyclopaedia of Birds.* George Allen and Unwin, London, 1985.

Perrins, Dr Christopher and Cameron, Ad, *Bird Life.* Peerage Books, London, 1984.

Perrins, Dr Christopher, *Illustrated Encyclopaedia of Birds of the World.* Headline Books, London, 1990.

Piechocki, Rudolph, *Eye Catalogue of European Birds.* Bochum, Germany, 1979.

Ridges, Bob, *The Decoy Duck.* Dragon's World, London, 1988.

Scholz, Floyd, *Birds of Prey.* Stackpole Books, Mechanisburg, PA, 1993.

Shourds, Harry and Hillman, Anthony, *Exotic Decoys for the Woodcarver.* Dover Publications, New York, 1984.

Shroeder, Roger, *How to Carve Wildfowl,* Vols 1 and 2. Stackpole Books, Harrisburg, PA, 1984 and 1986.

Shroeder, Roger and Muehlmatt, Ernest, *Songbird Carving with Ernest Muehlmatt.* Stackpole Books, Harrisburg, PA, 1987.

Soothill, Eric and Whitehead, Peter, *Wildfowl of the World.* Blandford Press, London, 1988.

Spielman, Patrick, *Making Wooden Decoys.* Sterling, New York, 1982.

Sprankle, James and Badger, Curtis, *Painting Waterfowl with James D. Sprankle.* Stackpole Books, Harrisburg, PA, 1991.

Sprankle, James and Shroeder, Roger, *Waterfowl Carving with James D. Sprankle.* Stackpole Books, 1985.

Tunnicliffe, Charles, *Tunnicliffe's Birds.* Gollancz, London, 1984.

Veasey, Tricia, *Championship Carving, Best in the World, 1985, 1986.* Schiffer Publications, West Chester, PA, USA, 1986.

Veasey, William, *Waterfowl Painting: Blue Ribbon Techniques.* Schiffer Publications, West Chester, PA, 1983.

Veasey, William, *Birds of Prey: Blue Ribbon Techniques.* Schiffer Publications, West Chester, PA, 1986.

Veasey, William with Hull, Carl Schuler, *Waterfowl Carving: Blue Ribbon Techniques.* Schiffer Publications, West Chester, PA, 1982.

Voous, Karel and Cameron, Ad, *Owls of the Northern Hemisphere.* Collins, London, 1990.

Weidensaul, Scott, *Ducks.* Portland House, New York, 1990.

Metric Conversion Table

Inches to Millimetres and Centimetres						
MM = Millimetres CM = Centimetres						
inches	**mm**	**cm**	**inches**	**cm**	**inches**	**cm**
1/8	3	0.3	9	22.9	30	76.2
1/4	6	0.6	10	25.4	31	78.7
3/8	10	1.0	11	27.9	32	81.3
1/2	13	1.3	12	30.5	33	83.8
5/8	16	1.6	13	33.0	34	86.4
3/4	19	1.9	14	35.6	35	88.9
7/8	22	2.2	15	38.1	36	91.4
1	25	2.5	16	40.6	37	94.0
1 1/4	32	3.2	17	43.2	38	96.5
1 1/2	38	3.8	18	45.7	39	99.1
1 3/4	44	4.4	19	48.3	40	101.6
2	51	5.1	20	50.8	41	104.1
2 1/2	64	6.4	21	53.3	42	106.7
3	76	7.6	22	55.9	43	109.2
3 1/2	89	8.9	23	58.4	44	111.8
4	102	10.2	24	61.0	45	114.3
4 1/2	114	11.4	25	63.5	46	116.8
5	127	12.7	26	66.0	47	119.4
6	152	15.2	27	68.6	48	121.9
7	178	17.8	28	71.1	49	124.5
8	203	20.3	29	73.7	50	127.0

INDEX

TITLES AVAILABLE FROM GUILD OF MASTER CRAFTSMAN PUBLICATIONS

BOOKS

Woodworking Plans and Projects	Guild of Master Craftsman Publications
40 More Woodworking Plans and Projects	Guild of Master Craftsman Publications
Woodworking Crafts Annual	Guild of Master Craftsman Publications
Woodworkers' Career & Educational Source Book	Guild of Master Craftsman Publications
Woodworkers' Courses & Source Book	Guild of Master Craftsman Publications
Woodturning Techniques	Guild of Master Craftsman Publications
Useful Woodturning Projects	Guild of Master Craftsman Publications
Green Woodwork	Mike Abbott
Making Little Boxes from Wood	John Bennett
Furniture Restoration and Repair for Beginners	Kevin Jan Bonner
Woodturning Jewellery	Hilary Bowen
The Incredible Router	Jeremy Broun
Electric Woodwork	Jeremy Broun
Woodcarving: A Complete Course	Ron Butterfield
Making Fine Furniture: Projects	Tom Darby
Restoring Rocking Horses	Clive Green & Anthony Dew
Heraldic Miniature Knights	Peter Greenhill
Make Your Own Dolls' House Furniture	Maurice Harper
Practical Crafts: Seat Weaving	Ricky Holdstock
Multi-centre Woodturning	Ray Hopper
Complete Woodfinishing	Ian Hosker
Woodturning: A Source Book of Shapes	John Hunnex
Making Shaker Furniture	Barry Jackson
Upholstery: A Complete Course	David James
Upholstery Techniques and Projects	David James
The Upholsterer's Pocket Reference Book	David James
Designing and Making Wooden Toys	Terry Kelly
Making Dolls' House Furniture	Patricia King
Making and Modifying Woodworking Tools	Jim Kingshott
The Workshop	Jim Kingshott
Sharpening: The Complete Guide	Jim Kingshott
Turning Wooden Toys	Terry Lawrence
Making Board, Peg and Dice Games	Jeff & Jennie Loader
Making Wooden Toys and Games	Jeff & Jennie Loader
The Complete Dolls' House Book	Jean Nisbett
The Secrets of the Dolls' House Makers	Jean Nisbett
Wildfowl Carving Volume 1	Jim Pearce
Make Money from Woodturning	Ann & Bob Phillips
Guide to Marketing	Jack Pigden
Woodcarving Tools, Materials and Equipment	Chris Pye
Making Tudor Dolls' Houses	Derek Rowbottom
Making Georgian Dolls' Houses	Derek Rowbottom
Making Period Dolls' House Furniture	Derek & Sheila Rowbottom
Woodturning: A Foundation Course	Keith Rowley
Turning Miniatures in Wood	John Sainsbury
Pleasure and Profit from Woodturning	Reg Sherwin
Making Unusual Miniatures	Graham Spalding
Adventures in Woodturning	David Springett
Woodturning Wizardry	David Springett
Furniture Projects	Rod Wales
Decorative Woodcarving	Jeremy Williams

VIDEOS

Dennis White Teaches Woodturning:

Part 1	Turning Between Centres
Part 2	Turning Bowls
Part 3	Boxes, Goblets and Screw Threads
Part 4	Novelties and Projects
Part 5	Classic Profiles
Part 6	Twists and Advanced Turning

Jim Kingshott	Sharpening the Professional Way
Jim Kingshott	Sharpening Turning and Carving Tools
Ray Gonzalez	Carving a Figure: The Female Form
David James	The Traditional Upholstery Workshop, Part 1: Drop-in and Pinstuffed Seats
David James	The Traditional Upholstery Workshop Part 2: Stuffover Upholstery
John Jordan	Bowl Turning
John Jordan	Hollow Turning

Guild of Master Craftsman Publications regularly produces new books and videos on a wide range of woodworking and craft subjects, and an increasing number of specialist magazines, all available on subscription:

MAGAZINES

WOODCARVING WOODTURNING BUSINESSMATTERS

All these publications are available through bookshops and newsagents, or may be ordered by post from the publishers at 166 High Street, Lewes, East Sussex BN7 1XU. Telephone (01273) 477374. Fax (01273) 478606.

Credit card orders are accepted.

Please write or phone for a free catalogue.